Journalism, Democracy and Civil Society in India

Since independence in 1947, India has remained a stable and functioning democracy in the face of enormous challenges. Amid a variety of interlinking contraries and a burgeoning media – one of the largest in the world – there has been a serious dearth of scholarship on the role of journalists and dramatically changing journalism practices. This book brings together some of the best-known scholars on Indian journalism to ask questions such as Can the plethora of privately run cable news channels provide the discursive space needed to strengthen the practices of democracy, not just inform results from the ballot boxes? Can neoliberal media ownership patterns provide space for a critical and free journalistic culture to evolve? What are the ethical challenges editors and journalists face on a day-to-day basis in a media industry which has exploded? In answering some of these questions, the contributors to this volume are equally sensitive to the historical, social and cultural context in which Indian journalism evolved, but they do not all reach the same conclusion about the role of journalism in Indian civil society and democracy. This book was originally published as a special issue of *Journalism Studies*.

Shakuntala Rao is a Professor in the Department of Communication Studies at the State University of New York, Plattsburgh, USA.

Vipul Mudgal heads the Common Cause and Inclusive Media for Change organisations. He is the founding Director of Publics and Policies Programme and has been a Visiting Senior Fellow at the Centre for the Study of Developing Societies, Delhi, India. He works on the intersections of media, democracy and political violence.

Journalism Studies: Theory and Practice

Edited by
Bob Franklin, *Cardiff School of Journalism, Media and Cultural Studies, Cardiff University, UK*

The journal, *Journalism Studies,* was established at the turn of the new millennium by Bob Franklin. It was launched in the context of a burgeoning interest in the scholarly study of journalism and an expansive global community of journalism scholars and researchers. The ambition was to provide not only a forum for the critical discussion and study of journalism as a subject of intellectual inquiry but also an arena of professional practice. Previously, the study of journalism in the United Kingdom and much of Europe was a fairly marginal branch of the larger disciplines of media, communication and cultural studies; only a handful of universities offered degree programmes in the subject. *Journalism Studies* has flourished and succeeded in providing the intended public space for discussion of research on key issues within the field, to the point where in 2007 a sister journal, *Journalism Practice,* was launched to enable an enhanced focus on practice-based issues, as well as foregrounding studies of journalism education, training and professional concerns. Both journals are among the leading ranked journals within the field and publish six issues annually, in electronic and print formats. More recently, 2013 witnessed the launch of a further companion journal *Digital Journalism* to provide a site for scholarly discussion, analysis and responses to the wide ranging implications of digital technologies for the practice and study of journalism. From the outset, the publication of themed issues has been a commitment for all journals. Their purpose is first, to focus on highly significant or neglected areas of the field; second, to facilitate discussion and analysis of important and topical policy issues; and third, to offer readers an especially high quality and closely focused set of essays, analyses and discussions.

The *Journalism Studies: Theory and Practice* book series draws on a wide range of these themed issues from all journals and thereby extends the critical and public forum provided by them. The editor of the journals works closely with guest editors to ensure that the books achieve relevance for readers and the highest standards of research rigour and academic excellence. The series makes a significant contribution to the field of journalism studies by inviting distinguished scholars, academics and journalism practitioners to discuss and debate the central concerns within the field. It also reaches a wider readership of scholars, students and practitioners across the social sciences, humanities and communication arts, encouraging them not only to engage critically with, but also to interrogate, the specialist scholarly studies of journalism which this series provides.

The Places and Spaces of News Audiences
Edited by Chris Peters

Theories of Journalism in a Digital Age
Edited by Steen Steensen and Laura Ahva

Cultural Journalism and Cultural Critique in the Media
Edited by Nete Nørgaard Kristensen and Unni From

Journalism, Democracy and Civil Society in India
Edited by Shakuntala Rao and Vipul Mudgal

Journalism, Democracy and Civil Society in India

Edited by
Shakuntala Rao and Vipul Mudgal

LONDON AND NEW YORK

First published 2017
by Routledge
2 Park Square, Milton Park, Abingdon, Oxon, OX14 4RN, UK

and by Routledge
711 Third Avenue, New York, NY 10017, USA

Routledge is an imprint of the Taylor & Francis Group, an informa business

© 2017 Taylor & Francis

All rights reserved. No part of this book may be reprinted or reproduced or utilised in any form or by any electronic, mechanical, or other means, now known or hereafter invented, including photocopying and recording, or in any information storage or retrieval system, without permission in writing from the publishers.

Trademark notice: Product or corporate names may be trademarks or registered trademarks, and are used only for identification and explanation without intent to infringe.

British Library Cataloguing in Publication Data
A catalogue record for this book is available from the British Library

ISBN 13: 978-1-138-24016-2

Typeset in Myriad Pro
by diacriTech, Chennai

Publisher's Note
The publisher accepts responsibility for any inconsistencies that may have arisen during the conversion of this book from journal articles to book chapters, namely the possible inclusion of journal terminology.

Disclaimer
Every effort has been made to contact copyright holders for their permission to reprint material in this book. The publishers would be grateful to hear from any copyright holder who is not here acknowledged and will undertake to rectify any errors or omissions in future editions of this book.

Contents

Citation Information	ix
Notes on Contributors	xi
Introduction: Democracy, civil society and journalism in India *Shakuntala Rao and Vipul Mudgal*	1
1. Indian Journalism in the Colonial Crucible: A nineteenth-century story of political protest *Prasun Sonwalkar*	10
2. Popular Cinephilia in North India: *Madhuri* shows the way (1964–78) *Ravikant*	23
3. A Media Not for All: A comparative analysis of journalism, democracy and exclusion in Indian and South African media *Shakuntala Rao and Herman Wasserman*	37
4. Phantom Journalism: Governing India's proxy media owners *Saima Saeed*	49
5. Shaming the Nation on Public Affairs Television: Barkha Dutt tackles colorism on *We the People* *Radhika Parameswaran*	66
6. Playing Reporter: Small-town women journalists in north India *Disha Mullick*	78
7. The Potential and Limitations of Citizen Journalism Initiatives: Chhattisgarh's CGNet Swara *Kalyani Chadha and Linda Steiner*	92
8. Connecting Activists and Journalists: Twitter communication in the aftermath of the 2012 Delhi rape *Thomas Poell and Sudha Rajagopalan*	105

CONTENTS

9. How Well do India's Multiple Language Dailies Provide Political Knowledge to Citizens of this Electoral Democracy? 120
   Bella Mody

10. Our Media, Our Principles: Building codes of practice for community radio in India 136
    Kanchan K. Malik

    Index 151

Citation Information

The chapters in this book were originally published in *Journalism Studies*, volume 16, issue 5 (October 2015). When citing this material, please use the original page numbering for each article, as follows:

Introduction
Introduction: Democracy, civil society and journalism in India
Shakuntala Rao and Vipul Mudgal
Journalism Studies, volume 16, issue 5 (October 2015) pp. 615–623

Chapter 1
Indian Journalism in the Colonial Crucible: A nineteenth-century story of political protest
Prasun Sonwalkar
Journalism Studies, volume 16, issue 5 (October 2015) pp. 624–636

Chapter 2
Popular Cinephilia in North India: Madhuri *shows the way (1964–78)*
Ravikant
Journalism Studies, volume 16, issue 5 (October 2015) pp. 637–650

Chapter 3
A Media Not for All: A comparative analysis of journalism, democracy and exclusion in Indian and South African media
Shakuntala Rao and Herman Wasserman
Journalism Studies, volume 16, issue 5 (October 2015) pp. 651–662

Chapter 4
Phantom Journalism: Governing India's proxy media owners
Saima Saeed
Journalism Studies, volume 16, issue 5 (October 2015) pp. 663–679

Chapter 5
Shaming the Nation on Public Affairs Television: Barkha Dutt tackles colorism on We the People
Radhika Parameswaran
Journalism Studies, volume 16, issue 5 (October 2015) pp. 680–691

CITATION INFORMATION

Chapter 6
Playing Reporter: Small-town women journalists in north India
Disha Mullick
Journalism Studies, volume 16, issue 5 (October 2015) pp. 692–705

Chapter 7
The Potential and Limitations of Citizen Journalism Initiatives: Chhattisgarh's CGNet Swara
Kalyani Chadha and Linda Steiner
Journalism Studies, volume 16, issue 5 (October 2015) pp. 706–718

Chapter 8
Connecting Activists and Journalists: Twitter communication in the aftermath of the 2012 Delhi rape
Thomas Poell and Sudha Rajagopalan
Journalism Studies, volume 16, issue 5 (October 2015) pp. 719–733

Chapter 9
How Well do India's Multiple Language Dailies Provide Political Knowledge to Citizens of this Electoral Democracy?
Bella Mody
Journalism Studies, volume 16, issue 5 (October 2015) pp. 734–749

Chapter 10
Our Media, Our Principles: Building codes of practice for community radio in India?
Kanchan K. Malik
Journalism Studies, volume 16, issue 5 (October 2015) pp. 750–764

For any permission-related enquiries please visit:
http://www.tandfonline.com/page/help/permissions

Notes on Contributors

Kalyani Chadha is an Assistant Professor in the Philip Merrill College of Journalism at the University of Maryland, USA. As a teacher and a researcher, she has focused on analysing trends in international communication as well as television programming and its impact on society. She is presently working on a book project that examines the consumption of Hindi films by young Indian Americans.

Kanchan K. Malik is an Associate Professor in the Department of Communication at the University of Hyderabad, India. Her research interests include print journalism, community media, gender media and development, and media laws and ethics. She is the coauthor of *Other Voices: The Struggle for Community Radio in India* (with Vinod Pavarala, SAGE, 2007).

Bella Mody is the Professor Emerita and the former De Castro Chair in Global Media at the University of Colorado, Boulder, USA. Her current research investigates journalism's supply of political knowledge to citizens in India's democracy. Her most recent books include *Geopolitics of Representation in Foreign News* (Rowman & Littlefield, 2010) and *International and Development Communication: A 21st Century Perspective* (SAGE, 2003).

Vipul Mudgal heads the Common Cause and Inclusive Media for Change organisations. He is the founding Director of Publics and Policies Programme and has been a Visiting Senior Fellow at the Centre for the Study of Developing Societies, Delhi, India. He works on the intersections of media, democracy and political violence.

Disha Mullick is the Director of Outreach for the Women, Media and News Trust, New Delhi, India. The organisation trains rural women from marginalised communities to produce and distribute a local language newspaper called *Khabar Lahariya*, providing rural populations with access to information on local issues, rights and government resources.

Radhika Parameswaran is an Associate Professor in the School of Journalism at Indiana University, USA. Her areas of research are feminist cultural studies, gender and media globalisation, South Asia, qualitative methods and postcolonial studies. She is currently working on two projects: an analysis of magazine cover representations of globalising India and the gender politics of Indian tabloid print journalism.

Thomas Poell is an Assistant Professor of New Media and Digital Culture and Program Director of the Research Master Media Studies at the University of Amsterdam, The Netherlands. His research is focused on social media and the transformation of public communication around the globe. He has published on social media and popular protest in Canada, Egypt, Tunisia, India and China, as well as on the role of these media in the development of new forms of journalism.

Sudha Rajagopalan is an Assistant Professor in East European Studies, and teaches in the Media Studies department at the University of Amsterdam, The Netherlands. Her research interests include Russian cultural studies, cultural history, historical media and new media cultures. She is the editor of *Digital Icons: Studies in Russian, Eurasian and Central European New Media*.

Shakuntala Rao is a Professor in the Department of Communication Studies at the State University of New York, Plattsburgh, USA. Her research and teaching interests are in the areas of global media, journalism ethics, postcolonial theory and popular culture.

Ravikant is an Assistant Professor at the Centre for the Study of Developing Societies, Delhi, India. His ongoing social history project, 'Words in Motion Pictures', navigates intermedia sites such as print, broadcasting and web in an effort to offer creative connections between these media forms and their diverse publics.

Saima Saeed is an Associate Professor in the Centre for Culture, Media and Governance at Jamia Millia Islamia University, New Delhi, India. Her research interests include news and broadcast journalism, television studies, media and democracy, political communication, development communication, community and public service media, and the dynamics of transnational media and globalisation. She is the author of *Screening the Public Sphere: Media and Democracy in India* (Routledge, 2013).

Prasun Sonwalkar is the editor (UK and Europe) of the *Hindustan Times*. He has published in the area of media and political violence, reporting conflict, international journalism and journalism history.

Linda Steiner is a Professor in the Philip Merrill College of Journalism at the University of Maryland, USA. She studies how and when gender matters in news and newsrooms and how feminists use media. Her current projects include researching a book about women war reporters and coediting a handbook on gender and war. She is the editor of *Journalism and Communication Monographs*.

Herman Wasserman is a Professor of Media Studies at the University of Cape Town, South Africa. His most recent books include *Reporting China in Africa* (Routledge, 2014) and *Press Freedom in Africa: Comparative Perspectives* (Routledge, 2013). He is also the editor of the academic journal *Ecquid Novi: African Journalism Studies*.

INTRODUCTION
Democracy, civil society and journalism in India

Shakuntala Rao and **Vipul Mudgal**

An emerging economic superpower, India is courting high growth while battling poverty, corruption, and precariously poor governance. Political violence, disorder, and social conflicts are some of its recurring problems. "India has law and China has order, but a successful nation needs both," writes Das (2012) in his book *India Grows at Night*. As India embraces the neoliberal economic and media model, the need is to answer the question that haunts critics like Das: can the country be governed effectively and remain the world's biggest democracy?

Since independence in 1947, India has remained a stable and functioning democracy in the face of enormous challenges. Proving the Western pundits wrong, India not only survived as a democracy but also evolved its own institutions of a diverse multi-party political system, strong judiciary, and vibrant media. It has managed to hold relatively free and fair elections and transitions of power have been peaceful. Unlike the more mature Western democracies, India's political landscape had always been shaped by a strong electoral presence. For instance, voter turnout has, from the first elections held in 1952, been high with the more historically disadvantaged groups voting most steadily. Since 1962 voter turnout in India, for general and regional assembly elections, hovered between 55 and 64 percent. By 1989, voter turnout was higher in rural than urban areas and increased among the backward castes, dalits (the erstwhile untouchables), and tribals who were more likely to vote than upper-caste Hindus; this was also true of the poor and very poor relative to upper classes (Tudor 2013). Clearly, democracy had established very deep roots in what was to some critics the inhospitable soil of India. But despite its obvious advantages, democracy had not transformed the lives of the majority of its people. Excessive politicization of institutions at the grassroots has catalyzed clashes of conflicting interests, leading to what Kohli (1990, 27) describes as India's growing "crisis of governability." The egalitarian and liberal principles of governance enshrined in India's constitution have come into direct conflict with historically rigid systems of disempowerment and exclusion.

Since the country embarked on a path of economic restructuring in the early 1990s, the development trajectory of the world's largest democracy has undergone dramatic transformations. New avenues for prosperity and mobility—social and physical—have opened up, and new technologies have shaped the imaginaries of rural and urban Indians in novel ways. Economic growth, rising income levels, and consumerism, coupled with technological advancements and policy initiatives taken by the Indian government, which encouraged the inflow of external investment, became the key drivers in the rise of a new transformed India. The stereotypical image of India in the West as an impoverished nation with Socialist leanings has gradually changed. "The political economic changes began to materially and discursively construct a new India," writes Oza (2006, 11), "They forced the country to shed its image of a cumbersome bureaucracy of the "license-permit-raj" in favor of a vibrant new economy that welcomed foreign investment."

Scholars argue that the biggest beneficiary of the economic growth has been the new urban, educated, and English-speaking middle classes whose identities and practices have begun to constitute the meaning and boundaries of citizenship by reproducing and intensifying historical exclusions based on hierarchies such as caste, religion, and gender. India has witnessed many fiery debates on poverty estimates; the erstwhile Planning Commission has often locked horns with civil society over the rise of inequalities since the liberalization of the economy in the 1990s. Some of these inequalities and exclusions provide a fresh perspective on poverty (India Exclusion Report 2013—2014) through widespread discrimination faced by dalits, tribals, and members of minority communities, women, and persons with disabilities. The Xaxa committee report (2014) on the state of the socio-economic, health, and educational status of tribal communities in India, notes that the tribals constitute only 8.6 percent of India's population, and yet, they are around 40 percent of all Indians displaced due to "development" projects. Despite that, the increased participation of these communities in elections at all three levels—Panchayats, State Assemblies, and Parliament—is reflective of peoples' faith in democratic processes.

However, it is equally true that the new middle classes have begun in the neoliberal era, to "claim democracy from demands of subaltern and marginalized groups" (Fernandes 2006, 197). Political democracy, Fernandes argues, had to be disassociated from the corrupting influence of mass-based participation and mobilization. The political assertion of the middle class has unfolded by redefining the boundaries of citizenship in the public sphere and gaining access to the state through practices and discourses that do not need to rely directly on electoral processes. The middle classes began to shape democratic trajectories as well as broader processes of globalization in ways that are often "disproportionate with their numerical strength in late-industrialized countries" (122). As an outcome, the exclusion of the majority of people from the benefits of the neoliberal economy is merely intensified. Fernandes argues that while traditional caste discrimination has been reduced as an effect of the liberal provisions of India's rights-based constitution, it appears that this has been accomplished at a certain cost. "Economic inequality generated by the expansion of capitalist production has not taken center stage in the debates of equality", Kaviraj (2000, 93) writes, "Two different forces, emanating from different directions and using very different arguments, are creating a discursive climate suited to the rapid development of capitalist inequality." Narendra Modi's Bharatiya Janata Party government, with its overtly capitalist agenda, has won over voters from even the lowest rungs of society, proves the abandonment of the provision of opportunities for poorer social and economic groups. Social inequality of the traditional type, such as the caste system, has been to a certain extent (though not fully) undermined by the power of democratic politics, but the logic of democracy has not opposed the logic of capitalist development and inequalities associated with that process. The Indian state has shifted from a reluctant pro-capitalist state with a socialist ideology, to an enthusiastic pro-capitalist state with a neoliberal ideology. This state–capital alliance, writes Varshney (2013), has led to widening inequalities along a variety of dimensions, suggesting that future patterns of development will be even more unequal.

It is important to unpack the democratic processes which are enormously influential but outside the domain of the state, governance, or corporate entities. These largely concern the civil society, citizens' associations, and peoples' movements which are manifest either as an agency of change from below or as eruptions of public action. The Indian media has been playing an important role in articulating these processes while mediating in multiple public spheres. The role of civil society is quite central in sustaining the vibrancy of democracy in general and that of the media in particular. We are applying the term "civil society" as a moral civil community of individual citizens, their associations and movements, or coalitions of non-state and non-market forces. It is formed largely by the middle classes who, according to Kaviraj (2001, 322) have "a natural taste for Liberty." In India, both civil society and the media have been part of the struggle for Independence and still continue to be prime movers of citizens' pursuit of freedom, civil rights, and social justice. Both civil society and the media work within severe limitations and their political economies raise legitimate questions but it is beyond doubt that they both gain from each other's strengths.

India has witnessed the expansion of civil society and the democratic public sphere from the presence of disparate voices, social and political movements, and in a variety of public interventions. Civil society has a definite role in recovering the liberal ground by monitoring areas like the environment, peace, human rights, feminism, alternative science, and technologies (Nandy 2003, 13). Civil society often finds in media willing collaborators for articulating alternative imaginations for the common good as against those of the state and markets. In the development sector, just as in areas of the environment, human rights, and feminism, the Indian media largely depend on civil society for contesting the state's policy choices. The media coverage against the Armed Forces Special Powers Act in Jammu and Kashmir and North Eastern States and that of human rights violations in tribal areas have a lot to do with the presence of a vigilant civil society.

India's communication revolution, in the post-liberalization era, has been well documented (Denyer 2014; Kamdar 2013; Singhal and Rogers 2001; Jeffrey 2000). Beyond the explosion of newspaper and magazine sales, television and new media have played a powerful role in the country's transformation. With 600 million viewers, India now claims to be the second largest television market in the world. Sixty percent of Indian households, approximately 119 million, have a television, and 42 percent of those have cable services. The growth of internet and social media, small in comparison to China, has been impressive, with 89 percent increase in connectivity in the past five years (Parthasarathi et al. 2012). India had 825 registered television channels in all languages and over 80,000 newspapers as of March 31, 2010, according to official figures released by the Registrar of Newspapers of India and the Telecom Regulatory Authority of India. India's media business is among the most profitable media businesses in the world, where each one of the top 10 media companies grew at least twice in size in the five-year period between 2003 and 2008 (Vanita Kohli-Khandekar 2010). According to FICCI-KPMG (2014), the Media and Entertainment sector registered a growth of almost 12 percent in 2013 to touch Rupees 918 billion (US$14 billion) and is slated to grow at a healthy combined annual growth rate of 14.2 percent to reach Rs 1785.8 billion (US$28.3 billion) in 2018. In the 2000s, as revenues continued to rise, the media industry began to concentrate in fewer hands with the rise of big media oligopolies, a trend which is likely to continue for some time in the present decade.

Such a massive media market and the world's largest functioning democracy also continues to struggle with multiple variants: the task of figuring out how prosperity can coexist with poverty, and how the service sector can live side by side with a failed agrarian system; how patterns of poverty and social exclusion along the lines of caste, class, region, and gender often reproduce themselves in relative isolation from the overall patterns of economic transformation; and why, while prosperity has not yet touched the lives of millions, the big story in the international media is about India's prospering classes. Recent changes in media suggest a growing contradiction: a desire for advocacy of the politics of redistribution and giving voice to the voiceless, on one hand, and the growing power of business in politics and media, on the other. For last two decades the Indian state has increasingly prioritized economic growth and the economic and political importance of indigenous business groups within India has grown. The Indian business sector has successfully and lucratively invested in the media business. As the media environment has become corporatized and commercialized, some media outlets have tried to foster a culture of investigative journalism and have tried to hold power accountable and give voice to the marginalized (Rao 2008); many others have gone down-market and emulated Western tabloid-style journalism by exclusively focusing on, in Thussu (2005b) words, "the three Cs of Indian journalism … cricket, crime and cinema." However, the overall trend is that the top circulation newspapers devote only a miniscule portion (2 percent) of their coverage to rural India's crises and anxieties, almost ignoring issues of malnutrition, hunger, displacement, or farmers' suicides (Mudgal 2011). India maybe an IT powerhouse for the rest of the world but its projects under successive governments to bridge the gap between its digital haves and have-nots have fallen woefully short of the stated targets (Mudgal 2014, 43–44).

Amid such interlinked contraries and burgeoning media, there remains a dearth of serious scholarly research on the role of journalists and the dramatically changing journalism practices in the weakening or consolidation of democracy, social movements, and civil society in India. While a few scholars have written about the specifics of journalism practices in India (Chattopadhyay 2014; Friedlander, Jeffrey, and Seth 2001; Ninan 2007; Ramaprasad, Liu, and Garrison 2012; Rao 2009; Somerville 2012; Thussu 2005a), more needs to be done. For instance, as the state broadcaster (Doordarshan) weakens and fails to provide the essential scaffolding for an informed democratic society, can the new media take its place as the vanguard of public good and reasoned deliberation? Can the plethora of privately run cable news channels provide the discursive space needed to strengthen the "practices of democracy" (Sen 2009, 218), not just inform results from the ballot boxes? Can neoliberal media ownership patterns provide space for a critical and free journalistic culture to evolve? What are the ethical challenges editors and journalists face on a day-to-day basis in a media industry which has exploded? In answering some of these questions, the contributors of this volume are equally sensitive to the historical, social, and cultural context in which Indian journalism evolved but they do not all reach the same conclusion about the role of journalism in Indian civil society and democracy.

Sonwalkar and Ravikant's essays explore the historical intersections of democracy and journalism. For Sonwalkar, India's democracy had, historically, been enhanced by its roots in the ancient tradition of dialog, debate, and argument, which had been transformed by the growth of print journalism since the late eighteenth century. His essay focuses on the period of India's modern political history when the idea of a free press became the locus of constitutional agitation. The agitation included the daring act of Rammohun Roy, social activist and journalist, to close his Persian journal, *Mirat-ul-Akhbar*, in protest against restrictions imposed by then acting governor-general John Adam. Recalling this chapter of political protest, Sonwalkar suggests, can help understand the dominant theme of the free press in Indian media, a tradition practiced today despite rampant commercialization and corruption. In a similar vein, Ravikant explores the evolution of film magazine journalism by studying the impact of *Madhuri*, a Hindi film magazine, which was highly popular in 1960s and 1970s India. *Madhuri*, Ravikant argues, acted as a crucial bridge between several disparate segments of society: film-makers, viewers, stars, fans, state, industry, litterateurs, directors, and exhibitors. It not only educated Hindi readers about the intricacies of the film medium but, in essence, invented a new form to narrate in words some of the classics of Hindi literature. The author argues that the restraint, irony, as well as exuberance in its editorial choices, content, and design were very much grounded in, but not circumscribed by, the aspirations of an expanding middle class nurtured on a print universe marked by Hindi nationalistic and democratic sensibility of the 1960s and 1970s.

Essays by Rao and Wasserman, Saeed, Parameswaran and Mullick directly tackle questions of exclusion in media and journalism practices. In comparing Indian and South Africa media, Rao and Wasserman conclude that the press in neither of these two countries represent voices of the majority and perpetuate practices of delegative democracy. By giving limited attention to the deep divisions present in society, and predominantly centered around class, gender, race, and caste, Indian and South African media perpetuate exclusion. The authors conclude that Indian and South African media do not represent the needs, rights, and duties of the majority of its citizens. Saeed focuses on the political economy of contemporary Indian media and concludes that media ownership patterns have resulted in the practice of what she labels as "phantom journalism" where sham transactions, fraudulent trade practices, and black money is used to fund news media, resulting in a lack of transparency in how news businesses are run and financed. In exploring the notion of "phantom journalism", Saeed notes a sharp decline in quality journalism, focused on public good, as a consequence of a disconcerting nexus between influential politicians, powerful corporates, and news organizations. Parameswaran's textual analysis of the show *We the People* on NDTV (New Delhi Television), a national cable news network, addresses the discrimination against dark-skinned Indians who are viewed as inferior to and less valued than light-skinned Indians. Parameswaran analyzes the content of two episodes (in 2008 and 2013) of this public affairs television program which tackled the growing problem of commodity colorism. The textual analysis examines the ways in which the journalist-host, Barkha Dutt, takes up and creates a forum for debate on the incendiary issues of colorism and explores perspectives on anti-colorism that either gain visibility or get marginalized in the televised terrain of democracy and civil society. Mullick's extensive ethnographic study is about the lives of women reporters in *mofussil* (small towns) in four central Indian states. Through in-depth face-to-face interviews with women reporters, Mullick documents and analyzes the experiences of women about their work environments and policies that inhibit women from entering or staying in the profession. The study concludes that even in an environment where the media were seen to be highly patriarchal, commercial, partisan, political, and seen as a "dirty business," women were knowledgeable about how to navigate their work sphere, how to challenge its norms, and how to find a professional place for themselves. Mullick argues that by engaging in media production—and knowing fully well the deeply embedded class, caste, and gender conventions of this institution—many of the women challenged the status quo and played out the notion of an engaged citizenship.

Rao and Wasserman and Saeed argue that changes at the level of elections and elected institutions are of little consequence in India and elsewhere so long as the social and economic inequalities of civil society remain unaltered and the non-elected institutions—bureaucracy, corporate entities, and police—continue to act either in an authoritarian manner or to exert undue influence on the media. Unlike Rao and Wasserman and Saeed, Parameswaran and Mullick's work suggests that there are spaces of democratic debate in media for those who are excluded—dark-skinned and women—and that Indian democracy is neither a "sham" (Bose and Jalal 2011, 87) nor a "mere ritual" (Beteille 2012, 141), as suggested by some scholars, with no space for critical resistance.

The essays by Chadha and Steiner and Poell and Rajagopalan are careful and much needed studies about the role of new and social media, Twitter, and citizen journalism, in evolving journalism practices. Comparatively smaller than Europe, the United States, and China, Web connectivity in India has risen dramatically in the past decade. Chadha and Steiner's paper focuses on CGNet Swara, an online citizen journalism initiative, which has attempted to enable rural and tribal communities to obtain and report news, and to facilitate coverage of their concerns, by acting as a bridge between those communities and professional news outlets. Historically, Chadha and Steiner, argue that the concerns of poor, rural, and marginalized people have been excluded from mainstream news outlets. Their research on the relationship between CGNet Swara and mainstream news outlets in central India finds that while at least some mainstream news journalists endorse the ideals of citizen journalism, they reject the idea that CGNet Swara can assist them. Authors suggest that there ought to be a re-evaluation of the role of citizen journalism in poor democracies to fully understand the potential of citizen journalism as a transformative and democratizing force. In such an environment, mainstream media continues to hold enormous power in news-making and news-framing compared to new online initiatives such as CGNet Swara. Poell and Rajagopalan's study examines how feminist activists, women's organizations, and journalists in India connected with each other through Twitter following the gang rape incident in Delhi in December 2012. Connecting via Twitter, Poell and Rajagopalan suggest, facilitates the current transformation of public discourse on gender violence and helps to keep the issue consistently on the front burner. In this sense, a significant shift from the past has occurred, when media coverage typically died out after an incident ceased to be news. Yet, their findings also reveal that connectivity is tempered by Twitter's limited Indian user base, and users' continued focus on the crime of the day.

India's Maoist insurrection has received significant media attention, in and outside of the country, in the past few years. The contemporary Maoist movement, Bose (2013, 166) suggests, will be remembered for its one positive contribution, "the role it has played in foregrounding poverty as the central problem and challenge for India's democracy." In her essay, Mody analyzes the content of the highest circulation dailies in five languages—Hindi, Telegu, Bengali, Urdu, and English—and the ways in which these news-dailies covered this armed struggle, seen by its leaders as the alternative to electoral democracy, and a movement that both Manmohan Singh and the Narendra Modi government consider India's greatest internal security threat. Mody's findings reveal significant regional inequalities in political knowledge supply to linguistic electoral constituencies. However, even with the regional differences, more than 90 percent of the news articles on the movement in all five dailies were framed as individual episodes or events with no explanation addressing causes, remedies, or context. Description of the event, as isolated incident, was the common frame: who, what, when, and where, but no why. By and large, there was no criticism of the government for its neglect of tribal concerns, consistent with the belief among scholars (see Saeed's article in this issue) of an increase in the use of the news media as tools of crony capitalism by their owners. Any historical analysis of the

Maoist movement was completely absent, as was any discussion of deep-seated poverty and depravation in the regions where the movement had taken shape.

Malik's essay stands out in this issue for its exclusive focus on community radio as a viable alternative to the private and commercial world of Indian media. While still nascent in the large Indian media market, with only 148 operational stations, community radio has come to represent itself as a tool for social justice and platform for community voices. Malik describes the purpose of the community radio movement and how community radio needs to counter the hegemony of mainstream media and move away from the commerce-driven negative tendencies of journalism such as sensationalism, tabloidization, celebrity-worship, the unrestrained use of hidden cameras, and paid news. As India witnesses an endeavor to develop a nationwide network of thousands of autonomous, locally orientated community radio stations, Malik suggests a set of ethics codes of practice for this third tier of broadcasting so that it does not become a clone of mainstream media. The essay explores some of these suggested principles that the community radio sector must hold as sacred in order to strengthen civil society and democracy. The arguments also strengthen the social value aspect of radio frequencies and telecom spectrum which must not always be allocated to the highest bidders solely on the basis of their market value. Community radio stations may never be able to compete with their commercial counterparts even though they contribute immensely to community causes by creating social capital and by deepening democracy.

In this issue, we have a multiplicity of theoretical and empirical perspectives to draw from as discussions of media, democracy, and civil society in India continues. The coverage of the 2014 general elections and the resounding electoral victory of Narendra Modi were not entirely disconnected from the way the media presented Modi as a political candidate. An exhaustive post-election study by the Center for Media Studies (2014) in Delhi shows that television content was overwhelming driven by Modi's personality while his opponents, Arvind Kejriwal of the Aam Admi Party and Rahul Gandhi of Congress, received less than half of the television coverage time compared to Modi. While it is premature to conclude that Modi was elected with the *help* of a neoliberal media which saw in him the strongest proponent of a pro-capitalist, anti-environment, and anti-minority rights agenda, it is now, more than ever, necessary to study the practices of one of the world's largest news media.

If there is a common theme among these essays it is that India needs to deepen its democratic institutions, including developing and fostering a public sphere where free and ethical journalism practices might flourish; journalists have to critically assess old systems of hierarchy and exclusions; media owners and state actors honor India's historic commitment to a free press; and journalists seek accountability from the powerful and give voice to marginalized in society. T. N. Ninan (2011, 14), well-respected and veteran editor, observes, "[India's] media has gotten bigger and richer and yet more vulnerable. Its survival as a powerful and free voice is not because the Constitution guarantees freedom of speech; Constitutions can get rewritten. The primary source of strength for the media is the trust contract that it has with its public." Indian journalism must make every effort to re-capture the full credibility of an institution that can be called the Fourth Estate even metaphorically.

REFERENCES

Beteille, Andre. 2012. *Democracy and Its Institutions*. Delhi: Oxford University Press.

Bose, Sugata, and Ayesha Jalal. 2011. *Modern South Asia: History, Culture, Political Economy*. London: Routledge.

Bose, Sumantra. 2013. *Transforming India*. Cambridge, MA: Harvard University Press.

Center for Media Studies. 2014. Unpublished Report. http://www.cmsindia.org/publications/Monograph_Coverage_2014_LokSaha_Polls.pdf.

Chattopadhyay, Saayan. 2014. "Online Journalism and Election Reporting in India." In *Online Reporting of Elections*, edited by Einer Thorsen, 101–117. London: Routledge.

Das, Gurcharan. 2012. *India Grows at Night: A Liberal Case for a Strong State*. New York: Penguin Books.

Denyer, Simon. 2014. *Rogue Elephant: Harnessing the Power of India's Unruly Democracy*. New York: Bloomsbury Press.

Fernandes, Leela. 2006. India's New Middle Class: Democratic Politics in an Era of Economic Reform. Minneapolis: University of Minnesota Press.

FICCI-KPMG. 2014. "Indian Media and Entertainment Industry Report 'The Stage is Set.'" Accessed January 5, 2015. https://www.kpmg.com/IN/en/Topics/FICCI-Frames/Documents/FICCI-Frames-2014The-stage-is-set-Report-2014.pdf.

Friedlander, Peter, Robin Jeffrey, and Sanjay Seth. 2001. "Subliminal Charge: How Hindi Language Newspaper Expansion Affects India." *Media International Australia* 100: 147–66.

India Exclusion Report. (2013–2014). Accessed January 5, 2015. http://www.im4change.org/law-justice/social-justice20500.html?pgno=3#india-exclusion-report-2013-14.

Jeffrey, Robin. 2000. *India's Newspaper Revolution: Capitalism, Politics and the Indian Language Press*. New Delhi: Oxford University Press.

Kamdar, Mira. 2013. *Planet India: How the Fastest Growing Democracy in the World Is Transforming America and the World*. New York: Scribner.

Kaviraj, Sudipta. 2000. "Democracy and Social Inequality." In *Transforming India: Social and Political Dynamics of Democracy*, edited by Francine Frankel, Zoya Hasan, Rajeev Bhargava, and Balveer Arora, 90–119. Delhi: Oxford University Press.

Kaviraj, Sudipta. 2001. "In Search of Civil Society." In *Civil Society: History and Possibilities*, edited by Sudipta Kaviraj and Sunil Khilnani, 287–323. New Delhi: Cambridge University Press.

Kohli, Atul. 1990. *Democracy and Discontent: India's Growing Crisis of Governability*. New York: University of Cambridge.

Mudgal, Vipul. 2011. "Rural Coverage in the Hindi and English Dailies." *Economic and Political Weekly* XLVI (35), August 27.

Mudgal, Vipul. 2014. "Union Budget and the Digital Divide: New Wine in Old Bottle." *Economic and Political Weekly* XLIX (31), August 2.

Nandy, Ashis. 2003. *The Romance of the State and the Fate of Dissent in the Tropics*. New Delhi: Oxford University Press.

Ninan, Sevanti. 2007. *Headlines from the Heartland: Reinventing the Hindi Public Sphere*. Delhi: Sage.

Ninan, T. N. 2011. "Indian Media's Dickensian Age." *Center for the Advanced Study of India Working Paper Series*. https://casi.sas.upenn.edu/sites/casi.sas.upenn.edu/files/research/Indian%2BMedia%27s2BDickensian%2BAge%2B%2BT.%2BN.%2BNinan%2B%28CASI%2BWorking%2Baper%2B%2526%2BKhemka%2BLecture%29.pdf.

Oza, Rupal. 2006. *The Making of Neoliberal India: Nationalism, Gender, and the Paradoxes of Globalization*. New York: Routledge.

Ramaprasad, Jyotika, Liu, Yu, and Garrison, Bruce. 2012. "Ethical Use of New Technologies: Where Do Indian Journalists Stand?" *Asian Journal of Communication* 22 (1): 98–114.

Rao, Shakuntala. 2008. "Accountability, Democracy and Globalization: A Study of Broadcast Journalism in India." *Asian Journal of Communication* 18 (3): 193–206.

Rao, Shakuntala. 2009. "Glocalization of Indian Journalism." *Journalism Studies* 10 (4): 474–488.

Sen, Amartya. 2009. *The Idea of Justice*. Cambridge, MA: Harvard University Press.

Singhal, Arvind, and Everett Rogers. 2001. *India's Communication Revolution: From Bullock Carts to Cyber Marts*. Delhi: Sage.

Somerville, Keith. 2012. "Indian Media: Global Approaches." *Journalism Studies* 13 (4): 652–653.

Thussu, Daya. 2005a. "Media Plurality or Democratic Deficit? Private TV and the Public Sphere in India." In *Journalism and Democracy in Asia*, edited by Angela Romano and Michael Bromley, 54–65. London: Taylor and Francis.

Thussu, Daya. 2005b. "The Three Cs of Indian News." The *Hoot:* Watching the Media in the Subcontinent. http://thehoot.org/web/ThethreeCsofIndiannews/1864-1-1-34true.html.

Tudor, Maya. 2013. "The Historical Inheritance of India's Democracy." In *Routledge Handbook of Indian Politics*, edited by Atul Kohli and Prema Singh, 23–36. New York: Routledge.

Vanita Kohli-Khandekar. 2010. *The Indian Media Business*. New Delhi: Response (Business Books from Sage).

Varshney, Ashutosh. 2013. *Battles Half Won: India's Improbable Democracy*. New York: Penguin/Viking.

Vibodh, Parthasarathi, Alam Srinivas, Archna Shukla, Supriya Chotani, Anja Kovacs, Anuradha Raman, and Siddhartha Narain. 2012. "Mapping Digital Media: India." http://www.opensocietyfoundations.org/sites/default/files/mapping-digital-media-india-20130326.pdf.

Xaxa, Virginius. 2014. *Report of the High-Level Committee on Socio-Economic, Health and Educational Status of Tribal Communities of India*. New Delhi: Ministry of Tribal Affairs, Government of India. http://www.kractivist.org/wp-content/uploads/2014/12/Tribal-Committee-Report-May-June-2014.pdf.

INDIAN JOURNALISM IN THE COLONIAL CRUCIBLE
A nineteenth-century story of political protest

Prasun Sonwalkar

India's imperfect democracy may be underpinned by an equally imperfect journalism, but the symbiotic relationship between the two is rarely acknowledged or highlighted. The fact remains that India's democracy is enabled and enhanced by its roots in the ancient tradition of dialogue, debate and argument, which was transformed by the growth of print journalism since the late eighteenth century. In the modern sense, this tradition matured in the acid bath of India's freedom struggle, when journalism and journalist-leaders such as Gandhi and Nehru played a central role before independence in 1947. This paper focuses on a forgotten chapter in India's modern political history, when the idea of a free press became the locus of the earliest example of constitutional agitation. In the colonial cauldron of the early nineteenth century, protest by Indian and British liberals against press licensing and other restrictions imposed by the East India Company took the form of "memorials" (petitions) addressed to the Supreme Court in Calcutta[1] and to the King-in-Council in London. The agitation begun in Calcutta in 1823 was carried forward in London, which later curbed the Company-state's restrictive acts towards the press in India, until the Mutiny of 1857. The agitation also included the daring act of Rammohun Roy to close his Persian journal, Mirat-ul-Akhbar, *to protest against restrictions imposed by acting Governor-General John Adam. Recalling this chapter of political protest enhances our understanding of the dominant theme of politics in Indian journalism, which continues today, despite rampant commercialisation and corruption.*

Introduction

The 2014 general elections in India—considered the largest democratic exercise in the world—provide a convenient backdrop to explore the symbiotic and deep relationship between politics and journalism in India. Superlatives are often used to describe various aspects about India, from its 1.2 billion plus population, to levels of poverty, to the growing number of millionaires and billionaires. Superlatives are also used to describe the ways in which the Indian news media covered—or did not cover—the 2014 elections. In the context of deepening of the corporate–politician nexus since the liberalisation of India's economy in the early 1990s, there are indications that the 2014 elections witnessed unprecedented levels of commerce and compromise on the part of the news media. Large numbers of candidates, constituencies, parties and issues were systematically marginalised in news discourse in favour of certain politicians and their parties. American-style branding of candidates and parties was taken to new highs of manufacturing consent as thousands of techno-savvy volunteers lent their expertise (including holograms) to selectively influence the discourse. Manoj Ladwa, who was the head of public relations of Bharatiya Janata Party's campaign, said after the party's landslide electoral victory: "We studied the Barack Obama and Tony Blair campaigns, but this was a [Narendra] Modi campaign and it will be seen as a benchmark in political communication on media courses" (Sonwalkar 2014, 11).

The news coverage of the elections presents itself as a rare case study of professionalisation of political communication and western-style methods being deployed in a traditional society that is undergoing transformation at various levels, but continues to face serious challenges of poverty, health, education and security. If the news coverage of the 2014 elections is seen as plunging new depths of corruption, misuse and manipulation—partly captured in the phrase "paid news", which means politicians paying for propaganda masquerading as news content—it also reflects and reiterates a reality that is so banal and boring that it is rarely acknowledged or noticed. It is the reality of politics being the default setting of Indian journalism, an aspect that defies Murdoch-style dumbing down of news content for commercial gains. Since the early 1990s, news content has become light as part of the "Murdochization" of Indian journalism (Sonwalkar 2002), with increasing focus on celebrities, cinema, crime and cricket, but the historical hard-wiring of politics in Indian society, as reflected in journalism, has retained its salience. Political events and issues are often narrated in Bollywood-style imagery and idioms, particularly on television, but despite the rapacious pursuit of profit and corruption by news organisations and some journalists, the dominance of politics, party leaders and issues has continued across the news media, including print, radio, television and the rapidly expanding social media. This article focuses on this core, umbilical link between journalism and politics in India, and recalls the first—but largely forgotten—chapter of protest in the early nineteenth century that set the template for subsequent political agitations, culminating in India's independence in 1947.

The origin of modern journalism in India in the late eighteenth century presents a unique case study of the idea of "British journalism abroad", of how the ways of doing journalism travelled from England to various colonies of the British Empire, how the "model" was received, adopted and constructively adapted by the local elites, and how journalism of this period prepared the groundwork for the use of the press as a powerful weapon during freedom struggles, particularly in non-Dominion or non-Settler colonies such as India. According to standard historical accounts, Indian nationalism began in 1885 with the formation of the Indian National Congress, or during the preparatory phase of agitational politics in the preceding decade. However, the vast material comprising hand-written records of the East India Company (EIC) and surviving copies of the first English and Indian-language journals suggest that by as early as 1835, print journalism had emerged as a site where the first impulses of Indian nationalism were being expressed. Journalism had also become an effective tool for social and religious reform. It had become a key aspect of what was then a new form of political protest—constitutional agitation—which included petitions to EIC officials, town hall meetings in Calcutta, seeking legal alternatives and raising issues through the press. Later, Mahatma Gandhi, Jawaharlal Nehru and other leaders of India's freedom struggle followed the example set by the the first leader-journalists such as Rammohun Roy, H. L. V. Derozio and Bhabani Charan Bandopadhyay, and used journalism to powerful effect. By 1835, Indians were already using print journalism to lecture to the British on how to run their empire, and writing extensively about the Irish and the revolutionary struggles in Spain and Italy as part of veiled attacks on the company's rule in India. This focus on politics in the early phase of Indian journalism helps partly explain the persistence of politics as the dominant theme in modern India's news media.

The next section places the origins of modern journalism in India in historical context and summarises key developments until the early nineteenth century. Journalism itself became the focus of the first political struggle in the colonial cauldron at the time, as top officials of the EIC saw the press as a threat and imposed severe restrictions. Matters came to a head in 1823, when acting Governor-General John Adam took two steps: deporting the irrepressible editor John Silk Buckingham, whose *Calcutta Journal* often launched scathing attacks on the Company government and its leading individuals; and issuing a Press Ordinance that imposed severe restrictions on the press. It is the response to this Press Ordinance by leading Indians in Calcutta that provides a remarkable and first example of modern ideas and the press being used in political protests in colonial India. As Gaonkar (1999, 17) observed, "Modernity is more often perceived as a lure than as threat, and the people (not just the elite) everywhere, at every national or cultural site, rise to meet it, negotiate it, and appropriate it in their own fashion". The Indian response to the Press Ordinance took the form of two memorials (petitions)—one addressed to the Supreme Court in Calcutta and the other to the King-in-Council (so-called when the sovereign is acting on the advice of the Council); and in an act described as "daring" at the time, social reformer Rammohun Roy closed his Persian journal, *Mirat-ul-Akhbar*, in protest. As historian R. C. Dutt put it, "It was the start of that system of constitutional agitation for political rights which their countrymen have learnt to value so much in the present day" (Majumdar 1965, 234). The response also included transnational protest when Buckingham, deported to England, continued his diatribe in print against the Company government from London. This article, however, focuses on the Indian response: the two memorials and the closure of Roy's journal.

The Context of Early Indian Journalism

This period in Indian journalism history was marked by political flux, when the Mughal Empire was in decline and a commercial enterprise from England—the East India Company—was coming to terms with the reality of having assumed political power over most of the sub-continent. It was a period of much uncertainty, when nothing was a given. In mid-eighteenth century Mughal India, slowly but surely, the old was giving way to the new in complex ways. The Mughal Empire was losing its influence, while the EIC gained political power and influence after the Battle of Plassey (1757), Battle of Buxar (1764) and the Treaty of Allahabad (1765), in which the Mughal Emperor formally acknowledged British dominance in the region by granting EIC the *diwani*, or the right to collect revenue, from Bengal, Bihar and Orissa. The Supreme Court was founded in Calcutta in 1774. The EIC ceased to be simply a trading company and transformed into a powerful imperial agency with an army of its own, exercising control over vast territories with millions of people. As Thomas B. Macaulay said during a speech in the House of Commons on 10 July 1833: "It is the strangest of all governments; but it is designed for the strangest of all empires". Elsewhere, the close of the eighteenth century was a period of cataclysmic change: American and French Revolutions had a profound influence not only on rulers in England but also on officials of the EIC. Radical politics began to emerge in England from the 1750s, which was strongly resisted by the forces of status quo. The same fears gripped the early officers of the expansionist EIC as it established itself in Calcutta and spread its influence across India.

Journalism emerged amidst such conditions and uncertain attempts by the Company government to introduce new, modern ways of governance and other measures, most of which proved controversial and faced opposition from Indians. The Company government, at the time engaged in battles across India, watched uneasily as English-language journals were launched from 1780 onwards, when James Augustus Hicky published the first journal, *Hicky's Gazette Or Calcutta General Advertiser*. Alert to the dangers of Jacobinism, the EIC tried to control the press and prevent its growth from as early as 1799, by when British entrepreneurs and agency house came together to launch more journals. The question of freedom of the press first exercised colonial authorities at the time of Richard Wellesley's governorship (1798–1805), when the Company government interpreted any criticism in journals as lurking Jacobinism. In 1799, Wellesley introduced regulations for the press, which stipulated that no newspaper be published until the proofs of the whole paper, including advertisements, were submitted to the colonial government and approved; violation invited deportation to England. Until 1818, the regulations applied only to the English journals, because until that year, there were no journals in Indian languages.

The Company government succeeded in controlling the press until 1818, by when the combination of a proliferating commercially driven print culture, a growing British community, a new generation of British editors and administrators, Christian missionaries and Indian elites alert to new ideas and impulses, ensured the growth of journalism and the idea of a free press. Several English-language journals followed Hicky's journal, as members of the small British community in Calcutta sought to recreate the British world and cultural conditions in England: "[As] the German demands his national beverages wherever he settles, so the Briton insists on his newspaper" (Mills 1924, 103). Calcutta became the setting for the origins of Indian journalism and the crucible of the first sustained cultural encounter between Indian intellectuals and the west. In the late eighteenth century (1780), the white population in the town was less than 1000; in the 1837 census, 3138 English were returned, with soldiers forming the main element of the community. A part of Calcutta came to be known as the "white town", where the British based themselves and sought to recreate British cultural life through news, goods, music, theatre and personnel that arrived and left for England by sea. As Marshall (2000, 308–309) noted, the "vast majority of the British were not interested in any exchange of ideas with the Indians. They did not expect to give anything, still less to receive. They were solely concerned with sustaining British cultural life for themselves with as few concessions as possible to an alien environment".

Yet, members of the Indian intelligentsia, such as Rammohun Roy, living in Calcutta responded in creative ways to aspects of European culture that became available to them. Some members of the British community, on their own, developed cultural contacts with the local population, notably Sir William Jones, Nathaneil Halhed, Charles Wilkins and, for evangelical reasons, the Baptist missionaries in nearby Serampore. Indian scholars employed at the Fort William College also brought them in close contact with the British. As EIC's presence spread and grew in its influence, Calcutta became the centre of governance, attracting unofficial Britons seeking to make a fortune, thus setting the scene for discursive interactions with the local population at various levels, including in the field of journalism (such as it was then). Indian intellectuals such as Roy were quick to absorb new ideas from the west. At the time, as Raichaudhuri (1988, 3) noted, "The excitement over the literature, history and philosophy of Europe as well as the less familiar scientific knowledge was deep and abiding".

At the heart of this "excitement" was the technology of print, which enabled the flow of ideas and news from the metropole to the colonial periphery, *vice versa*, and slowly beyond Calcutta to the other two presidencies of Madras and Bombay and elsewhere. The printing press first arrived in India in Goa with Portuguese missionaries in the mid-sixteenth century. Several religious texts were later printed in Konkani, Tamil and other Indian languages, but it was not until the late eighteenth century that the first English-language journals were launched in Calcutta, followed by journals in Bengali, Persian and Hindi in Calcutta, and in other Indian languages in Madras and Bombay. In the last two decades of the eighteenth century, "Calcutta rapidly developed into the largest centre of printing in the sub-continent … appropriate to its paramount importance to the British as an administrative, commercial and social base" (Shaw 1981, ix).

Hicky catered to the small but expanding British community, which was able to sustain more English journals, some of them launched with the support of the EIC. As Marshall (2000, 324) noted, "White Calcutta sustained a remarkable number of newspapers and journals in English. Between 1780 and 1800, 24 weekly or monthly magazines came into existence … The total circulation of English-language publications was put at 3000 … These are astonishing figures for so small a community". It was the era of journalist as publicist, as editors—in England and in colonial India—stamped their personalities on their journals, often entering into vicious attacks against rival editors and officials of the EIC. Hicky bitterly attacked Governor-General Warren Hastings, chief justice of the Supreme Court Sir Elijah Impey and others in the British community in Calcutta. The English journals were mainly non-political in character, sustained by advertising and had the British community as its audience. Besides some criticism of the EIC by mostly anonymous letter writers to the editor, the journals published orders of the colonial government, Indian news, personal news, notes on fashion, extracts from papers published in England, parliamentary reports, poems, newsletters and reports from parts of Europe. Editorials and other content would mainly interest the British community.

If Hicky's journal is better known historically for publication of scandals, scurrilous personal attacks and risqué advertisements selling sex and sin, he was also the first to fight against the colonial government, then almost single-handed, to defend the liberty of the press. He wrote: "Mr Hicky considers the Liberty of the Press to be essential to the very existence of an Englishman and a free G-t. The *subject* should have full liberty to declare his principles, and opinions, and every act which tends to *coerce* that liberty is *tyrannical* and injurious to the COMMUNITY" (Barns 1940, 49, italics and capitals in original; in the days of letter press, "G-t" stood for "Government"). Hicky was soon hounded by Hastings and Impey, fined, imprisoned and his journal closed in March 1782. He died in penury in 1802. He was the first of several editors of English journals to invite the wrath of EIC officials who were wary of the effects of the ideas spawned by the French Revolution in India, and were highly sensitised to any threats to the existing order. By 1800, some journals closed for want of advertising and subscription, while others closed when British editors were deported to England after publishing material that was considered unacceptable by the EIC. Editors who attracted EIC's ire and found themselves on ships back to England included William Duane, editor of *Bengal Journal*, removed as editor and almost deported in 1791, and finally deported as editor of *Indian World* in 1794; Charles Maclean, editor of *Bengal Hurkaru*, deported in 1798; James Silk Buckingham, editor of *Calcutta Journal*, and his assistant, Sandford Arnot, deported in 1823; and C. J. Fair, editor of *Bombay Gazette*, also deported in 1823.

The year 1818 had witnessed developments that catalysed the growth of journalism in an expanding colonial India. As noted above, deportation remained a key instrument to discipline British editors, but the measure could not be applied to editors who were Indians or to Europeans born in India. To remove the anomaly, the Marquess of Hastings, who was governor-general from 1813 to 1823, removed the 1799 censorship and issued a new set of rules in 1818. In a circular to all editors and publishers in Calcutta, he set out guidelines with a view to prevent the publication of topics considered dangerous or objectionable, or face deportation. But his new rules did not possess the force of law as they were not passed into a Regulation in a legal manner, which meant that in practice there were no legal restrictions on the press. The Marquess of Hastings was soon hailed in Calcutta as a liberator of the press. In the same year, the first journals in an Indian language—Bengali—were launched, the precursors of several Indian-language journals in other parts of India. There is a dispute about which was published first, the *Bengal Gejeti* edited by Harachandra Roy with the assistance of Gangakishore Bhattacharya, or *Samachar Darpan*, launched by the Baptist missionaries at Serampore—both were launched in May 1818 (some scholars claim that *Bangal Gejeti* was launched in 1816). The missionaries had earlier launched the monthly *Digdarsan* in April 1818, but due to the missionary context, nationalist historians credit *Bangal Gejeti* as the first journal in an Indian language, but it did not last for more than a year (none of its issues are known to exist). The year 1818 also saw the launch of Buckingham's *Calcutta Journal*, on 2 October, a biweekly of eight quarto pages, which was to come into frequent conflict with EIC and also encourage the growth of the indigenous press by often publishing extracts from the Indian-language journals and commenting favourably on their growth. A Whig, Buckingham propagated liberal ideas and views through his journal that almost reached the record daily circulation figure of 1000 copies. As the editor, he wrote, he conceived his duty to be "to admonish Governors of their duties, to warn them furiously of their faults, and to tell disagreeable truths" (Barns 1940, 95). Setting himself up as a champion of free press, Buckingham saw a free press as an important check against misgovernment, especially in Bengal, where there was no legislature to curb executive authority.

By the beginning of the nineteenth century, a "multifarious culture of the print medium" had come into existence in India:

> It was the first fully formed print culture to appear outside Europe and North America and it was distinguished by its size, productivity, and multilingual and multinational constitution, as well as its large array of Asian languages and its inclusion of numerous non-Western investors and producers among its participants. (Dharwadker 1997, 112)

Print journalism had found a fertile soil in colonial Calcutta, but it also generated near-panic among colonial officials about its potential subversive effect on the army. Expressing "intense anxiety and alarm", Chief Secretary John Adam (1822) wrote in a lengthy minute on the press: "That the seeds of infinite mischief have already been sown is my firm belief". When the Marquess of Hastings sailed for England on 9 January 1823, he was temporarily succeeded as governor-general by John Adam, whose first act was to deport Buckingham to England, which led to the closure of *Calcutta Journal*. Secondly, Adam promulgated a rigorous Press Ordinance on 14 March 1823, which made it mandatory for editors and publishers to secure licences for their journals. To secure the licences, they had to submit an affidavit to the chief secretary under oath. For any offence of discussing any of the subjects prohibited by law, the editor or publisher was liable to lose the licence.

The following sections set out the Indian response to the Press Ordinance, mainly directed by Rammohun Roy (1772–1833), who is less known for his contribution to Indian journalism than for his reformist initiatives in the realm of religion, education and social awareness (in particular, for his campaign to abolish *sati* or widow burning). Considered in hagiographic and nationalistic accounts as the founder of modern India, most of his reformist initiatives were conducted through the technology of print in the form of pamphlets, translations, tracts and journals. He was closely associated with at least five journals: *Bengal Gejeti* (Bengali, 1818), *The Brahmunical Magazine* (English–Bengali, 1821), *Sambad Kaumidi* (Bengali, 1821), *Mirat-ul-Akhbar* (Persian, 1822) and *Bengal Herald* (English, 1829). Roy—easily one of the foremost examples of an "argumentative Indian" (Sen 2005)—often engaged in lengthy debates with Baptist missionaries and used his polemical skills to oppose the Press Ordinance.

Press Ordinance and Two Memorials

Before the Press Ordinance was issued on 14 March 1823, officials in the governor-general's administration were clamouring for legal restrictions on what they saw as "excesses" of the press. In a lengthy minute dated 14 August 1822, John Adam (1822) wrote: "My objection is to the claim of that class of persons to exercise in this country, the privileges they are allowed to assume at home, of sitting in judgement on the acts of Government, and bringing public measures and the conduct of public men, as well as the concerns of private individuals, before the bar of what they miscall public opinion". Another senior official, W. B. Bayley, wrote on 10 October 1822: "Feeling as I do that the Native Press may be converted into an engine of the most serious mischief, I shall … state the grounds on which I consider it essential that the Government should be vested with legal power to control the excesses of the Native as well as the European Press".

The Marquess of Hastings, who had tolerated much criticism from Buckingham and had refrained from taking action, was faced with an increasingly belligerent group of officials, who wanted more powers to clamp down on the press. The Marquess of Hastings finally wrote to London in October 1822 for more such powers, but before any progress could be made on the issue, he returned to England on 9 January 1823. Adam, the senior-most official at the time, took over as the acting governor-general, and as stated above, his first two acts in office were deporting Buckingham to London, and issuing the rigorous Press Ordinance. Under the laws of the time, every new executive measure had to be submitted to the Supreme Court for registration before it could come into force. Adam's Press Ordinance was submitted to the court on 15 March 1823, and two days later, Rammohun Roy and four others submitted a memorial, asking the court to hear objections against it. Besides Roy, it was signed by three Tagores (Chunder Coomar, Dwarkanath, Prosunno Coomar), Hurchunder Ghosh and Gowree Churn Bonnergee.

The memorial discussed in a logical manner the general principles on which the claim of freedom of the press was based in all modern countries, and recalled the contribution Indians had made to the growth of British rule. It created a sensation at the time and came to be described as the "*Aeropagitica of Indian history*" (Collet 1988, 180, italics in original). The memorial pointed out the aversion of Hindus to undertaking an oath because of "invincible prejudice against making a voluntary affidavit, or undergoing the solemnities of an oath". Using the rhetorical strategy of professing loyalty and attachment of the Indians to British rule, the memorialists wrote that they were "extremely sorry" to note that the new restrictions would put a "complete stop" to the diffusion of knowledge, promoting social progress, and keeping government informed about public opinion. It pointed out that the natives "cannot be charged with having ever abused" freedom of the press in the past, and went on to audaciously state:

> Your memorialists are persuaded that the British government is not disposed to adopt the politician's maxim so often acted upon by Asiatic Princes, that the more a people are kept in darkness, their Rulers will derive the greater advantages from them; since, by reference to History, it is found that this was but a short-sighted policy which did not ultimately answer the purpose of its authors. On the contrary, it rather proved disadvantageous to them; for we find that as often as an ignorant people, when an opportunity offered, have revolted against their Rulers, all sorts of barbarous excesses and cruelties have been the consequence … Every good Ruler, who is convinced of the imperfection of human nature, and reverences the Eternal Governor of the world, must be conscious of the great liability to error in managing the affairs of a vast empire; and therefore he will be anxious to afford every individual the readiest means of bringing to his notice whatever may require his interference. To secure this important aspect, the unrestrained Liberty of publication, is the only effectual means that can be employed. And should it ever be abused, the established Law of the Land is very properly armed with efficient powers to punish those who may be found guilty. (Collet 1988, 392–393)

The memorial was read in court, but the judge, Francis Macnaghten, dismissed it, but admitted that before the Press Ordinance was entered or its merits argued in court, he had pledged to the government that he would sanction it. The ordinance was registered in the court on 4 April 1823. The memorial was much appreciated but failed to prevent the ordinance from becoming law. The only other recourse Roy and his group had was to appeal to the King-in-Council in London. Roy then drafted another memorial, more sophisticated in its logic and arguments, and sent copies to Lord Canning (then Foreign Secretary and Leader in the House of Commons) and to the EIC's Board of Control, in London. Over 55 numbered and lengthy paragraphs, Roy repeated the opposition to the Press Ordinance. Describing the second memorial, Collet (1988, 183) wrote: "Its stately periods and not less stately thought recall the eloquence of the great orators of a century ago. In a language and style for ever associated with the glorious vindication of liberty, it invokes against the arbitrary exercise of British power the principles and traditions which are distinctive of British history". Continuing the rhetorical strategy of mixing fulsome praise with caution, warning and criticism, the second memorial recalled world history and put it to the King:

> Men in power hostile to the Liberty of the Press, which is a disagreeable check upon their conduct, when unable to discover any real evil arising from its existence, have attempted to make the world imagine, that it might, in some possible contingency, afford the means of combination against the Government, but not to mention that extraordinary emergencies would warrant measures which in ordinary times are totally unjustifiable, your Majesty is well aware, that a Free Press has never yet caused a revolution in any part of the world because, while men can easily represent the grievances arising from the conduct of the local authorities to the supreme Government, and thus get them redressed, the grounds of discontent that excite revolution are removed; whereas, where no freedom of the Press existed, and grievances consequently remained unrepresented and

unredressed, innumerable revolutions have taken place in all parts of the globe, or if prevented by the armed force of the Government, the people continued ready for insurrection. (Collet 1988, 407)

In parts of the memorial, Roy lectured to the King in polite language on the importance of freedom of the press and its relevance to the continuation of British rule in India. He also reproduced the eight restrictions under the Press Ordinance, and recalled that *Friend of India*, a publication by the Baptist missionaries from Serampore, had appreciated the role of the native press and had stated in a recent issue: "Nor has this liberty been abused by them [the native press] in the least degree". Roy then eloquently pointed out that the Ordinance, issued after Buckingham's deportation to England, gave the impression that the Indian press was being punished for the actions of one individual, and stated: "Yet notwithstanding what the local authorities of this country have done, your faithful subjects feel confident, that your Majesty will not suffer it to be believed throughout your Indian territories, that it is British justice to punish millions for the fault imputed to one individual". A key aspect of the memorial was Roy's recall of Mughal history and the *akhbarat* (newsletters) system instituted during their rule. In two paragraphs (43 and 50), the memorial regretted the new press restrictions, made veiled criticism of British rule and stated:

> Your Majesty is aware, that under their former Muhammadan Rulers, the natives of this country enjoyed every political privilege in common with Mussalmans, being eligible to the highest offices in the state, entrusted with the command of armies and the government of provinces and often chosen as advisers to their Prince, without disqualification or degrading distinction on account of their religion or the place of their birth … Notwithstanding the despotic power of the Mogul Princes who formerly ruled over this country, and that their conduct was often cruel and arbitrary, yet the wise and virtuous among them, always employed two intelligencers at the residence of their Nawabs or Lord Lieutenants, *Akhbar-navees*, or news-writer who published an account of whatever happened, and a *Khoofea-navees*, or confidential correspondent who sent a private and particular account of every occurrence worthy of notice; and although these Lord Lieutenants were often particular friends of near relations to the Prince, he did not trust entirely to themselves for a faithful and impartial report of their administration, and degraded them when they appeared to deserve it, either for their own faults or for their negligence in not checking the delinquencies of their suordinate officers; which shews that even the Mogul Princes, although their form of Government admitted of nothing better, were convinced, that in a country so rich and so replete with temptations, a restraint of some kind was absolutely necessary, to prevent the abuses that are so liable to flow from the possession of power. (Collet 1988, 413, 416–417)

The memorials were an example of the confluence of themes of history, earlier Indian administrations (notably Mughal) and modern ideas, notably the utilitarianism of Jeremy Bentham, with whom Roy had been in touch. Roy cited the intelligence network of the Mughal rules to emphasise the use of various ways of communication to the rulers. At a time of weak international communication, Roy demonstrated remarkable understanding of world politics, and referred to examples to support his opposition to imposing restrictions on the press. The memorials, or public petitions, were addressed to British authorities, but drew on earlier traditions, *akhbarat,* of alerting the ruler to the moral infractions of his servants. In the process, Roy and his co-petitioners reframed the form and substance of the memorials but not its essential purpose that was often used in the past. This confluence of the past and the then colonial present was best exemplified by Roy, who, as Bayly (2004, 293) put it, "made in two decades an astonishing leap from the intellectual status of a late-Mughal state intellectual to that of the first Indian liberal … he independently broached themes that were being simultaneously developed in Europe by Garibaldi and Saint-Simon".

The memorials failed to overturn the Press Ordinance; they were couched in courteous language of the time, but included covert and not-so-covert warnings that the future of British rule in India was in danger if the new rulers did not allow Indians many of the privileges available to people in England. The memorials were seen as a daring act by Roy and his group at a time when expanding colonial rule was marked by arbitrary official decisions, racism, punishment, imprisonment and the rapacious extraction of resources. But Roy took another daring step at the time: closing his Persian journal, and setting down the reasons for doing so in its last edition.

Closure of *Mirat-ul-Akhbar*

In his minute of 10 October 1822, Bayley devoted much attention to the contents of Roy's *Mirat-ul-Akhbar* (Mirror of News) to justify demanding more powers to curb the press. Noting Roy's "known disposition for theological controversy", Bayley recalled an article in the journal on the death of Thomas Middleton, bishop of Calcutta. He wrote: "After some laudatory remarks on his learning and dignity the article concludes by stating that the Bishop having been now relieved from the cares and anxieties of this world, had 'tumbled on the shoulders of the mercy of God the Father, God the Son and God the Holy Ghost'. The expression coming from a known impugner of the doctrine of the Trinity, could only be considered as ironical, and was noticed … as objectionable and offensive". In subsequent issues, Roy went on to defend the article in his style described by Bayley as the "polemical disposition of the editor". On 4 April 1823, the day the Press Ordinance was registered in the Supreme Court and became law, Roy closed *Mirat-ul-Akhbar* in protest. In the final issue, he set out the reasons for doing so:

> Under these circumstances, I, the least of all the human race, in consideration of several difficulties, have, with much regret and reluctance, relinquished the publication of this Paper (*Mirat-ool-Ukhbar*). The difficulties are these:
>
> First—Although it is very easy for those European Gentlemen, who have the honour to be acquainted with the Chief Secretary to Government, to obtain a License according to the prescribed form; yet to a humble individual like myself, it is very hard to make his way through the porters and attendants of a great Personage; or to enter the doors of the Police Court, crowded with people of all classes, for the purpose of obtaining what is in fact, already [? Unnecessary] in my own opinion. As it is written—
>
> Abrooe kih ba-sad khoon i jigar dast dihad
>
> Ba-oomed-I karam-e, kha'jah, ba-darban ma-farosh
>
> (The respect which is purchased with a hundred drops of heart's blood
>
> Do not thou, in the hope of a favour commit to the mercy of a porter).

Secondly—To make Affidavit in an open court, in presence of respectable Magistrates, is looked upon as very mean and censurable by those who watch the conduct of their neighbours. Besides, the publication of a newspaper is not incumbent upon every person, so that he must resort to the evasion of establishing fictitious Proprietors, which is contrary to Law, and repugnant to Conscience.

Thirdly—After incurring the disrepute of solicitation and suffering the dishonour of making Affidavit, the constant apprehension of the License being recalled by Government which would disgrace the person in the eyes of the world, must create such anxiety as entirely to destroy his peace of mind, because a man, by nature liable to err, in telling the real truth cannot help sometimes making use of words and selecting phrases that might be unpleasant to Government. I, however, here prefer silence to speaking out:

Guda-e goshah nashenee to Khafiza makharosh

Roo mooz maslabat-i khesh khoosrowan danand

(Thou O Hafiz, art a poor retired man, be silent,

Princes know the secrets of their own Policy).

I now entreat those kind and liberal gentlemen of Persia and Hindoostan, who have honoured the *Mirat-ool-Ukhbar* with their patronage, that in consideration of the reasons above stated, they will excuse the non-fulfilment of my promise to make them acquainted with passing events.

Once again, the confluence of themes of religion, language, personal honour rooted in the past and the colonial present are evident in Roy's last note to his readers. He invoked Persian couplets to make courteous attacks on the British and the restrictions imposed in the Press Ordinance. He pointed out the differential access Indians and the British had to officials of the Company government, and recalled the embarrassment rooted in religion and tradition faced by Indians to the act of taking an oath. Taken together, even though the two memorials and closing Roy's journal were couched in courteous terms and some rhetoric, they were essentially an act of political defiance, which was delivered in the language and discourse of the new rulers. The opposition to the Press Ordinance won new converts among the British (such as Lieutenant Colonel Leicester Stanhope), and provided a template for future political opposition on other issues, such as the controversial Jury Act, Indian property and labour, the rights of Britons in India, taxes, education and making English the medium of instruction.

Conclusion

Roy closing his journal in protest and the two memorials did not succeed in changing policy, but their significance lies in the ways in which the colonial authorities dealt with the press subsequently. The memorials were much appreciated in England, where Buckingham had continued his campaign in print against the EIC and its exercise of arbitrary powers in India. Lord Amhurst, who took over from John Adam as the governor-general of India in 1823 (he was in office until 1828) did not implement the Press Ordinance rigorously, neither did his successor, Lord Bentinck. The memorials, closure of Roy's journal and Buckingham's activities in London had generated much publicity on the issue of freedom of the press in colonial India, with governors-general choosing to avoid taking major action against the fast growing press. In 1835, it was another acting governor-general, Charles Metcalfe, who, aided by Macaulay, removed Adam's licensing and other restrictions on the press through Act No. XI. By then, the idea of a free press had become a key element of a growing public sphere in Calcutta and elsewhere in colonial India. Metcalfe, who was later penalised by EIC authorities in London for removing the press restrictions, was hailed as a liberator of press and immortalised in Metcalfe Hall, a major landmark in Calcutta, which was built with public subscription in the style of imposing empire architecture in his honour. The press had become a key site of discussion and protest as the Company government introduced new laws and initiatives to govern India. The largely permissive situation for the press continued until the 1857 rebellion, by when opinions and positions had hardened on both sides, as Indian journals openly criticised the British and the EIC imposed new restrictions on the press.

But the press had grown all over colonial India, despite new repressive measures. As Majumdar (1965, 233) put it, "[The] daring act of Rammohan and his five associates marks the beginning of a new type of political activity which was destined to be the special characteristic of India for nearly a century". The significance of Roy's two memorials was highlighted soon after the Round Table Conference was held in London in 1930–1931 to discuss India's future: "It might never have come about had the great Ram Mohan Roy not taken the lead, and three Tagores, a Ghose, and a Banerji, not joined him in the starting the process that led to it" (O' Malley 1941, 198). This forgotten chapter of protest focused on the idea of a free press provides a key insight into the continuation of politics as the dominant theme in Indian journalism today. Politics and political protest occupied the centre-stage in early Indian journalism, and continued during the long freedom struggle, which further entrenched politics as the dominant theme, which continued after independence, up to the present. The form, structure and discourse of politics in Indian journalism has changed, reflecting corresponding changes in political structures and themes, but the symbiotic link between journalism and politics in India has never been in question.

DISCLOSURE STATEMENT

No potential conflict of interest was reported by the author.

NOTE

1. British/Colonial spellings have been used for people and places in the paper.

REFERENCES

Adam, John. 1822. Minute No. 3, British Library, Bengal Public Consultations, P/10/55.
Barns, Margarita. 1940. *The Indian Press: A History of the Growth of Public Opinion in India*. London: Allan & Unwin.
Bayley, W. B. 1822. Minute No. 8, British Library Bengal Public Consultations, P/10/55.
Bayly, C. A. 2004. *The Birth of the Modern World: 1780–1914*. Oxford: Blackwell.
Collet, Sophia D. 1988. *The Life and Letters of Raja Rammohun Roy*. Calcutta: Sadharan Brahmo Samaj.

Dharwadker, Vinay. 1997. "Print Culture and Literary Markets in Colonial India." In *Language Machines: Technologies of Literary and Cultural Production*, edited by Jeffrey Masten, Peter Stallybrass, and Nancy J. Vickers, 108–133. London: Routledge.

Gaonkar, Dilip P. 1999. "On Alternative Modernities." *Public Culture* 11 (1): 1–18. doi:10.1215/08992363-11-1-1.

Majumdar, R. C. 1965. *British Paramountcy and Indian Renaissance. Part II*. Bombay: Bharatiya Vidya Bhavan.

Marshall, P. J. 2000. "The White Town of Calcutta under the Rule of the East India Company." *Modern Asian Studies* 34 (2): 307–331. doi:10.1017/S0026749X00003346.

Mills, J. S. 1924. *The Press and Communications of the Empire'*. London: W. Collins Sons.

O'Malley, L. S. S. 1941. *Modern India and the West: A Study of the Interaction of Their Civilisations*. Oxford: Oxford University Press.

Raichaudhuri, Tapan. 1988. *Europe Reconsidered: Perceptions of the West in Nineteenth Century Bengal*. New Delhi: Oxford University Press.

Sen, Amartya. 2005. *The Argumentative Indian*. London: Allen Lane.

Shaw, Graham. 1981. *Printing in Calcutta to 1800*. London: The Bibliographical Society.

Sonwalkar, Prasun. 2002. "Murdochization of the Indian Press: From By-line to Bottom-line." *Media Culture & Society* 24 (6): 821–834. doi:10.1177/016344370202400605.

Sonwalkar, Prasun. 2014. "Narendra Modi's Victory Compared to '1979 Thatcher Moment' in UK." *Hindustan Times*, June 2.

POPULAR CINEPHILIA IN NORTH INDIA
Madhuri shows the way (1964–78)

Ravikant

Amongst the Hindi film magazines Madhuri *stands out as an engaged, earnest and agenda-driven journalistic intervention. It acted as a crucial bridge, an effective mediator between several disparate segments and stake-holders: the film makers, viewers, stars, fans, state, industry, litterateurs, directors, "Urdu" and "Hindi", music makers, listeners, exhibitors, theatre-patrons, "commercial" and "art" cinema types, regional, national and world cinema-lovers, and so on. It also continued with the ongoing task of educating Hindi readers about the intricacies of the film medium and its evolving history, ran vigorous campaigns advocating adoption of Nagri (Hindi) script for credit-rolls, and identified progressive literature waiting to be scripted; excavated new locations for shooting films, and more generally, invented a new form to narrate in words some of the classics of Hindi cinema. This paper argues that the restraint, irony as well as exuberance evident in its editorial choices, content and design were very much grounded in but not circumscribed by the aspirations of an expanding middle class nurtured on a print universe marked by Hindi nationalistic sensibility of the 1960s and 1970s. All the same,* Madhuri's *unique crowd-sourced campaigns lent a sense of civic identity to its readers, who started clamouring for better sonic, visual and hygienic facilities and comforts at cinema halls.*

Introduction

In the hitherto scarce history of ephemeral Hindi film magazines, *Madhuri* (named so from the sixth issue after its launch as *Suchitra* on the Republic Day, 1964) enjoyed a remarkably robust health in a longish career spanning close to three decades. Reduced to a shadow in translation, it still survives in its new avatar as Hindi *Filmfare*, but I propose to revisit its long founding decade to analyse its effort at finding a foothold and gaining respectability as a family film magazine speaking to a literature-loving north Indian public.[1] Run by a small band of journalists with Arvind Kumar as the editor, the magazine made innovative use of what is today known as crowd-sourcing. It turned its readers into contributors by soliciting comments on a range of issues such as: how happy they were with the films being made and what could be done to improve their quality and "purposefulness", and even more importantly, how good/bad/adequate were the cinema halls in their respective cities/towns/*qasbas*—each named and described in detail, giving us the sense of an expanding cartography of cinematic pleasure and civic desires. Since cinema in South Asia has always been a listening experience too, *Madhuri*'s generous focus on film music, lyrics and story-telling provided a lot of gramophone, radio and audio-tape listeners and recyclers with an instant connect. To absorb, record and comment on the unmistakable echoes of cinema as an ever-changing technology, art, craft, trade and cultural experience, *Madhuri* kept renewing itself in terms of content and design in the entire period under discussion.

"Going to cinema was considered a sin (*qufra*) when I took over as the editor", ruminated Arvind Kumar several decades later (interview with the author, 5 May 2009). And here is his editorial written within two years of its launch:

> Cine-journalism in Hindi has been more or less neglected by its well-educated and highbrow elite. Even cinema has not been completely accepted by our families. Going to movies is taken for a sign of defiance and indiscipline by the elders, and some film makers have only confirmed this belief by making cheap films. Gaining a respectable foothold in this social context was not easy at all for a film magazine.
>
> Cinema has become the most important and essential means of entertainment. So a society would do no good to itself by running away from it. On the contrary, we need to take a deeper interest in order to improve it, and make it worthy of our developing nation. Our youth if armed with a new understanding of cinema may be better equipped to welcome healthy entertainment. In a project like this the role of responsible magazines and journals cannot be overemphasised. I am making an effort to play this role by providing the right kind of information about films. And the kind of reception I have received in the families assures me that I am on the right path. (*Madhuri*, February 11, 1966)

Written in the first-person singular, the editorial was a direct address by the magazine to its readers. In the first place it was a gentle critique of the highbrow and well-educated Hindi elite, familiar from as early as the 1930s (Joshi 2009). Secondly, it was a manifesto of its editorial ambitions. Thirdly, struggling with the entrenched prejudices of the past, it addressed the youth, the next generation. Fourthly, it was not satisfied with the way cinema was, but wanted it to become worthy of the developing nation. All these catchphrases of the 1960s thus projected the picture of a magazine that meant business. Finally, it wanted to be a popular family filmzine, and to that successful end it exercised tremendous self-restraint, so much so that notwithstanding its radical views on several other issues, it could not become as bold as *Filmfare* in the period under study, even though it gradually and cleverly pushed the normative boundaries of permissiveness on or off-screen. To that extent, *Madhuri*'s editorial stance was broadly contoured though by no means limited by the diversity of stances its readership offered, but it was quite sure-footed about the kind of cinema it wanted India to have.

Arvind Kumar recalled that he took its first issue around for feedback to several friends and some big names of the film industry and how V. Shantaram's comment about it being under the undue influence of *Filmfare* struck a chord. So *Madhuri* charted out its own Hindi route. Kumar, an autodidact without a regular higher education, had picked up the skills of printing and publishing as an apprentice typographer at his father's press in Meerut, and had acquired editorial acumen working with a couple of Delhi Press Group magazines such as *Sarita* in Hindi and *Caravan* in English, for which he wrote film reviews (A. Kumar, interview with the author, 7 September 2014; Anurag 2011). He came to Bombay on a call given by the Jains of the Times of India Group, then contemplating the publication of a Hindi film magazine along the lines of *Filmfare*.

Armed with a small team, his friendship with Raj Kapoor via lyricist Shailendra, a resourceful insider Ram Aurangabadkar, and a good *Times of India* infrastructure, Arvind Kumar thus set out on a memorable personal journey lasting for 14 years.[2] Almost immediately it gained the reputation of a dependable magazine for the fast growing number of middle-class households in the big and small urban centres of north India and beyond. By presenting a wholesome fare in terms of content and colourful pages in the form of photographs of film players as blow ups, centre-spreads and even calendars, it became more popular than the other Hindi film magazines, and even its sisterly *Filmfare*.

The lavish pictoriality of a filmzine forces us to look beyond the notion of a middle-class literate readership. In South Asian contexts marked by resourcelessness and a certain cultural habit, sharing has been a norm rather than an exception: from community listening to radio and neighbourhood television watching down to the public phone booths, e-cafes and e-chaupals. So we must imagine a larger itinerant readership at the roadside tea-stalls, barbers' salons, doctors' clinics, public libraries or even the train compartments for *Madhuri*. Part of this readership would simply ogle at the images, unless read to by a helpful friend or stranger. This non-reading readership rarely wrote back, so we have to work with the outpourings of a writerly readership in which the opinionated middle classes disproportionately dominated the proceedings. But Shiv Lal Arya (Nai or barber) from Yevetmal, already on the listening map for sending song requests to radio stations, did after all write back, jolting us out of our lazy assumptions:

> In the issue dated May 29, Raj Mishra of Lucknow writes, "*Madhuri* carries more photographs than matter, which might be of special interest to barbers and teenagers (*chhokras*) ['and certainly not to the enlightened readers']." As far as I can imagine there are barbers in every corner of India, and *Madhuri* is subscribed to in each salon. Once he has read it the barber leaves it for people from all classes visiting the salon to read. On the basis of my experience at "Savita Keshbhusha Griha" I can say that all kinds of people read *Madhuri* with great interest, especially the non-Hindi speaking people. This must be because ordinary people understand its language. The profusion of images in the magazine is matched by the amplitude of [reading] matter. The magazine sheds light on diverse aspects of cinema and provides reviews of the latest films. The distaste of the letter-writer for such a beautiful magazine runs so deep that she has chosen to rage against the barbers, which must have shocked other barbers like me. To say that the barbers are like teenagers in age and wisdom looks like her own original piece of wisdom. But we would like to inform Mishraji that along with *Madhuri* we read literature of the most serious kind, and would like to know from her if she has read Pantji's "Chidambara" or Prasad's "Kamayani"? (*Madhuri*, July 10, 1970, 46)

This no-holds-barred exchange, somewhat typical of the Hindi public domain, is packed with a wealth of socio-cultural meanings. At one level, it showcases the divergent expectations the readers of a hierarchically divided society could pile up on film magazines. At another it demonstrates that the intellectually dominant upper-caste attitude towards cinema had not changed radically; the stock language of derision, however residual, was still in currency. While Miss Mishra betrays an elitist Brahmanical bias in her response to the so-called morally corrupt world of Hindi films, and in the larger text she launches into a cynical attack not only on the editor for his "abject apologia", but the entire industry "without exception" ("and I challenge you to name that exception") for being given to "drinking, womanising, and income tax evasion" before slipping into a generalised casteist and ageist vilification (*Madhuri*, May 29, 1970; May 1, 1970, 46). Little wonder that Arya was shocked and hurt, and to bolster his claim for aesthetic tastefulness he took recourse to a bibliographical terrorism of a high literary kind! His conjecture was right: the morally high-brow "enlightened" position of Miss Mishra was very much sourced from, or at least widely shared by the high literary domain. So he took the battle to where it belonged. All the same, isn't it worth speculating if Miss Mishra was not insinuating a clientèle with a lustful male gaze in some of the public spaces we listed above? Perhaps. One must also note that the editor made a clever selection from a number of responses he must have received to Mishra's uncouth outpourings. In any case, Arya's rebuttal was the one that effectively challenged the elite assumptions about film literacy, on the one hand, as it also reinforced *Madhuri*'s campaign against those who regarded cinema as less than respectable. It thus showcased cinema's, and *Madhuri*'s own, potential outreach.

Making a careful selection from the past and existing popular features and columns of its predecessors, *Madhuri* recycled them under new names. The letters to the editor column dealt strictly with film-related "respectable" queries. Humorous and ironical responses of writers in rival film journals like Baburao Patel (*filmindia*), or anecdotal understatements of the Dehlavi (*Shama-Sushma*) flavours were replaced by cryptic answers by movie icons like I. S. Jauhar, Dev Anand and Mahmood in a chronological succession (Mukherjee 2013). Publishing poetry as caption for the stars' photographs persisted, the critical difference with contemporary *Shama-Sushma* being that *Madhuri* was more inclined towards using Hindi lyrical poetry or even blank verse than Urdu couplets. Urdu came to the magazine mainly via the film lyrics and dialogues, and an ugly debate raged over whether the language of Bombay films be designated Hindi or Urdu when iconic poet and lyricist Sahir Ludhyanvi proclaimed that 97 per cent of the film vocabulary was Urdu, and campaigned for it being given the second state language status in Uttar Pradesh. The editorials were sharp and focused, but the editor wrote an additional column "Chale pawan ki chal" (or "Blows Like a Wind")—borrowed from a philosophical Pankaj Mulick song—to comment on the burning cinematic issues, under the pseudonym Filmeshwar (God of Films). One abiding feature that had traditionally connected the three worlds of music records, oral performance and print—*swarlipi*/notations—and had made an easy transition after the film songs edged out non-film genres into niche occupations from the mid-1930s onwards was a regular. The column with the photographs of the featured lyricist, music director and the singer/s forked into a collectible sub-column called "Raag Madhuri" in which notations of the raga-inspired film songs were described with the beats of instruments used. This had been a speciality of a magazine like *Film Sangeet*, which *Madhuri* happily incorporated, making it a readers' request feature. On the popular side, it published political, social and cultural parodies of popular film songs, written by such veterans as Kaka Hathrasi and Barsanelal Chaturvedi. The trend soon caught on and a slew of excellent parodists emerged from amongst the readers, which beautifully indexed the practice of popular remixing of cinematic content, a paradoxical instance being the sacred "kanvariya" or "Bhagwati Jagran" cassettes and CDs taking off on such ribald items as "choli ke peechhe kya hai?" [what is under the blouse?] in more recent times.[3] Each issue of *Madhuri* published a four-page newspaper "cinesamachar" or cinema news with reports on seminars, awards, musical nights, charity shows, policy statements, trade disputes, strikes, technical innovations, and on the making of very select national and international films. Like *Filmfare*, *Madhuri* had allocated a couple of pages for Hollywood film stories, with colour transparencies mostly of actresses in skimpy attire, which might be understood as a pact of conformity in the home and the world mould, because readers rarely objected to these culturally-offshore-therefore-safe images. Coverage of major national and international film festivals was rigorously pursued in consonance with the magazine's stated policy of promoting serious-realist-meaningful cinema. By contrast, the readers looking for star-related gossip were likely to be thoroughly disappointed as the two columns—"Around the Stars", and "Second Sunday is a Holiday" by Itwarilal that could potentially provide juicy scoops hardly delivered any. Cartoons drawn by a distributed authorship often spoke to the text on the page which could be an ironical take on the "purposeless" run-of-the-mill commercial films, on censors' inconsistent policy, everyday situations about writing for films, history of film making, going to the cinema, watching cinema—the whole film culture. The play of ironical humour must have appealed to the part of the readership still morally ambivalent about for-profit films.

Crowd-sourcing

Madhuri's true editorial acumen, however, lay in the unprecedented amount of contributions it could source from its readers. It headed out to engage with the most articulate sections of society in a series of roving discussions—"Cinema and Society"—on the state of film-making in general. Typically, a local writer or journalist would meet four to six people (students: makers of tomorrow and teachers: makers of the nation's future) asking certain basic questions, such as: how significant was cinema's impact; were they happy with the films being made; what did they expect from cinema, the films they would rate as good, etc. Most respondents predictably expressed unhappiness with the standard of films being made, criticised Hindi films for being obscene, formulaic, repetitive, and full of unnecessary songs and dress changes, and wanted the filmwallas to embrace literary plots and design socially uplifting, realist treatments. The respondents from Kolkata produced overwhelming evidence for good cinema in the literary names of the cinema halls in the city and the linguistic fact of a single word "boi" carrying a double meaning for book and film, as well as the numerous adaptations Bengali film makers had made from the works of litterateurs like Sharatchandra and Tagore.[4] The survey was clearly skewed as we do not see *Madhuri* visiting any non-middle-class household or a semi-public space such as a barber's salon, but the subaltern presence could sometimes be heard behind the respondents' voices. Explaining the delay in opening the door, Mrs. Kalpana of Jamshedpur complained, "Forgive me, our Baisakhu [servant] has gone to see *Haqeeqat* today, and I was taking milk from the milkman at the back door. These servants are so intoxicated on cinema that they do not care for their duties. They watch 3–4 films every month even in these inflationary times and you can hear them singing those juicy songs at work all the time!" (November 5, 1965, 26). The drawing room discussions took a hypocritical, highbrow position which helped *Madhuri* shape its own reformist agenda of making cinema socially useful. For the respondents the films were rarely good, the names were those that we would hear time and again in the Hindi *avant-garde* magazines and souvenir volumes produced on 50, 75 or 100 years of cinema. Thus a whole new cannon of "good" films was also being built through a survey like this.

However, the debate was on with the younger generation coming out in support of the mainstream films. Shyamli Bose of Patna, a student of classical music, found in cinema a repository of folk forms and idioms, and denied any negative energy to cinema. But Mrs. Manjurani Verma, a lecturer who sang *ghazals* by Sahir and Shakeel, pointed out that cinema handed to young men certain songs as legitimate tools to harass women on the street. Indicating its deeply undesirable impact, she also related an apocryphal—for her downright scandalous—tale of a fashionable lady who would take her tailor to see films! A third instance of a science college student, Santosh Singh Thakur, brought out the hypocrisy of such positions rather succinctly, thanks to Rajkamal Choudhary, the celebrated Hindi fiction writer of morally uncertain repute, the man conducting the interview. Thakur admitted the bad influence of cinema, "Go to any room and you will find a student lost in the imaginary, colourful, luxuriant, almost Kashmir-like dreams found in the films, often fantasizing himself in the company of a heroine…" Thakur stopped midway as Choudhary's eyes panned to the wall with Vyjayanti Mala's calendar on the one side and a Kashmiri figure in the shape of Sharmila Tagore sitting with a radio on the other. Thakur blushed "inadvertently" (*Madhuri*, September 24, 1965, 21–22). Another student, Manjushree Sharma, pointed out that cinema entertained the common people, and if they found it good enough, we should not listen to the ivory tower intellectuals. Speaking for herself, she extolled Gemini's old *Chandralekha* for showcasing some thrilling circus feats, *Jhanak Jhanak Payal Baje* for presenting Indian dance in various colourful styles; "*Junglee* made it possible for us to see the beauty of Kashmir for the first time, and *Shahar aur Sapna* made us encounter the complex dilemmas of a metropolitan existence. How can you say that our cinema is neither beautiful nor new?" Gulshan Oberoi of Ujjain was so inspired by *Haqeeqat* that she enlisted herself for the National Cadet Corps (NCC) the very next day (*Madhuri*, February 11, 1966, 31). Yogkar Jha, a student schooled in historical materialism, talked about De Sica's films, and saw in cinema the tool most suited for a post-feudal industrial society that helped the world come closer to us. In general terms one can notice a generation gap in the enthusiasm or lack of it in the respondents and the Delhi discussion was a good example of this (*Madhuri*, September 10, 1965). Admitting an inherent weakness for romantic films and female stars, an unmarried Dr Upreti from Agra loved Meena Kumari in *Chitralekha* and Saira Bano in *Junglee*, and loathed Ashok Kumar as Kumargiri, thought Hindi films should get rid of certain unrealistic conventions such as "showing a hero sing in a jungle with the full orchestra, as if he carried it in his pocket! And how does it happen that the heroine sings at her rooftop, and the hero sitting hundreds of miles away sings along with her!" (*Madhuri*, October 22, 1965, 19–20). One could cite an apocryphal story in response to Dr Upreti's crude realism. S. D. Burman was once asked a hard realist question: where does music come from in an otherwise deserted scene in a film? His characteristic response: from the same source as the camera!

The roving seminar was dynamic also in another sense that the focus of discussion kept changing with location. Dehradoon discussed the possibility of nationalisation of the industry, the thorny question of mindless imitation of the West, and disproportionately lavish budgets splurged on advertising films through Radio Ceylon, posters and itinerant bands and rickshaws, and wondered why Satyajit Ray Moshai did not consider making a Hindi film (*Madhuri*, June 3, 1966, 20–21). Kanpur picked up the purported relationship between cinema and crime, while Mathura appropriately evaluated the genre of *bhakti* films (*Madhuri*, January 28, 1966, 33–34). Depending on the place and the person, the discussion could veer around Bhojpuri, Marathi or Bengali films as well.

Satellite of Cinema in a Hindi Literary Orbit

If the Urdu–Hindi journalism of rival magazine *Shama-Sushma* used Urdu poetry and fiction to create a familiar literary context for localising cinema, Hindi *Madhuri* took recourse to a whole range of old and new poetic forms to accomplish the same objective. Easily remembered compositions from medieval devotional poets were parodied and remixed with film-derived content. For example, a *chaleesa* is a *bhasha* form of Sanskrit devotional prayer (*stotra/stuti*) and cinema merely produced a fresh playing field, a *leelabhumi* as it were, for a new set of avatars in the film players whose achievements and virtuosities were listed in the following "film *chaleesa*" which followed the *tarz*/metre/tune of the most accomplished and popular of all—the *Hanuman Chaleesa*, written by the best-selling Tulsidas. Sample the following lines for the flavour:

> Jai jai Shri Ramanand Sagar, Satyajit sansar ujagar [Victory to Ramanand Sagar, Satyajit [Ray] is known to the whole world]
>
> Dara Singh atulit baldhama, Randhawa jehi bhrata nama [Dara Singh is a powerhouse, Randhawa is his brother]
>
> Dilip "Sangharsh" mein ban Bajrangi, pyar karai Vyjayanti sangi [Dilip played Bajrangi and romanced Vyjayanti [Mala] in Sangharsh]
>
> Mridul kanth ke dhani Mukesha, Vijay Anand ke kunchit kesha... [Mukesh has a sweat voice, while Vijay Anand got curly hair] (Godhra 1972, 15)

For a hagiographic roll call of film celebrities like this, the *chaleesa* is quite representative. Producer-directors, heroes, villains, singers, music directors, item dancers and comedians are all listed here. A triumvirate of heroines are packed up in the all-important concluding couplet, the exception being Meena Kumari, whose death was still fresh in memory, and whose career and persona combined literary and social genres, two clear favourites with the *Madhuri* readers. And it is not a mere celebration via substitution of a single monkey-god by so many film players; the penultimate passage is a tongue-in-cheek critique listing the fair and unfair "rewards" of a career in films—bungalow, car, male and female servants, fan mail, black money, good food and alcohol. Bombay is the place to be in, but the ultimate destination for every film devotee is a pilgrimage to Marilyn Munroe's grave. Notice also how the parodist demands work in the film industry like the saint poets would ask their deities for liberation (*moksha*) from the cycle of birth and death. In other words, the parodist is not singing from an uninterested outsider's high pedestal, he is a devotee like so many other readers of the magazine, wishing to get as close as they can to their idols.

Parodies quite often acquired explicit political overtones: the following one, inspired by the *Sangam* title song, dealt with the eternally excruciating theme of inflation. With one ironical difference that Indira Gandhi does not speak up at all here, unlike the situation in the film where the bagpiper-playing-modern-avatar-of-Krishna-stealing-*gopis*'-garments Raj Kapoor blackmails Vyjayanti Mala into a u-turn: her initial emphatic "no" (*nahin, nahin, nahin*) becomes a "yes" (*hoga, hoga, hoga*) in the end:

> Bol Indira Bol
>
> Rising price of rice, and rising price of wheat
>
> Tell us Indira, if the prices will go down or not!
>
> Hours I spend in the ration shop everyday
>
> The boss invariably scolds me on the delay
>
> Will these clashes ever come to an end or not
>
> Tell us Indira, if the prices will go down or not!
>
> We live to die, like the goat in the abattoir
>
> On each breath we take, kindly load tax one more

Won't you breathe easy, if half the people are no more?

Tell us Indira ... (Shukla 1967, 10)

Modern lyrical literature too was generously deployed to domesticate cinema. Old and new Hindi lyricists came together in the print versions of the poetry meets on festive occasions, so the readers could watch the stars playing Holi or lighting lamps while reading their favourite poets in the same issue. It was a clever attempt at creating a common platform for cultural identification for three discursively disparate and differentially glamorous domains of the star, the literary/film poet and the amphibian reader.

Madhuri also worked hard to dispel the misapprehensions about cinema amongst Hindi littérateurs by organising round tables on "the status of writers in Hindi films" (August 29, 1975) or on the differential formal features between Hindi literary lyrics and film lyrics (June 2, 1967). Similarly, some prominent ones like Pant, Bachchan and Dinkar were invited to watch films and record their experiences (June 2, 1967; February 24, 1967). It was natural for *Madhuri* to provide generous coverage to the literary adaptations such as *Teesri Kasam* (Renu), *Usne Kaha Tha* (Guleri), *Uski Roti* (Mohan Rakesh) and *Sara Akash* (Rajendra Yadav). Since the film makers often complained of lack of good stories, and since the mountain had steadfastly refused to go to Mohammed, the magazine ran a series on the classical and new fictional works it thought film-worthy in the desperate hope that they would be filmed.

Cinematic Civic Consciousness

By all accounts, cinema halls continued to grow in number in the post-independence period but there was no proportionate improvement in the viewing conditions, comforts or basic conveniences offered by them.[5] As Krishna Shah's film *Cinema Cinema* (1979) was to show, even the exhibitors did not treat their clients with much respect till the late 1980s, which in a way mirrored the larger social attitude. *Lathi* (baton) charge by the police or the hall management, the people jumping queues, jostling against or riding over each other's bodies to get tickets, black marketing, stinking toilets, cat calls in the theatre—these were scenes so generic that we would not even notice. The halls themselves were often ramshackled makeshift arrangements, modified godowns or cold storages, with creaky rickety seats infested with bloodsucking bugs and mosquitoes, and the roofs covered with tarpaulin, asbestos or tin. The insides were equipped with run-down second-hand projectors, sound boxes and torn, faded or patchy screens. Power cuts were routine and the generator took time to restore the supply, giving the phrase "cinema of interruptions" an entirely different purchase (Gopalan 2002). Spoilt as we have been by the luxurious, royal comforts of the multiplex cinema halls, it is not easy for us to imagine that the people watched films sitting for all three hours on carpets or wooden or iron benches without backrests, sweating all the way in sultry conditions. Smokers could smoke anywhere they pleased, paan or tobacco chewers could spit into every possible corner, and viewers at large could sit in any possible position they fancied. Might was often right, and rogue men walked with a swagger, with their collars up, brushing meek men, and groping women on the way. In short, going to the cinema at least in the small towns of north India in the 1970s and 1980s was nothing less than an adventure, rife with the possibility of being molested, assaulted, humiliated or at least disgusted. The Upahaar cinema fire tragedy with 53 deaths and 103 injured made for shocking news in the capital of India in 1997, so we can imagine the state of safety and security in the rest of the country in the 1960s.[6]

It was this underclass predicament of the cine-goers against which *Madhuri* raised a systematic and thorough public campaign lasting for the entire period under discussion.[7] The obduracy on the part of cinema owners must have been really strong and the government will equally fickle for the unfair arrangement to have lasted for as long as it did. Going by NDTV anchor Raveesh Kumar's (2010) blog report on what he called *khomcha*plex in the suburbs of Delhi, such conditions might still be prevalent in some godforsaken parts or even in the backyards of the shiny multiplexes we go to. The inspiration for *Madhuri*'s campaign seems to have come from the readers themselves whose complaints appear first in trickles in the letters to the editor column. Very soon the frequency rose to torrential proportions, and then *Madhuri*, alert as ever, grabbed the opportunity to formalise it as a column, following a special comprehensive issue on the history of cinema halls and their current state in different parts (June 30, 1967). To get a sense of travails the cine-goers have historically undergone, let us go through a selection from these hilariously ironical reports sent in by the readers.

From Chakradharpur in Bihar somebody wrote that betel leaf stains and peanut shells were a common site in the theatre and people lit up their cigarettes and *bidis* the moment the "No Smoking" sign came up. The Films Division documentaries were invariably in English and the people responded to nature's calls just as the national anthem played. In the same issue, the news from Hoshangabad read that somebody had converted a warehouse into a cinema hall, providing no drinking water, but free water could be had by buying food. The letter writer made a modest appeal for disinfectants being sprayed at least once a month, and the toilets be kept clean, and the waiting period be made a little comfortable by facilitating sitting lounges. Jhansi said that in a population of approximately a quarter of a million, there were as many as seven cinema halls in the town, but all but one were in complete disarray with tattered seats and yellowing screens; the audience jeered "kaun hai be [Who is hell is that]" or whistled at the power cuts or breaks in reels. The gatekeeper sold tickets informally, and flexed muscles if objected to; the parking was a good place to get tickets, only if you parked your cycle there. Films—English or Hindi—took their own sweet time in coming to this town, and if the concerned authorities did not act, warned the revolutionary resident of the town of the Rani Lakshmibai, the local people would have to quit watching films altogether. A resident of Bikaner boasted of three cinema halls, but felt uncomfortable with one adjacent to a college, with the queues of the ticket-seekers spilling over to the road and the noise into the college premises, disrupting the classes. Even the seats in the first class were designed with sadistic intentions, just as the air conditioning —"it was better to stand in the sun"—and there was absolutely no cleanliness on the hall campus. The balcony in the other cinema hall was worse than the first class, "The viewer, immersed in the film suddenly feels a sting, when he looks around he finds a rodent in the seat. Little wonder: there are several rat-holes in the hall" (*Madhuri*, September 8, 1967, 21).

A film-goer from Sardar Shahar complained that the entrance was really narrow, and two pillars stood right between the audience and the screen. The horrible acoustics were competitively matched by the loud noises from the fans. When it rained it poured right into the hall, and the chairs had lost at least one of their arms or feet, and even the back rests. Getting the licence for a new hall was not easy. Darbhanga reported that three out of four halls were simply not fit for the higher classes, the National Talkies being a pigeonhouse. People just barged in and ordered tickets right from their seats. At the screening of *Mera Saya*, a shadow of the rod of the fan fell over the screen, and such being the nature of the film, we kept waiting for some diegetic secret to unravel. "This is however not a laughing matter. Who will solve these problems—the government or the managers? I am afraid none, because their coffers are getting filled in any case. Boycotting the cinema hall seems to be the only way." A viewer expressed his anguish with fellow viewers after what he saw during an *April Fool* show in Gurdaspur, "People surpass all moral limits by raising a hullabaloo over love scenes. That is the reason why rarely do gentlemen venture out with their mothers and sisters ... The doors of the hall are left open during the national anthem, so people sneak out and the ones remaining inside either scratch themselves all over or yawn endlessly ... The good successful films that come to some other parts of the Punjab at the beginning of the year reach here by the end, with the result that we get to see the Republic Day News Reels by the Independence Day! And as can be expected we still wait for *Anupama* and *Aaye Din Bahar Ke*." According to a report from Khadagpur in West Bengal, during *Aai Milan ki Vela* our reporter was dumbstruck at the beating received by Dharmendra at the hands of Rajendra Kumar because the projectionist had run the reels in reverse order resulting in a cause–effect confusion—as the "subsequent" reel showed, the former had kidnapped Saira Bano! (*Madhuri*, December 29, 1967, 22).

A writer came back from Ara to say:

Had gone to Ara for the vacations. Was really upset with the apathy of the management in the cinema hall there. Tickets are for sale at the paan shop nearby while the people line up in vain at the counter. A romantic scene brings out the worst cacophony of shouts and whistles. There is no fixed time for the film to begin. If an officer is to visit with his family, the film will begin only after their arrival. And young fellows are in such a hurry to get inside that they often barge into the family suits. (*Madhuri*, December 29, 1967)

The scene looks like a straight lift from David Dhawan's *Raja Babu*, in which a rich and spoilt young brat Govinda roams about in a plumy red Enfield Bullet with his sidekick Shakti Kapoor, and when they reach late for the show, he makes the projectionist rewind the film, and goes on to insist on rewinding his choicest scenes, the protest by the audience notwithstanding. That the real small-town *babus* [bureaucrats] would not hesitate in throwing their weight around impervious of the inconvenience caused to the people they were meant to serve is borne out by several other accounts as well. It could be worse, as another reader complained, several years down the line, during The Emergency, when the movie was stopped after 45 minutes, only to be rewound for the local Superintendent of Police and after several balcony seats were vacated to accommodate his entourage (*Madhuri*, November 21, 1975, 55).

Also the big cities did not always offer narratives substantially different from the small towns:

Some of the old Delhi cinema halls are in a horrible condition. The women here are privileged only in one sense that they get tickets rather easily. Enter inside and what you see is that people at the back are resting their feet, as a matter of their right, on the front seats. The audience chitchats about their domestic worries even while the film is on. If you forbid them they would start a quarrel, and sitting as you are with your mother and sister, you would not want to attract undue attention. And hear them go berserk with choicest expletives when a love scene comes along. To say nothing of the wolf-whistles that look like preloaded in sync with the background music. They would not let an opportunity of molesting a woman go by. All this happens because the audience in the cinema hall wants a two-way entertainment. Not even a tolerant person will like watching films in such an ambience. (*Madhuri*, December 29, 1967, 22)

A lot of these letters, it is obvious, were as much about the "uncouth" nature of public male behaviour in a common public space such as the cinema hall. What the complainants failed to see was that the show in the hall was quite simply an extension of the shows available outside—whether a *Ramleela* (musical performance around the Rama story), *yagna* (a fire sacrifice) or a *mujra* (peformance by professional dancers). That is one way in which one can explain the widely reported incidence of the audience throwing coins at the *Jai Santoshi Maa* screenings. Or for that matter, the ritual of worshipping the television screens during *Ramayana* telecasts in the 1980s. This is still benign and innocent, ridiculous to some, but still understandable. What about the wolf-whistles and other abominable acts the complainants felt justifiably incensed about? Part of the explanation lay in the complainants' own hypocrisies. We cannot help noticing that all of them, without fail, went to cinema with mothers and sisters! Clearly, the middle-class men had not yet developed the language of heterosexual companionship. It is also borne out by the memoirs of going to cinema in the 1980s in Bihar, in which young women were ritually taken to the cinema by their brothers-in-law, not without considerable anxiety from the matriarchs in the household (V. Kumar 2013) The *jeeja-saali* relationship represented that liminal zone where family norms were relaxed just a wee bit; a younger brother was still sent along on double duty of the chaperon and the watchful eye. The publicness of the cinema hall gave the elders added assurance that things could not go really too far. From the other end of the spectators' spectrum, the atomised individual, or even a youth collective in a male-bonding situation, felt liberated enough in the darkness of the hall to let their suppressed steam out the moment they saw in public, on the screen that is, what was not permissible in family situations. So the middle-class invocation of the asexual family (mother, sister) of the *Madhuri* letters represent only the flip side of the same coin. Suppression and outlet are not eternal antonyms, but determined by context and company.[8]

In any case, *Madhuri*, the middle-class film magazine which wanted to be popular in the family while educating the youth, had to take up the cause of better cinema halls, and in the effort it exhibited the tireless optimism of a believing activist. It did want these complaints to reach out to the last man, to use a gendered term. Also it seems from the odd letters praising a rare cinema hall, or the management writing back to the magazine, and sometimes action in the shape of the suspension of the licence of Bombay's Novelty, that at least some of the concerned authorities were listening (*Madhuri*, August 3, 1973). Theatres in bigger towns at least did get better with time: the provision of enclosed spaces like balcony, dress circle, boxes, and the presence of bouncers and separate waiting areas for women cordoned them off from the rogue male gaze and touch. Ashok Cinema in Patna, self-styled "The Pride of Patliputra", was widely acknowledged as the ideal family hall not only because it put up social films, but enforced the civic norms *that Madhuri's* readers were clamouring for. Several cinema halls emerged as architectural wonders and exemplars of good public behaviour in the period under study, so much so that visitors to those cities also went to see those halls only to return with celebratory accounts.[9]

Conclusion

"Perhaps [the film magzines] have been neglected because they seem too trivial, not about films at all, but consisting instead of stories of the exciting and scandalous lifestyles of the stars of the film world presented in a manner guaranteed to titillate bored, middle-class metropolitan housewives", lamented Rachel Dwyer (1993, 253) in the early 1990s, while S. V. Srinivas referred to some early struggles to democratise the film exhibition space in class and caste terms in south India. *Madhuri*'s own efforts in the 1960s and 1970s in the north suggest that in order to wash the social stigma attached to the film world, it pitched the category of "family" as the principal addressee to win the confidence of the critical and articulate sections with morally high-strung stances towards cinema. Scandal or gossip could not have been the agenda for such a project, so it took recourse to what Neepa Majumdar (2009) has labelled "reticence and literary innuendo" as stylistic strategies for the journalism of the pre-independence period. Literature was profusely used to package and naturalise the cinematic content, including colourful images of the film players, and campaigns for Nagri credits were used to assure the Hindi-reading public that the magazine was actually working towards extending the frontiers unconquered by Hindi. All the same, *Madhuri* insisted on the cine-viewers' democratic and civic rights, and deployed their energy to shape a film culture that was at once socially responsible and realist in a nationalist sense.

DISCLOSURE STATEMENT

No potential conflict of interest was reported by the authors.

ACKNOWLEDGEMENTS

The author would like to thank the following for their help, hospitality, and wisdom: staff at NFAI, Pune, colleagues at CSDS; Prabhat, Sanjeev, Saumya, Vibhas, Karunakar, Pankaj and Vandana Raag, Sangeeta and Rajesh Ranjan, Piyush Daiya and Shahid Amin. The usual disclaimers apply.

NOTES

1. One of the pioneers amongst film scholars writing on film journalism through *Stardust*, Rachel Dwyer (1993, 253), is simply inaccurate about *Madhuri* when she says, "Filmfare had a Hindi version (*Filmfare Madhuri Samahit*) from 1964 but it was not very successful and soon ceased publication". This name was given to the magazine in the 1990s, just before it closed down after a successful run. See my article (Ravikant 2011) for a fuller account of *Madhuri*'s stellar contribution in shaping the film culture in north India. To be sure, film scholars have always used film magazines, especially *filmindia* and *Filmfare* as sources, and in spite of some recent efforts made by Debashri Mukherjee (2013, 2014) and Neepa Majumdar, film journalism is yet to have an independent monograph-length study in English, though survey essays have kept appearing on what may be called jubilee occasions of cinema in India; Ramchandran (1985), Shrivastava (1976) and Murai (2013) are good examples. Although Lalit Joshi (2009) made a notable start, the wealth of *bhasha* film journalism is yet to be explored fully.

2. The issue dated June 2–18, 1978 was the last one edited by him and appropriately enough it has Raj Kapoor on a photoframed cover with the story, "Why do I make films?" See also Arvind Kumar (2013).
3. There are examples galore in Hindi films of parodies based on earlier film songs. *Johar in Bombay* (Shantilal Soni, 1967) showcases one such medley of four different *mukhras* in Rafi's own voice parodying "teri pyari pyari surat ko kisi ki nazar na lage [May your lovely face be protected from evil eye]". *Madhuri*'s film review took note of the parodies in the film (see "Parakh", September 7, 1967, 35; also Manuel 1993).
4. *Madhuri*, July 30, 1965, 11–12. The teachers of Chandigarh too praised Bengali films. Literary critic Indernath Madan said he could not sit for more than 15 minutes in a film show and one respondent held cinema responsible for the rise in drinking habits among the girls (*Madhuri*, December 17, 1965, 27–28).
5. According to the figures presented in the Government Annual Reports, there was a steady increase in the permanent as well as touring cinema facilities; from 2807 in 1956, the total number had almost trebled to 7588 in 1972. Yet, *Madhuri*'s readers often cited the demographic figures from their own towns to suggest inadequacy in the sheer number of halls that could cater to the rising local demands.
6. See http://en.wikipedia.org/wiki/Uphaar_Cinema_fire
7. S. V. Srinivas (1999) mentions some early journalistic campaigns for caste-equality in terms of the non-Brahmin audience's entry into the cinema halls in south India for a period as early as the 1940s. His argument that the democratic potential that cinema represented in terms of public co-habitation cutting across caste lines had to be actually fought for is well taken, even though we do not see much of caste conflict in the pages of *Madhuri*.
8. This came to me while watching *Peepli Live* (Anusha Rizvi, 2010) in Pune, in an area inhabited by software programmers. Each time the rustic characters in the film used those raw expletives, a part of the audience burst out. It was obvious that the film was regurgitating in them a reconnect with a suppressed and linguistically detached past, and they could not help but laugh uncontrollably, otherwise a taboo in those sanitised weatherproof buildings they worked in.
9. Sanjeev Kumar (2013) has recorded the excitement of growing up in the neighbourhood of a cinema hall.

REFERENCES

Anurag. 2011. "Rukna Mera Kam Nahin [There is No Stopping Me]." http://lekhakmanch.com/2011/01/16/; and Lagan se kiye Sapne Sach [I Worked Hard to Realise My Dreams]. http://lekhakmanch.com/2011/01/17/.

Dwyer, Rachel. 1993. "Shooting Stars: The Indian Film Magazine *Stardust*." In *Pleasure and the Nation: The History, Politics, and Consumption of Public Culture in India*, edited by Rachel Dwyer and Christopher Pinny, 247–285. Delhi: OUP.

Godhra, Virendra Singh. 1972. "Film Chaleesa." *Madhuri*, 15 September.

Joshi, Lalit. 2009. "Cinema and Hindi Periodicals (1920–47)." In *Narratives of Indian Cinema*, edited by Madhu Jain, 19–52. New Delhi: Primus Books.

Kumar, Arvind. 2013. "Raj Kapoor aur mere Sangam ki vah Shaam [That Evening of Sangam with Raj Kapoor]", *Naya Path: Hindustani Cinema ke Sau Baras*, January-June, 309–314.

Kumar, Raveesh. 2010. "Khomchaplex: Cinema ka naya Adda [Khmochaplex: A New Avenue for Cinema]." http://naisadak.blogspot.in/2010/10/blog-post_13.html.

Kumar, Sanjeev. 2013. "Dastan-e-Vaishali [Narrating Vaishali Cinema Hall]." *Naya Path: Hindustani Cinema ke Sau Baras*, January-June. 322–333.

Kumar, Vineet. 2013. "Cinema Vahi jo Jeejaji Dikhayein." *Naya Path: Hindustani Cinema ke Sau Baras*, 343–345.

Majumdar, Neepa. 2009. *Wanted Cultured Ladies Only: Female Stardom and Cinema in India, 19302–1950s*. Chicago: University of Illinois Press.

Manuel, Peter. 1993. *Cassette Culture: Popular Music and Technology in North India*. New York: OUP.

Mukherjee, Debashree. 2013. "Notes on a Scandal: Writing Women's Film History against an absent Archive." *Bioscope* 4 (1): 9–30.

Mukherjee, Debashree. 2014. "Creating Cinema's Reading Publics: The Emergence of Film Journalism in Bombay." In *No Limits: Media Studies from India*, edited by Ravi Sundaram, 165–198. Delhi: Oxford University Press.

Murai, Ram. 2013. "Film Patrikaon ka Itihas." *Naya Path: Hindustani Cinema ke Sau Baras*, January-June, 349–354.

Gopalan, Lalitha. 2002. *Cinema of Interruptions: Action Genres in Contemporary Indian Cinema*. London: British Film Institute.

Ramchandran, T. M. 1985. "Film Journalism in India." In *70 Years of Indian Cinema (1913–1983)*, edited by T. M. Ramachandran, 309–315. Bombay: Cinema India-International.

Ravikant. 2011. "Hindi Film Adhyayan: Madhuri ka Rashtriya Rajmarg [Hindi Film Appreciation: Madhuri takes the National Highway]." *Lokmat Samachar Deep Bhav*, 184–189. Reproduced online at http://kafila.org/2011/12/05/.

Shukla, Shrilal. 1967. "Itna Mehenga Genhun [Fancy Price of Wheat]." *Madhuri*, September 22, p. 10.

Shrivastava, Bachchan 1976. "Filmi Patrakarita [With additional photographs]." In *Hindi Patrakarita: Vividh Aayam*, edited by Dr. Ved Pratap Vaidik, 312–321. New Delhi: National Publishing House.

Srinivas, S. V. 1999. "Gandhian Nationalism and Melodrama in the 30s' Telugu Cinema." *Journal of the Moving Images* Autumn (1): 14–36.

A MEDIA NOT FOR ALL
A comparative analysis of journalism, democracy and exclusion in Indian and South African media

Shakuntala Rao and **Herman Wasserman**

This paper provides a comparative analysis between the media of India and South Africa, two emerging regional economic powerhouses and emerging democracies. The analysis is macro. The paper describes and analyzes media content and journalism practices in each country and how Indian and South African media have given limited attention to the deep divisions—centered around class, gender, race, and caste—which mark day-to-day life in each society. Consequently, we conclude, that delegative democracy, characterized by the exclusion of the voices of the poor and marginalized, is perpetuated by a globalized, liberalized, and privatized media.

Introduction

One is often referred to as the world's largest democracy, while the other is often celebrated as an example of a country that managed to overcome centuries of colonial and racial oppression to make a peaceful transition to democratic rule. Both these countries also boast of vibrant and independent media. However, India and South Africa continue to share the challenges of social, political, and economic inequality that are characterized by widespread poverty, which raises questions about the access to and participation of the majority of the population in the mediated public sphere.

For all its limitations, India remains the world's largest constitutional democracy with a functioning parliament, a free press, numerous political parties, and free elections for which millions of citizens turn out to vote. Furthermore, democracy has served India well because it has provided the glue that holds together this polyglot nation that has a population of over a billion people, 20 major languages, and an impenetrable checkerboard of identities. The dominant issue in India is no longer whether democracy can survive but whether it can become a meaningful way for diverse sections of society to exercise collective influence over public decisions that affect their lives. There are constant concerns about the "quality" of India's democracy, as exemplified by Zakaria's (2004, 22) epithet, "Democracy is flourishing, liberty is not," a view widely shared by intellectuals and policy-makers. What we find in India is a form of governance that deliberately combines the rhetoric of liberal democracy with illiberal rules of religion and caste. For example, Zakaria notes that although regular and competitive elections are held, which qualifies the country as an electoral democracy, the everyday practices of the state are marked by arbitrariness and abuses (28). The challenge for Indian journalists today is the rise of private media, which comes with its own set of constraints. Some media organizations totally surrender to market forces by sensationalizing news and falling to the lowest common denominator of reporting. Big advertising and circulation revenues have increasingly interfered with good investigative journalism and at times have prevented news media from reporting negative news to protect commercial interests. Yet new investigative techniques and technologies, such as hidden cameras and surreptitious taping, have allowed journalists and media organizations to hold politicians accountable and to reassert the general belief that the information so gained would benefit the larger public.

In post-apartheid South Africa, the mediated public sphere is determined to a large extent by the forces of capital. Although the media now enjoy constitutionally guaranteed freedom, and debate is much more open and critical than was ever allowed under the restrictive conditions of the apartheid state, the dominance of commercial media over public service and community media has implications for the depth and quality of democracy. The fact that commercial imperatives largely circumscribe the terms of engagement between citizens to those interactions which yield commercial value means that participation in democratic deliberation in the public sphere remains limited. The media may position itself as a watchdog over the young democracy, but because audiences with commercial value hold sway, the issues on the media's agenda are largely informed by what Friedman (2011, 107) called a "view from the suburbs."

We define India and South African democracies, to use O' Donnell's (1994, 56) phrase, as "delegative democracies" where elected officials are held accountable only vertically (by voters every few years) but not horizontally, where autonomous institutions within or without the government do not adequately or effectively monitor their conduct and punish wrongdoing. In delegative democracies, horizontal accountability is "extremely weak or non-existent," and elected presidents or prime ministers rule in highly personal, paternalistic, and majoritarian fashion, with few effective constraints on their exercise of constitutional authority. Formal political institutions (e.g., judiciary and legislative) and media are rendered weak, and governance rests "on the premise that whoever wins election is thereby entitled to govern as he or she sees fit," constrained only by the practical reality of terms of office (57). Delegative democracies are prone to high levels of corruption and clientism and are less effective at overcoming protracted economic, material, and social problems.

A comparison between media systems and journalism practices in these two countries is justified not only on the basis of economic and political similarities, but also because of their shared history of colonialism and migration, which has resulted in a presence of the respective countries in each other's media. South African's Indian diasporic community is one of the largest in the world, and reporting on India can therefore be expected (Hofmeyr and Williams 2009, 5). The economic relations between the two countries and public policies aimed at supporting interaction between them attest to their position as middle-ranking economies in the Global South with strong traditions of public debate, press freedom, and vibrant civil societies (6). It is not unusual to see appearances of South African sports personalities on Indian television, just as it is common to read about and watch Bollywood film stars and celebrities in South African media. Such political, economic, and cultural intermingling and commonalities increasingly necessitates comparison.

India and South Africa Embrace (Media) Globalization: Unshackling the Private Sector

India's post-1991 rapid economic reforms and global integration have helped the economy grow at more than 6 percent per year, on average, since 1992. This has laid to rest the ghost of the anemic "Hindu rate of growth" of 3.5 percent under which India seemed perennially trapped from the early 1950s to the early 1990s (Rao 2008, 193). If, as expected, India maintains this growth momentum over the next several years, it will make the country's $80 billion economy (the tenth largest in the world, third largest in Asia) into the fifth largest in the world by 2020. South Africa, although recently overtaken by Nigeria as the biggest African economy, still has the largest gross domestic product (GDP) per capita on the continent—three times that of Nigeria. And although South Africa's growth rate, at 1.9 percent in 2013, is much lower than Nigeria's 6.4 percent (Bisseker 2014), it has better infrastructure and financial services sector. As part of the BRICS (Brazil, Russia, India, China, and South Africa) grouping of emerging states, South Africa also has an influential position in a new geopolitical alignment. These two countries, in post-liberalization and post-apartheid systems, have wholeheartedly embraced a globalization characterized by an intensification of industrial growth, reduced barriers for multinational companies, free trade, and high-velocity and high-intensity communication interaction.

In a high-growth era, the expansion of Indian media has been spectacular. In the aftermath of the collapse of the Soviet Union in the late 1980s, the government of then-Prime Minister P. V. Narasimha Rao was faced with a fiscal crisis that forced them to introduce policy changes that relaxed restrictions on multinational corporations; such companies in turn were quick to invest in the Indian media market. The arrival of international, satellite-based television—with the debut in India of CNN International in 1991 as the young network covering the first Gulf War—signaled an onslaught from the skies that radically changed the Indian media landscape. A few months later, Hong Kong-based Star TV, a subsidiary of News Corporation, began broadcasting five channels into India using the ASIASAT-1 satellite. Between 1991 and 1995, several Indian satellite-based television services were launched, most prominent among them being Zee TV and Sony TV. As a result, the Indian broadcast media economy underwent a dramatic change. The sale of television sets increased at a nominal rate of 13.9 percent from 2005 to 2010—a period that saw India emerge as the third-largest cable television-viewing audience in the world, after China and the United States, with more than 130 million cable television households by the end of 2013. Having previously depended for their news solely on Doordarshan, the state-owned and state-operated television network, post-reform Indian audiences have been able to choose from among hundreds of 24-hour news channels (Mehta 2008; Thomas 2014). The Indian Information and Broadcasting Ministry today boasts of more than 800 cable channels available for audiences, of which roughly 300 are around-the-clock, all-news channels that provide news-based programming in multiple languages. In addition to this widespread and expanding access to broadcast media, newspaper circulation in India has remained robust, with daily circulation of various publications totaling some 330 million copies. A staggering 750 million people—approximately 75 percent of the population—have access to mobile phones, a figure second only to China (Parthasarthy et al. 2012). India has entered an era of intense media saturation as consumers are increasingly able to access global and satellite television, the internet, social networking services, and the ever-proliferating new media and technologies that now co-construct and disseminate major events as they unfold.

The majority of media in India is now privately owned, and ownership is increasingly concentrated in the hands of a few. "Despite impressive numbers of publications, radio stations and television channels, the media in India is possibly dominated by less than a hundred large groups or conglomerates, which exercise considerable influence on what is read, heard, and watched," writes Guha Thakurta (2012). Liberalization and privatization has concerned critics. "In the absence of cross-media ownership laws, private media companies use their media holding to lobby for their non-media business interests," writes Guha. "Some large media groups have been able to diversify their business activities, thanks to the profits generated by their media business." Owners of private media companies are not only politically well-connected but, because of such connections, have been able to build subsidiary business interests in sectors as varied as aviation, hotels, shipping, steel, education, automobiles, textiles, information technology, and real estate (see the article in this issue by Saeed 2015). For example, the Dainik Bhaskar group, which in 1958 ran a single edition of a Hindi newspaper from Bhopal in the central state of Madhya Pradesh, as of 2012 has a market capitalization of $133 million, owns seven newspapers, two magazines, and 17 radio stations, and has a significant presence in the printing, textiles, petroleum, real estate, and power-generation industries (Guha Thakurta 2012).

Similarly, in South Africa the end of apartheid saw the demise of an erstwhile strong anti-apartheid alternative newspaper sector and the increased dominance of commercial media. Although regulatory frameworks that were adopted with the rise of democracy made provision for a three-tiered media system—public, commercial, and community—the public and community sectors remain beset by problems of funding, management, and constant political interference. Commercial media has benefited greatly from the new democratic and capital-friendly environment, which not only opened up new markets domestically—for instance, the rise of a black middle-class consumer market that provided the readership for the rapid growth and huge commercial success of new tabloid newspapers (Wasserman 2010)—but also allowed South African media companies to break out of their isolation and penetrate new markets on the African continent and abroad. For instance, the South African company of Naspers has profited significantly from its investment in the Chinese social media platform, TenCent (Steyn 2012), alongside investments in Brazil, India, Russia, and elsewhere. While the rapid growth of commercial media, including digital satellite television and online media, indicate to some extent the vibrancy of the South African media industry, the major growth areas remain limited among those who can either pay for access or those who are viewed as lucrative constituents for advertisers. The public and community broadcasting tiers, which were meant to provide a counterbalance to commercial media, have been less robust in the first 20 years after democracy. The public broadcaster, the South African Broadcasting Corporation (SABC), has been beset by allegations of political interference, mismanagement, and corruption. Moreover, the public broadcaster also relies on revenue from advertisements as the license fee and government subsidy is not enough to support its operations. While the Media Diversity and Development Agency has been established to support community media, many of these smaller outlets struggle to remain sustainable or to compete with their commercial counterparts. The result is that while the South African media industry has grown in scope and reach since the end of apartheid, the mediated public sphere in the broader sense is still marked by significant exclusions. In India, Doordarshan, like SABC, has been running at a loss since the late 1990s, some estimate a loss of $1 billion in five years. Highly subsidized by the state, Doordarshan has lost most of its urban and middle-class viewers. It is often perceived as a mouthpiece of the ruling government and seen as catering to the lowest of the socioeconomic sections. Such audiences do not appeal to advertisers, and instead of emerging as the next BBC or Al-Jazeera, Doordarshan is now perceived as a "dead channel" (Guha Thakurta 2014).

The rapid rise of the Indian and South African private media, as well as the simultaneous decline of public broadcasting, raises concerns about how such a media environment could foster democratic values.

Inequality in Society (and in Media)

All countries have different inherent inequalities with which they must contend. India, like South Africa, is faced with a unique cocktail of lethal divisions and seemingly irresolvable disparities. Few countries have to contend with such extreme inequalities across so many sociocultural dimensions, including large economic inequalities as well as major disparities in caste, religion, class, and gender. The comparatively affluent in India's urban areas have been the main beneficiaries of the rapid economic growth of recent decades, and per capita income data indicate a growing concentration of income at the top; data on wealth, patchy as they are, also point to growing disparities between the urban upper and middle classes as well as the urban and rural poor and very poor. While the principles of European and American democracy were aimed at reordering the basic principles of an aristocratic society, the caste system in India had functioned differently. In caste society, there is a tendency toward differentiation, if not systematic asymmetry, which gives rise to the types of inequality specific to the Indian social form. The outcome is that Indian democracy has functioned in a way that has retained and perpetuated elements of the caste system instead of changing castism. A study of Uttar Pradesh, a northern Indian state, revealed the near-total grip the higher castes had on all positions of power and influence, including in press clubs, among university faculty, at major non-governmental organizations, in trade unions and media houses, among bureaucrats, and in the police force (Dreze and Sen 2013). The two upper-most castes, Brahmins and Kshatriyas, occupied 75 percent of the top jobs in these institutions, despite the two castes comprising only approximately 20 percent of the population in Uttar Pradesh. In her ethnography of political practices in India, Michelutti (2007) found that political parties routinely conduct ethnic headcounts in which they nominate only certain high-caste candidates, which guarantees votes from upper castes and leaves the lower castes with no choice but to vote for upper-caste candidates. Inequality in society filters down to inequality in journalism practices. The quantity of Indian and South African media, and the economic success story associated with their growth, has not been matched by an increase in quality or by the practicing of a more democratic journalism. Discourses of materialism and consumerism compete with political ideals of democracy and social justice in these countries' media (Hofmeyr and Williams 2009, 6).

Given the breadth and scope of its media, it would be impossible here to analyze the work being done in the Indian newsrooms of each of its 86,000 newspapers and weekly magazines and its 300 news channels broadcasting diverse content to the Indian television-viewing audience. There is, however, enough research available for us to conclude that Indian media have, in general, failed to challenge India's biggest and most intractable problems, including the disparities and inequalities that continue to characterize its society. Rather than confronting these issues, the media often have gone along with the established norms and what they consider to be easy to sell. The research of scholars such as Jeffrey (2000), Mudgal (2011), Rao (2009), Sainath (1996), Sonwalkar (2002), Thussu (2005), and others in this issue have highlighted but some of the biases that plague Indian media practices. These are complex biases having to do with media representation, but what is remarkable is the obvious lack of interest shown in the lives of India's poor, based on the balance of news selection. For instance, in Mudgal's study of the content of the three English and three Hindi daily newspapers with the broadest circulation, the author found that only 2 percent of reported news items addressed issues with which India's rural population was concerned (e.g., reporting on drought or floods, livestock, the price of grain, or issues surrounding land rights), which is all the more shocking given that approximately 70 percent of Indians live in rural settings. The majority of news coverage, according to Rao's (2009) research on broadcast news content, is devoted to crime, politics, and entertainment. Rao's (2012, 88) research conducted among local journalists found that these men and women spent more time cultivating relationships with top politicians than collecting actual information, and that they create the illusion of professional independence through the careful enacting of "performances of distance" (89). Rao argued that in so doing, journalists in India are able to reconcile a professional code that insists on objectivity and impartiality with a cultural code that places leaders—who often belong to a higher caste—at the center of Indian politics and political news reporting. The proliferation of "paid news"—the phenomenon of paying newspapers or television news channels to report certain facts as truthful accounts—has presented serious ethical concerns (Guha Thakurta 2010). In 2003, Bennett Coleman Company Limited (publishers of the newspapers *Times of India* and the *Economic Times* among other publications) started a "paid content" service that enabled them to charge advertisers for coverage of product launches or celebrity-related events. In the run-up to the 2009 general elections, this practice became widespread. The behind-the-scenes influence of corporate interests was made particularly apparent by the leaking of recorded conversations between Nira Radia, a powerful lobbyist with clients such as the Tata group and Reliance Industries, and a variety of business, politicians, and journalists. The tapes revealed what had long been an open secret: the collusion and uncomfortable closeness among corporate elites, politicians, and journalists, a world in which the line between politics and business, public relations and news, was increasingly blurred. The practice of "paid news" certainly has helped to disseminate misinformation, but troubling as it may be, the real harm is in the reduced space it leaves in its wake for public discussion of the less dazzling matters that are of importance to ordinary people—topics such as education, health, nutrition, and sanitation. The caste and class affiliation of many journalists, as mentioned earlier, also can play a vital role. In a 2006 survey of 315 Delhi-based editors and well-known journalists, not one of them reported that they belonged to the Dalit, the lowest caste of Indian society. In fact, about 85 percent belonged to one of the two top castes, which combined constitute only about 16 percent of India's population, and about half of these were Brahmins, the highest caste. The hold that certain castes and classes have on Indian media leads to the exclusion of concerns over and for India's poor, tribal groups, and otherwise marginalized populations (Chamaria, Kumar, and Yogendra 2006). The coverage of the 2012 rape incident in Delhi highlighted the exclusion of the poor more starkly than ever before. While there are four rape cases reported daily in Delhi, Rao's (2014) research showed that the only cases that receive continuous media coverage are those in which the victims are urban, educated, and middle class—as was the case in the incident of December 2012. The rape of poor and Dalit women, frequent and omnipresent, especially in rural areas, is ignored by the national and regional media. While one cannot assume that a more equitable representation of caste and gender will automatically lead to media content that is more sympathetic to the experiences of women in lower castes, one can conclude that the caste and class monopoly over the media is a huge problem created by the unequal society within which it exists. Its potentially corrective role in Indian social and political thinking is made that much more difficult by the society that has molded it.

Like India, South Africa has a middle class that is rising rapidly as a result of a globalizing economy, but with huge social and economic inequalities. Inequality in South Africa is an inheritance from centuries of colonialism and apartheid, systems predicated on the subjugation of the majority of the country's population as a source of labor for racist oligarchies. Twenty years after the beginning of democratization, South Africa remains one of the countries with the highest income disparity in the world (Hofmeyr and Williams 2009, 12). While India has a higher annual GDP growth rate (4.7 percent in 2012) than South Africa (2.5 percent in 2012), the poverty rate in India is higher (41.6 percent of the population living below $1.25 a day in 2005, compared to South Africa's 17.4 percent in 2006). The lowest 20 percent of the Indian population, however, share a bigger percentage of its income (8.5 percent in 2010) than that of South Africa (2.7 percent in 2009) (Hofmeyr and Williams 2009, 13). These levels of inequality have an impact on the ability of the media to help in strengthening a democratic public sphere where the voices of all citizens can be heard. As Heller (2009) points out, democracy conferred the legal "status" of citizenship on all South Africans when they became part of the new democratic polity in 1994, but the political economy of the media—which privileges elite voices and slants access to media agendas toward those with economic power—means that subaltern South Africans still cannot fully enjoy the "practice" of citizenship vis-à-vis the media. This media, despite its claims to centrality in the post-apartheid democracy, still do not afford all South Africans with the same ability to exercise a voice in the public sphere and, thus, do not impact decision-making processes that determine the quality of their daily lives. Critics have pointed out that although the South African political system was radically reformed after apartheid, economic policies continue to favor elites and marginalize the poor majority of South Africans, for whom economic justice remains evasive. The tension between the democratic right to freedom of expression and the imperative on the media to contribute to the restoration of the right to dignity remains at the center of debates about media in South Africa (Wasserman 2013).

While the South African media has embarked on a thorough and ongoing revision of its professional practices to reflect the new democratic environment, these revisions often remain limited to the level of procedures. In contrast, the structural demands of the media industry transformation that are necessary to provide more substantive opportunities for subaltern voices to impact policy-making remains a more difficult challenge to meet. Indian media has functioned similarly to South African media, where the expansion and privatization of media has led to a plethora of information on entertainment and soft news, but the voices of the majority of Indians who live in impoverished conditions remain unrepresented. Any representation of substantive justice and democratic equity is largely missing from media's day-to-day coverage.

Is Democracy a Universal Value? The Role of Journalism

Here, we refer to Indian economist and noble laureate Amartya Sen's provocative essay, "Democracy as a Universal Value," to discuss how journalism practices can undermine democracy if such practices are not attentive to the question of equality. Recognizing democracy's global value, Sen provides a normative definition of democracy:

What exactly is democracy? We must not identify democracy with majority rule. Democracy has complex demands, which certainly include voting and respect for election results, but it also requires the protection of liberties and freedoms, respect for legal entitlements, and the guaranteeing of free discussion and uncensored distribution of news and fair comment. Even elections can be deeply defective if they occur without the different sides getting an adequate opportunity to present their respective cases, or without the electorate enjoying the freedom to obtain news and to consider the views of the competing protagonists. Democracy is a demanding system, and not just a mechanical condition (like majority rule) taken in isolation. (Sen 1999, 4)

Stating that democracy is not a "mechanical condition," Sen emphasizes the notion of justice and a "flourishing life," where needs of all citizens are met, as integral to the democratic process. The value of democracy, according to Sen, is inherently diminished if the process does not take into account "freedom to obtain news and to consider the views of competing protagonists" as well as to protect all liberties and freedoms. Sen (1999, 5) does not understand democracy as purely a Western phenomenon—outlining elements of democratic practices in ancient Buddhism and Mughal dynasty in India—and suggests that there is general acknowledgment in every society that democracy is desirable and that no citizens of a democratic nation has clamored for "less democracy, more authoritarianism." In fact, the contrary is true. Sen advocates for the *intrinsic* importance of democracy, which values needs, rights, and duties, including political and economic rights.

This is true in India where the rhetoric of the Indian state has often been redistributive, emphasizing socialism, the abolition of traditional privileges in the reform of the caste system, and populism. Political practice, however, has been considerably different, eschewing any decisive redistribution. The Indian state has been criticized both for its excellent socialist commitments and for its failure at substantial redistribution. The political impact of these twin tendencies—radical in tone, conservative in practice—may have inadvertently strengthened democracy in some instances: the powerful in society feel well served by the system but weaker groups do not feel totally excluded or hopeless. The quality of governance, however, remains mixed. India is perceived as a democratic power in which ethnic diversity has been accommodated, the economy is growing, foreign and economic policies are sound, and where an educated middle class is flourishing. This image is valid but incomplete. First, this is a relatively recent image. Second, it is an image that is more likely to appeal to distant friends of India who do not deal with daily India, but less to a common office worker in Kanpur or a poor farmer in Andhra Pradesh. Many such Indian citizens, by contrast, experience the Indian state as relatively ineffective and corrupt, more of an obstacle than a source of solutions, even venal and just as often simply absent when needed. Indian leaders are increasingly focused on economic growth and political stability rather than equality and no downward penetration of state authority. A narrow alliance between technocratic and business elites has succeeded in steering India onto a higher growth path, but at the expense of widening inequalities.

The post-liberalized media and journalism practices in India have not led to a more participatory democracy or advocated democracy's universal value. A recent study by the Center for Media Studies (2014) in Delhi on the television news coverage leading up to the 2014 national elections in India showed a significant emphasis on personality-driven rather than policy-driven coverage. Important issues being discussed preceding the elections, such as corruption, poverty, and gender discrimination, completely disappeared from the news landscape when the election coverage began. The media coverage was dominated by surveys though the report states that there was no transparency in the surveys, the nature of the survey instrument, who was conducting the surveys, or who was paying for them. The report concludes that some of these surveys, like paid news, were "paid surveys" by political parties and corporate entities. The ruling party (Congress) received less than 30 percent of the entire television news coverage, including discussion of its key leaders, political platform, and legislative performance. While more research needs to be done to uncover the links among the Bharatiya Janata Party (BJP) that came to power following the 2014 general elections, media owners (many of whom publicly supported BJP), and the general tone and nature of press coverage, it is clear that Sen's advocacy for and emphasis on news and perspectives from all sides in order for democracy to flourish was overwhelmingly undermined.

Similarly in South Africa, the democratic process and institutions put in place after the end of apartheid in 1994 may well be seen as fulfilling merely the "mechanical" criteria of voting, meaning acceptance of the outcome and majority rule. The abolishing of apartheid's racist laws have bestowed the right of citizenship on all South Africans, but in practice, the country's vast economic inequalities and persisting social exclusions militate against the practice of such citizenship in daily life (Heller 2009). The widespread disillusionment with the low-yield democracy as produced in the lives of the poor, coupled with disgust in the widespread corruption and perceived lack of accountability among members of the government, has led to a malaise among citizens that undermines celebratory discourses of democracy. Furthermore, several developments in post-apartheid South Africa have given rise to fears that the protection of liberties and freedoms, respect for legal entitlements, and the guaranteeing of free discussion and uncensored distribution of news and fair comment—elements Sen (2009, 188) identifies as some of democracy's "complex demands"—are being eroded. These developments, signaling an increased intolerance for criticism of a ruling party, include the passing of the draconian "Bill on the Protection of Information," which has led to materials being classified (hidden from public scrutiny) and, thus, weakened the ability of civil society to hold the government to account. The African National Congress' support for a statutory media appeals tribunal, which would criminalize journalistic infringements, was also perceived as an indication of the diminishing space for critical debate in the country.

Perhaps the strongest indication of the disjuncture between formal democracy, based on procedures such as voting, and the normative values of participatory democracy, as outlined by Sen, has been the rise of community protests in post-apartheid South Africa and post-liberalized India. These protests, in popular journalism language, have been described as service delivery protests, but research has shown that these uprisings are related to a more widespread dissent and outrage at the persisting conditions of poverty as well as the sense that the government does not listen and respond to the demands of its citizens. What has been described as a "rebellion of the poor" should therefore be read as a deeper "disappointment with the fruits of democracy":

> The protests reflect disappointment with the fruits of democracy. While some people have gained, the majority are still poor. Levels of unemployment are greater than in 1994, and income inequality remains vast. People can vote, but all too often elected representatives are self-seeking and real improvements are few. (Alexander 2010, 37)

These protests, numbering more than one per day in South Africa (Grant 2014), should be seen as an attempt to participate in democratic policy-making on a level other than merely the ability to join in the electoral ritual of voting every five years. The fact that the government is increasingly clamping down on these protests—a total of 43 protesters had been killed by police in the decade between 2004 and 2014 in South Africa (Grant 2014)—is a further indication of how the space for democratic participation is shrinking even as the formal demands for democratic procedures such as elections continue to be met. In India, an entire social movement led by Gandhian activist Anna Hazare has taken shape and led to nationwide protests and marches, as well as to the evolution of an entirely new political party, the Aam Aadmi Party or the party of the common man. But this party failed to gain any national presence in the 2014 general elections and was largely shut out of political debates.

If Sen's normative definition of democracy, rather than a universal descriptor for procedures, was to be applied to post-apartheid South Africa and post-liberalized India, two countries and their media would fall far short of the complex set of demands he outlines.

Conclusion

For O' Donnell (1994), delegative democracy rests on the idea that the paternal figure of the state, embodied in the elected official, is supposed to take care of the whole nation, and his or her political base is a movement signified by the supposedly vibrant overcoming of the factionalism of a multiparty system. In this system, other institutions such as courts and legislatures are nuisances to governance and must be undermined. Delegative democracy is more democratic than an authoritarian state but is not intrinsically devoted to the needs, rights, and duties of all its citizens. O'Donnell rightly argues that in a representational democracy such is not the case, where accountability would run not only vertically but also horizontally and where a network of relatively autonomous institutions are able to work independent of political interference from the state. In representational democracy, media's work would involve representing all voices and holding the powerful accountable. We argue that India and South Africa, as examples of delegative democracy, instead foster a media and journalism culture that excludes the voices of many, based on race, gender, class, and caste, and in highlighting the victories in the ballot box, rarely seeks governmental effectiveness or political accountability.

It is clear from the existing research on India and South Africa described in this paper that democratic and journalism practices need to change. Media of both countries routinely and loudly celebrate the expanding economies of the two countries and their close economic proximity as now part of the BRICS alliance; what is left out of the media map are critical analyses of the quality of the lives of the majority of Indians and South Africans and what it means for the strengthening of key democratic institutions. The decisive importance of democracy, Sen argues, lies in its values of political participation and freedom in human life as well as in understanding the needs, rights, and duties of its citizens. The purpose of democratic journalism is to foster all such values. We suggest that Indian and South African media need to focus more on such values and make the ongoing political and economic reforms meaningful for the majority of their citizens.

DISCLOSURE STATEMENT

No potential conflict of interest was reported by the authors.

REFERENCES

Alexander, Peter. 2010. "Rebellion of the Poor: South Africa's Service Delivery Protests — A Preliminary Analysis." *Review of African Political Economy* 37 (123): 25–40. doi:10.1080/03056241003637870.

Bisseker, Claire. 2014. "'Wake-up Call' for SA as Nigeria's Economy Takes Top Spot." *Business Day BD Live*. http://www.bdlive.co.za/economy/2014/04/07/wake-up-call-for-sa-as-nigerias-economy-takes-top-spot.

Center for Media Studies. 2014. *Media Election Coverage 2014: A Recap*. Unpublished report. India: Center for Media Studies.

Chamaria, Anil, Jitendra Kumar, and Yadav Yogendra. 2006. *Survey of the Social Profile of the Key Decision Makers in the National Media*. Unpublished report. New Delhi: Center for the Study of Developing Societies.

Dreze, Jean, and Amartya Sen. 2013. *An Uncertain Glory: India and Its Many Contradictions*. Princeton: Princeton University Press.

Friedman, Steven. 2011. "Whose Freedom? South Africa's Press, Middle-class Bias and the Threat of Control." *Ecquid Novi: African Journalism Studies* 32 (2): 106–121.

Grant, Laura. 2014. "Research Shows Sharp Increase in Service Delivery Protests." *Mail & Guardian*. http://mg.co.za/article/2014-02-12research-shows-sharp-increase-in-service-delivery-protests.

Guha Thakurta, Paranjoy. 2010. "Paid News: The Buried Report." *The Outlook Magazine*. http://www.outlookindia.com/article/Paid-News-The-Buried-Report/266542.

Guha Thakurta, Paranjoy. 2012. "Media Ownership Trends in India." *The Hoot: Watching Media in the Subcontinent*. http://www.thehoot.org/web/home/story.php?storyid=6053.

Guha Thakurta, Paranjoy. 2014. "What Future of the Media in India?" *Economic and Political Weekly*. http://www.epw.in/web-exclusives/what-future-media-india.html.

Heller, Patrick. 2009. "Democratic Deepening in India and South Africa." *Journal of Asian and African Studies* 44: 123–149. doi:10.1177/0021909608098679.

Hofmeyr, Isabel, and Michelle Williams. 2009. "South Africa–India: Connections and Comparisons." *Journal of Asian and African Studies* 44 (1): 5–17. doi:10.1177/0021909608098674.

Jeffrey, Robin. 2000. *India's Newspaper Revolution: Capitalism, Politics, and the Indian-language Press, 1977–1999*. New Delhi: Oxford University Press.

Mehta, Nalin. 2008. *India on Television: How Satellite News Channels Have Changed the Way We Think and Act*. New Delhi: Harper Collins.

Michelutti, Lucia. 2007. *The Vernacularization of Democracy: Politics Caste and Religion in India*. London: Routledge.

Mudgal, Vipul. 2011. "Rural Coverage in the Hindi and English Dailies." *Economic and Political Weekly* 46 (35): 92–97.

O'Donnell, Guillermo. 1994. "Delegative Democracy." *Journal of Democracy* 5 (1): 55–69.

Vibodh, Pathasarathi, Alam Srinivas, Archna Shukla, Supriya Chotani, Anja Kovacs, Anuradha Raman, and Siddhartha Narain. 2012. "Mapping Digital Media: India." *Open Society Foundations*. http://www.opensocietyfoundations.org/sites/default/files/mapping-digital-media-india-20130326.pdf.

Rao, Shakuntala. 2008. "Accountability, Democracy and Globalization: A Study of Broadcast Journalism in India." *Asian Journal of Communication* 18 (3): 193–206. doi:10.1080/01292980802207041.

Rao, Shakuntala. 2009. "Glocalization of Indian Journalism." *Journalism Studies* 10 (4): 474–488. doi:10.1080/14616700802618563.

Rao, Shakuntala. 2014. "Covering Rape in Shame Culture: Journalism Ethics in India's New Television News Media." *Journal of Mass Media Ethics* 29 (3): 153–167. doi:10.1080/08900523.2014.918497.

Rao, Ursula. 2012. *News as Culture: Journalistic Practices and the Remaking of Indian Leadership Traditions*. New York: Berghahn Books.

Sainath, Palagummi. 1996. *Everybody Loves a Good Drought: Stories from India's Poorest Districts*. New Delhi: Penguin Books.

Saeed, Saima. 2015. "Phantom Journalism: Governing India's Proxy Media Owners." *Journalism Studies*. doi:10.1080/1461670X.2015.1054174.

Sen, Amartya. 1999. "Democracy as a Universal Value." *Journal of Democracy* 10 (3): 3–17. doi:10.1353/jod.1999.0055.

Sen, Amartya. 2009. *The Idea of Justice*. Cambridge, MA: Harvard University Press.

Sonwalkar, Prasun. 2002. "'Murdochization' of the Indian Press: From By-line to Bottom-line." *Media, Culture and Society* 24 (6): 821–834. doi:10.1177/016344370202400605.

Steyn, Lisa. 2012. "Naspers Rides Big Chinese Wave." *Mail & Guardian*. http://mg.co.za/article/2012-08-31-naspers-rides-big-chinese-wave.

Thomas, Pradip. 2014. "The Ambivalent State and the Media in India: Between Elite Domination and Public Interest." *International Journal of Communication* 8: 466–482.

Thussu, Daya. 2005. "Media Plurality or Democratic Deficit? Private TV and the Public Sphere in India." In *Journalism and Democracy in Asia*, edited by A. R. Romano and M. Bromley, 54–65. London: Taylor and Francis.

Wasserman, Herman. 2010. *Tabloid Journalism in South Africa: True Story!* Bloomington: Indiana University Press.

Wasserman, Herman. 2013. "Media Ethics in a New Democracy: South African Perspectives on Freedom, Dignity and Citizenship." In *Global Media Ethics: Problems and Perspectives*, edited by S. J. A. Ward, 126–145. Oxford: Wiley-Blackwell.

Zakaria, Fareed. 2004. *The Future of Freedom: Illiberal Democracy at Home and Abroad*. New York: W. W. Norton.

PHANTOM JOURNALISM
Governing India's proxy media owners

Saima Saeed

A key parameter of determining the changing nature of journalism is to address the question of who owns the media and why. Recent revelations of sham transactions, fraudulent trade practices and black money being used to fund the news media in India, suggest a lack of transparency in how news business are run and financed. Five cases involving leading news organizations in India are analysed to illustrate the argument. In conjunction with this, the corporate take-over of news space by non-media entities signals the rise of a press that can no longer serve as a watchdog of democracy. The paper outlines a decline in quality journalism as a consequence of a disconcerting nexus between influential politicians, powerful corporates and profit-maximizing news organizations. Corrupt funding procedures and concealed ownership patterns have orchestrated a crisis of credibility for journalism while posing fresh challenges for media governance and the nature of democracy.

Introduction

This paper addresses the old debate that has occupied much of the Marxist and later political economy approaches to studying communication—who owns the media and to what end? The answer, it is argued, runs beyond conventional explanations of the media being hegemonic tools of control and consensus-generation to more a reflection of the complex ways in which crony capitalism and systemic corruption have crept into every public institution, news media being no exception. Indeed, it is the media which may be more susceptible to it than other sectors of the economy, as this article demonstrates.

The ownership and financing pattern of contemporary news organizations in India reflect a dubious truce between the corporate world and the political class albeit with some new actors. So who are these new actors? These are not representatives of civil society, minorities, or poor and marginalised groups; instead, they are a bouquet of private firms in which money as well as owners change hands frequently, making the news business vulnerable to the very corruption which journalism seeks to expose. This in turn has led to a crisis of truth and trust in journalism, abstract virtues that at once distinguish the vocation and which, unlike other commodities, should not be bought at a price. With mounting instances of "black money" (non-taxed revenues) as a major source of media funding, the invisible causality of the relationship in which hidden corporate and political interests order the news content points to what this paper calls the rise of phantom journalism. The legitimizing format of the news genre that presupposes truth-telling, hegemonically conceals a complex web of funders and funding relationships in which the actual owners never stand up or are hard to identify. This makes the news product imaginary to the extent that it camouflages its real intentionality and a mode of production that impairs its criticality and editorial independence. The public is unable to connect the dots between ownership problems and content. In the absence of the knowledge of who is funding the media and to what end, with what interests and why, the journalistic practice itself becomes a phantasmagoria—the process is rendered into a chimera, a falsity, even as, ironically, it is in the business of being a watchdog of democracy. The phrase phantom journalism is symbolic of this inversion from tenets of objective truth-telling as a professional ethic to selling news and information as a business compulsion; and much like the phantom, the illusion remains powerfully infallible.

Power, Politics, Policy and Public Provisioning: Reviewing the Complex Field of Media Ownership

The question of who owns the media seems to be getting only more complicated as we realize its growing significance to democracies. Of late, scholars working within the political economy of media tradition are focused on the linkages between media and society. To that extent, there has been a larger strand of scholarship on media, society and democracy from the vantage point of print, more specifically the Indian-language press (Jeffrey 2000; Ninan 2007) and television (Rajagopal 2001; Roy 2011; Chakravartty and Roy 2013; Saeed 2013). Chakravartty and Roy (2013) assert that the historical, political and contemporary dynamics of liberalization in India have resulted in media ownership patterns that do not fit into the typology of the West, instead there arises a need to re-examine the relationship between television and democracy. Their contention is that the emerging media system and practices in India present a complex pattern of relationship with democracy with different levels of political parallelism and in the process have been forming new structures of political power and privilege acting as agents and enablers, not mere mirrors of politics. A second trope, at times emanating from the first, focuses on structural issues of media organizations, media systems and markets, and the impact of media policies and regulatory practices on them. The proximity of media to capitalism, both at national and global levels, has consistently attracted the attention of media scholars. For instance, McChesney (2003) points to the "crucial role of the profit motive in shaping media performance" (27). For him, a political economy of communication must begin first with a "recognition that all media systems are the direct and indirect result of explicit public policies" (28) which powerful interests shape to their own advantage, which in turn influence, "the nature of political debates over media and communication policies" (28). Critical scholars, particularly McChesney (1999, 2008), Schiller (1989), Bagdikian (2004) and Herman and Chomsky (1988), have been drawing attention to how the corporate media system in the United States and many other developed countries in the West are in variance with attempts at providing for social justice, good governance and healthy participatory democracy. Schiller (1989, 93–106) looks at how public expression has been corporatized as a result of the corporate take-over of museums and public television. Bagdikian (2004) gives an account of how the corporate ownership of the media (especially since the Reagan years' adoption of deregulation as a policy) aligned itself with the interests of the owners and not the individual readers. Baker (2002, 8) elucidates how media products have a "public good" aspect which means that unlike typical products, the use of communication products by one person does not affect its use or benefit to another person. Drawing on the tensions between economic and democratic theory when it comes to media products, Baker concedes that a free trade regime can seriously undermine attempts at creating a robust public sphere and a dialogic culture as aspired by nation-states (255). As free markets are not able to fulfil public needs, a more substantive looking at the legal, economic and social structures is required to serve democracies better and uphold journalistic freedom. Extending this framework, Baker (2007, 28) supports what he calls, "ownership dispersal" as it "reduces the risk of undemocratic dominance of the public sphere—the Berlusconi effect". Doyle (2002) contends that media ownership matters because of its impact on media pluralism and diversity. Concentrated media ownership raises the risk of "the abuse of political power by media owners or the under-representation of some significant viewpoints" posing a danger to the interest of society (6). This negative correlation between levels of market concentration and levels of pluralism would posit two media policy challenges—first, the "potential socio-political and cultural implications of media empire-building" and, second, "the economic implications of allowing media concentration to develop" (11–13).

Indian scholarship on the subject of media and ownership shows similar concerns. Jeffrey, while tracing the shift of the newspaper empires from traders to capitalists, succinctly draws on how most of the

> Indian language newspapers are family-controlled and not listed on the stock market. Of the twenty-one newspapers that controlled 70% of Audit Bureau of Circulations (ABC) daily circulation in the 1990s, only one—*Mathrubhumi*, the Malayalam daily of Kerala— was a public company whose shareholders were mostly unrelated. But even *Mathrubhumi*'s shares were held by a small clique. (Jeffrey 2000, 112)

Jeffrey (2000, 113) points out how the North India proprietors usually came from the "non-Brahmin but commercial caste families" like in the case of Ramnath Goenka, a Marwari born in Bihar, who set his base in Mumbai and established the *Indian Express* empire. The South India newspaper ownership which was a bit more varied was equally dominated by the Brahmin or upper-caste families, moneyed elites or influential castes like the Nadars in Tamil Nadu. The points relevant to this paper that Jeffrey (2000) makes are, first, that in India, 21 newspapers controlled 70 per cent of the circulation with the remaining circulation being shared by thousands of small dailies. Second, of these, only 9 had interests exclusively in media-related activities and 10 had "substantial other interest" (122–123). Third, as for the legal, financial and regulatory implications of such family ownership with shares doled out to family members, transparency became a big issue. In order to meet the prescribed governmental requirements and to gain the trust of the employees, many of them "created imaginative financial structures ... the most common device was to divide a newspaper's activities into a number of businesses which in theory were distinct and self-contained" (Jeffrey 2000, 123) but in reality were sub-units of a single complicated structure that came handy in protecting the interests of large businesses. By the 1990s, as newspapers broke into major war over advertising and readership, these newspapers had not yet listed themselves on the stock exchange!

Complicating the scenario was the arrival of private television which had a reverse pedigree—trans-border patrons and a massive advertising potential even before they could find a foothold in the market. So, unlike the traditional medium of the press which remained in the stranglehold of families like the Jains, the Birlas and Goenkas, post-1990s, the new medium of television revealed a propensity to being funded by large corporates and influential political families. The next two decades saw a quick demise of public service broadcasting and the entry of private players from within and outside the sovereign boundaries, most enduringly and inescapably in the form of Rupert Murdoch's bouquet of five channels (Thussu 1999, 2007; Sinha 1998). Chakravartty and Roy (2013, 352) suggest how, unlike the Western and American media ownership which was marked by consolidation and convergence, with a dominance of transnational corporate capital, the Indian media scenario, post-globalization, showed initial signs of vertical integration alongside "the presence of variegated forms of capital—transnational and domestic corporate and non-corporate". This "corporatization of the media of TV news in India" (Saeed 2013, 128) and the subsequent "entertainmentalization of news" has had a profound impact on content and one that is squarely based on the logic of profit-making, failing to represent and serve large sections of population that exist on the margins. These shifts have implications for political participation, the nature of content being fielded in the public sphere and the criticality of the public knowledge thus created (348–359).

Recent work on the subject of eroding media ethics includes *The Hoot Reader: Media Practices in the Twenty-first Century*, a collection of articles by editors, journalists and media watchers. Edited by Ninan and Chattarji (2013), it looks at the changing professional practices as a result of, among other things, cross-media ownership combined with political power. As in the case of the Sun TV, Ninan points out how the powerful Maran family has managed to have a father and a brother in the cabinets of two successive central governments of opposing political formations. This tremendous political clout explains the expansive network consisting of 14 television channels in four states, cable distribution, four magazines, two newspapers and FM stations (Ninan 2013a, 323). Bharat Bhushan's account in the same reader details how an entire industry is thriving based on the relationships between public relations departments of advertising-giving agencies and representatives of those seeking publication, with some money being routed back as bribes into the "pockets of key individuals in the advertisement-issuing government departments" (Bhushan 2013a, 332–333).

As for the literature on media regulation in India, there are three discernible thrusts—one, emanating from the need to make policymaking more transparent; a second has been fielded from a rather well-known position of aligning policy and regulation with the public right to know, with *access* becoming a buzzword, as in much of the Community Radio debates in 2006 and the Broadcast Services Regulation Bill in the same year (see Muralidharan 2007; Saeed 2009). A third cluster calls for stricter regulatory practices that can check and control the growing nexus between media, corporates and the political class. Such scholarship has lamented the blurring of the boundary between news and advertorials; information and propaganda; corporate lobbying and opinion-formation in what has been often termed as "manufacturing news", as by former NDTV journalist Sandeep Bhushan (2013b). Critics have looked at a more literal manufacture of news, following the surfacing of "paid news" in newspapers during the Lok Sabha and Assembly Election of 2009 and the subsequent interventions by the Election Commission, the Press Council of India, and the Securities and Exchange Board of India (see e.g. Thakurta 2011). Thakurta (2011) attributes part of the reason for such media practice to a weak regulatory mechanism while debating on the feasibility of self-regulation in such a market. Concerns over the corporate takeover of news have been echoed in Thakurta and Chaturvedi (2012). They read the entry of Reliance Industries Ltd (RIL) in the media sector and the subsequent TV18 and Eenadu deal as setting a dangerous precedent for the diversity and plurality of news in the country. Incidentally, this was just one among other such high-value deals that have been made public. Hardly surprising, that the FICCI-KPMG (2013) put on record that the year 2012 saw one of the highest deal-making activities in the media and entertainment sector. The total advertising spend across media in 2012 was a whopping INR (Indian Rupees)[1] 327.4 billion (US$5370 million) and made up to 40 per cent of media and entertainment industry revenues (FICCI-KPMG 2013, 8–9). This is up from a total advertising spend of INR 300 billion (US$4920 million) in 2011 and INR 221 billion (US$3624 million) in 2008. This means that there has been an increase of INR 100 billion (US$1640 million) in total advertising spend in merely four years. For instance, in the television sphere alone, at present, there are around 745 television channels of which a little over half are in news and current affairs. Another 600 channels have applied for licences. Clearly, there are rich dividends to be milked from owning news channels which explains the large investment.

Crony Capitalism and the News Net: Some Recent Evidence

What these numbers do not reveal is the money trail, the fraud transactions and complicated relations of exchange, many of them covert, between media, corporate and political elites which are incompatible with media's role as a watchdog. As more instances of paid news, private treaties and advertorials surface, there are enough reasons to worry about how free is the media in the world's largest democracy. This begs the questions: who owns the media and how does it impact the nature of the work journalists do? The following five cases demonstrate the entry of crony capital in the news media space and how it has transformed journalistic practices:

(1) the Zee extortion case;
(2) the Enforcement Directorate official and the Sahara blackmail case;
(3) the Chit Fund Scam;
(4) the Tejpal rape case; and
(5) the money trail in the sale of channel NewsX.

These cases and their implication for journalism in India are discussed below.

Editors as Extortionists and News as Ransom: The Zee Versus Jindal Case

The Zee extortion case laid bare the otherwise hidden economic dimension of editorial processes. On 27 November 2012, the Indian journalistic fraternity was left red-faced when the Crime Branch of the Delhi Police arrested Zee News editors Sudhir Chaudhary and Sameer Ahluwalia on charges of extortion and criminal conspiracy. The arrests came two months after Jindal Steel and Power Ltd (JSPL) owned by Congress Member of Parliament (MP), Naveen Jindal, filed a First Information Report (FIR) on the matter. The FIR (which is a written document recorded by the police reporting the commissioning of a cognisable offence and is the first step that sets in motion the criminal justice procedure) was filed on 2 October and alleged that, "the Zee executives had demanded INR 100 crore [US$16.40 million] in committed advertising from JSPL in return for dropping an investigation launched by their two channels on the alleged undue benefits accrued to Jindal in the allocation of coal blocks by the UPA government" (*Indian Express* 2012). JSPL had accused the Zee Group Chairman, Subhash Chandra, and his son, Puneet Goenka, of being part of this conspiracy (*Indian Express* 2012). In support of its claims, JSPL provided the police with audio-visual recordings of its officials with Chaudhary and Ahluwalia in mid-September 2012, in Delhi's Hyatt Regency Hotel (*Indian Express* 2012). The arrests were made after a forensic report testified to the inauthenticity of the clips. In turn, Zee cried foul, pointing to the political clout used by the powerful Congress Minister, Naveen Jindal, construing the matter as an attack on the freedom of the press. In a dramatic press conference that was interestingly dubbed as a "reverse sting" in an article in *The Hindu*, on 25 October 2012, Jindal Managing Director (CEO) Naveen Jindal showed, in his press conference, a 14-minutes video montage extracted from hidden recordings of the meetings between JSPL executives and Zee editors, giving evidence of Zee's attempt at extorting money from his company. An angry Jindal, pointing to this shocking case of media corruption, observed in the press conference, "The government gives channels a licence to show news. They are not given a licence for extortion or blackmail" (Jebaraj 2012). In the footage, the editors were heard telling the JSPL representatives how the entire deal would work. Mr Chaudhary is heard describing the relationship of an advertiser with a news outlet as "that of a client, where the management and the sales team will convince editorial to 'go soft' on a company which gives business with them" (Jebaraj 2012). Later, Mr Chaudhary is seen brandishing copies of *Times of India* supplements, alleging that *the Delhi Times* and *Bombay Times* are "completely paid for, with sponsored interviews and pictures, and Medianet arranging for positive film reviews" (Jebaraj 2012).

Sponsored content being passed off as news is rather well-documented in the chequered history of Indian journalism. Financial journalist and managing editor of *Moneylife*, Sucheta Dalal (best known for her investigative reportage that unearthed the Securities scam while she was at *the Times of India*) has in her articles unravelled how the largest selling English-language newspaper in the world, the *Times of India*, had set up a full-fledged division called Medianet that looks after paid news which she defines as the business of "selling news" (Dalal 2003). She points out how the Medianet division even maintains a rate card to sell this news content! Dalal (2003) explains how "the sale of news is different and distinct from paid advertisements, advertorials or special supplements, all of which are clearly identified as 'sponsored features,' while paid news is not". Paid news, therefore, cheats on the reader's sensibility in passing itself as news that assumes the characteristics of truth, fairness and accuracy. Dalal attributes such decline in journalistic ethics as contributing to incidents such as the arrest of two business journalists of the same publication group, the *Economic Times*, namely the arrest of Rishi Chopra with a fellow journalist accomplice, in an attempted extortion racket, wherein, the Mumbai police in March 2003 caught the duo accepting a bribe of INR 700,000 (US$11,512). This was a second instalment of an INR 2.5 million (US$41,113) pay-off, to kill a negative news report about Poonamchand Malu of Malu Financial Services (Dalal 2003).

Intimidation and Blackmail as Journalistic Practice? Making Sense of the Supreme Court Notice to the Sahara Group

Yet another case of intimidation and blackmail by another well-known media company, the Sahara Group, further substantiates the murkiness that has enveloped not just the news business but the editorial department, in its choice of stories, to the extent of using them as tools of coercion. On 6 May 2011, a Supreme Court bench, comprising Justices G. S. Singhvi and A. K. Ganguly, initiated *suo motu* contempt proceedings after the Enforcement Directorate (ED) stated that a Sahara Samay Television reporter had sent a questionnaire to investigating officer, Rajeshwar Singh, seeking personal information from Singh and his response to the charges against Sahara (Anand 2013). The court took notice of the fact that the questionnaire, with 25 questions, was sent soon after summons were issued to the Sahara Group's chief, Subrato Roy, under the Prevention of Money Laundering Act. In an article published on 6 May 2011, *The Hindu* reported that the Supreme Court of India issued show cause notices of criminal contempt to the Sahara MD, Subrato Roy, Upendra Rai, editor and news director of Sahara India and reporter Subodh Jain for allegedly interfering with the investigation into the 2G spectrum case (Venkatesan 2011). The notice was issued to find out whether there was a deliberate attempt to disrupt the probe into the high-profile 2G scam, one of the biggest corruption scandals to have rocked the government of the time, exposing deep-rooted corruption, as leaked telephone conversations (popularly known as the "Radia tapes") between tainted corporate lobbyist, Nira Radia, and politicians and news editors came to light (after leading Indian news magazine *The Outlook* uploaded them on the internet) and revealed an unholy truce between powerful ministers, bureaucrats and big corporates including some noted journalists. These conversations, surreptitiously taped by the income tax department of the government of India in 2008–2009, as part of their effort to locate instances of tax evasion, money laundering and restricted financial practices, created a massive furore as the taped transcripts spilled into the public domain. In these tapes, several prominent media persons were heard talking to lobbyist Radia regarding fixing of ministerial positions in government as well as brokering deals with regard to the 2G scam.[2]

That said, an *India Today* story on 7 May 2011 (Singh 2011) made apparent how the Sahara television channel reporter had sought to know about the investigating officer Rajeshwar Singh's assets, his proximity to politicians, the amount of money he spent on his daughter's birthday, the number of phones he had changed and other personal questions. The channel had purportedly threatened to do a series of stories against Singh. Furthermore, the Central Bureau of Investigation (CBI) is probing a complaint by the Enforcement Directorate alleging Rai had offered a bribe of INR 2 crore (US$328,906) for going soft on the corrupt corporate lobbyist Radia (Singh 2011).

Incidentally, at the time of writing this article, the chief of the Sahara Group, Roy, who runs a global media empire with several television channels and assets worth more than US$11 billion from a business conglomerate comprising more than 4700 establishments (Sasi and Bhattacharjee 2014) has been lodged in Delhi's Central Jail for a massive financial scam. Roy was arrested on 28 February 2014 for failing to appear at a Supreme Court hearing after the apex court's repeated attempts at trying to get the company to refund the INR 19,000 crore (US$3116) to millions of small investors who had been duped by the company. The court has asked Sahara to submit title deeds worth INR 20,000 crore (US$3280) to the market regulator, Securities and Exchange Board of India (SEBI), which it can then sell to refund the investors.

News Eclipsed by Shadow Finance: The Chit Fund Scam

What connects the Zee extortion case with the Sahara contempt notice is the dubious ways in which money is raised to finance newspapers and television news channels and the direct role that editors and reporters have played to facilitate it. This substantiates how fraudulent business practices have fundamentally redefined their product, the news story and the relation of news with the journalist itself. Another fraud with links to the media surfaced in 2013, in what came to be known as the Saradha Chit Fund Scam. The SEBI notice dated 23 April 2013, issued to the Saradha Group of companies (Mr Sudipa Sen, Chairman and Managing Director),[3] reveals the clandestine workings of shadow finance in

West Bengal, India's fourth most populous state located in the eastern part of the country. Notably, the state had witnessed over three decades of Communist rule (1977–2011) which was broken when All India Trinamool Congress (TMC), under the leadership of Mamata Banerjee, swept to power. The 2013 SEBI notice elaborates on how this group, Saradha Realty India Ltd, was collecting contributions of monies from the public, particularly in rural areas of the state. The contribution amount ranged from INR 10,000 (US$164) to INR 100,000 (US$1644) for tenures of 15–120 months. The investors had an option for a land or a flat allotment or get a refund. The notice charged the company of fraud in that this land/flat allotted was not pre-determined or identified. Moreover, the average return offered in lieu of the land, in case the investor opts for returns, were between 12 and 24 per cent which was more than double what any banks in India could offer. Saradha Realty, caught in this multi-million dollar scam, was therefore asked to wind up this scheme and submit a repayment report to SEBI.

The ruling TMC government's reaction to this fraud in West Bengal reveals yet again the close relationship between politicos, the media and the corporates. Popularly known as the Chit Fund Scam, such fraud occurred in the state and its adjoining areas despite the fact that as early as 2009 and then April 2010, the earlier Left Front government had sent a letter to the SEBI to investigate the group's activities. Instead of taking the SEBI order to its logical conclusion and making the Saradha Group pay back to all those people it had duped, Mamata Banerjee, the Chief Minister of the State of West Bengal, hurriedly announced an INR 500 crore (US$82 million) relief package for the small and medium depositors of Saradha to ensure that the entire scam was given a quite burial (*Business Standard* 2013). "I am very sorry, but I have to do this", Banerjee said in a press conference (*Business Standard* 2013). Interestingly, *The Hindu* reported on 25 April 2013 how the sop came on a day when Sudipta Sen had lobbed an explosive 18-page letter to the CBI, the country's top investigating agency, nailing two TMC MPs, Kunal Ghosh (notably the CEO of the Saradha Group's media wing) and Srinjoy Bose (owner of the *Pratidin* newspaper), explaining how they forced Sen to foray into the media business (Dutta and Singh 2013). The letter does not fully explain why Sudipta Sen was on a media acquisition spree from 2010 and how in a couple of years he had managed to own 18 newspapers and channels in Bengal and the adjoining state of Assam, most of which were unmistakably serving as mouthpieces of TMC. However, there is little doubt about the ruling TMC's patronage of the Saradha media network given that it had ordered all public libraries to subscribe to newspapers owned by the group, including a Bengali daily *Kolom* which Mamata Bannerjee had herself inaugurated (see Chowdhury 2013). She was also seen distributing ambulances, motorcycles and bicycles donated by the Saradha Group in 2011 in a publicized media event. Further, it was reported that Sudipto Sen bought a painting by Banerjee for INR 1.86 crore (US$305,883) (Chowdhury 2013). Even more significantly, it was Mamata Banerjee who nominated Kunal Ghosh, the CEO of the Saradha Group's media business, to *Rajya Sabha* (refers to the upper House of the Parliament in India).

Sudipta Sen's 18-page letter to the CBI suggests that perhaps the blackmail was reciprocal. More importantly, the contents of the letter reveal what benefits accrue out of media ownership. In his letter, Sen alleged that he was forced to start his media business in order to deter the attacks by Bengali newspaper, *Pratidin*. Consequently, he said he bought Channel 10 which was a regional news channel at the time for INR 24 crore (US$3.93 million) (Dutta and Singh 2013). Thereafter, a deal was struck with *Pratidin* wherein going by the agreement, *Pratidin* would be paid INR 60 lakh (US$98,672) and Ghosh would be appointed CEO at a monthly salary of INR 15 lakh (US$24,668) (Dutta and Singh 2013).

The extent of the fraud can be gauged from the fact that in May 2014, the Supreme Court handed over the Saradha scam probe to the highest investigating agency in the country, the CBI, asking the state government to co-operate in the probe, even as Saradha's defraud investment schemes are being looked into by the capital markets regulator, SEBI, and Saradha chief Sudipta Sen is behind bars. Not just impacting the quality of content, such unprincipled transactions in the news media space have resulted in a moral vacuity that has cost the media a crisis of credibility as the arrest of *Tehelka* editor, Tarun Tejpal, makes evident.

Crony Capitalists as Newswallas: Larger than Life Journalists, Lies and Videotapes

Tarun Tejpal's news magazine, *Tehelka*, redefined journalism, in particular investigative journalism, in many ways. He shot to fame when his investigative website Tehelka.com (launched in 2000) did a sting operation that blew the betting racket rife in Indian cricket, exposing the role of cricketer Manoj Prabhakar. The following year, he caught the attention of an alarmed nation that witnessed on tape, the corruption in defence deals in which the then Bharatiya Janata Party (BJP) President, Bangaru Laxman, was seen accepting a cash bribe from an undercover *Tehelka* reporter. Sting after sting, Tejpal as well as Shoma Chaudhury, an old associate of Tejpal and the managing editor of *Tehelka*, came to be recognized as vanguards of truth, transparency and trust, virtues that were becoming a thing of the past in the contemporary press. So when Tejpal's sexual assault case came to light on 7 and 8 November 2013 in Goa, the venue of the Think Fest (an annual event organized by the Tehelka group publicized as a platform where influential politicians, business personalities, actors, writers and the like get together to exchange ideas and connect in a festival setting), there was justified horror. Figurative of this shock within the media fraternity was the 9 December 2013 cover page of the leading news magazine, *India Today*. Titled, "Disgrace: A Fabled Media Star Falls Over Allegations of Rape" (Pradhan and Jayaraman 2013), it donned a black and white, close-up shot, of a worn-out and ominous looking Tejpal, sporting a grey beard. Given Tejpal's image of probity in the public, asking such a question would be a sacrilege until his fall in the Goa Think Fest. So clean was Tejpal's image that he would go gunning for every wrong in public life and report it unabashedly. Everyone feared his guts. So when he fell, it emerged that even his empire was built on clandestine deals, political connections and an uneasy concoction of glamour, hotel and tourism businesses, and event management.

India Today reported how Tejpal had built a network of eight firms aside of his publishing business (Pradhan and Jayaraman 2013). Nowhere is the phenomenon of proxy ownership we are discussing in this article rendered more visible than in the surreptitious deals that inked Tarun Tejpal's holding company, Anant Media, which publishes the *Tehelka* magazine. It had the following shareholders (sourced from Pradhan and Jayaraman 2013): Tarun Tejpal (19.25 per cent), Shoma Chaudhury (0.50 per cent), TMC MP Kanwar Deep Singh owned Royal Building and Infrastructure Pvt Ltd (66.75 per cent), Weldon Polymers (5.87 per cent), Tejpal family members (2.56 per cent), Ram Jethmalani (0.05 per cent) and others (5.02 per cent). Singh is an infamous TMC Rajya Sabha MP who was caught with INR 57 lakh (US$93,738) in cash at the Delhi airport on-route to Assam where elections were to be held soon after. Singh is the owner of the INR 10,000 crore (US$1641 million) Alchemist Group and had allegedly bought his way to be a member of *Rajya Sabha,* as revealed in an IBN-Cobrapost sting operation in 2010. Leading investigative newspaper, the *Indian Express,* reported on 13 December 2013 how from funders like the slain liquor baron, Ponty Chadha (who was dramatically shot by his brother at their farmhouse), to controversial TMC MP and businessman, K. D. Singh, the money route could be traced to two firms linked to a Jindal Group company named in the coal scam FIR which invested upwards of INR 28 crore (US$4.59 million) in Anant Media (Suresh 2013). The nature of businesses of some of the other firms controlled by Tejpal is worth examining, as Table 1 demonstrates.

Table 1 makes apparent that it is the husband and wife duo of Tarun Tejpal and Geetan Batra, along with sister Neena Tejpal and brother Minty Tejpal, that are major shareholders in most of the Tejpal-associated firms, making his business empire primarily family-owned and family-run. Besides, unlike the general perception that at the bedrock of Tejpal's dogged chase for truth was a genuine commitment to investigative journalism, the money mostly came from non-journalistic, even non-media, businesses including tourist resorts, hospitality and events management businesses, on the one hand, or through corporate and political partners who had a history of being involved in financial irregularities, as discussed in the foregoing account, on the other hand.

TABLE 1

Tarun Tejpal's business empire: dangerous liaisons

Name of the company	Type of business/sector	Shareholders
Tehelka.com Pvt Ltd	Digital version of *Tehelka* magazine	K. D. Singh (0.97%), Anant Media (97.1%), Tarun Tejpal (1.99%)
Chestnut Height & Resorts Pvt Ltd	Hospitality	Sheela Lunkad, Rajeev Lunkad, Tarun Tejpal and wife Geetan Batra (25% each)
Thinkworks Pvt Ltd (February 2010)	Organized annual Think Fest (the one in 2013 saw Tejpal being accused of raping a junior colleague, resulting in his arrest and imprisonment)	Tarun Tejpal (80%), sister Neena Tejpal (10%), managing editor and business partner Shoma Chaudhury (10%)
Thriving Arts Pvt Ltd (2013)	Business Prufrock Club (late liquor baron Ponty Chadha'sfirm. He invested INR 2 crore. Prufrock was supposed to cater to select,urban elite)	Tarun Tejpal (80%), Neena Tejpal (20%)
AOD Lodges Pvt Ltd	Hospitality	Geetan Batra (50%), Tarun Tejpal (50%)
Amaraman India Pvt Ltd	Media and entertainment services. The firm had controversially been awarded a 52-episode television series from Doordarshan, India's public service broadcaster, while Tejpal was its board member and had to forgo the position after the rape charges	K. D. Singh (10%), Tarun Tejpal (70%), Shoma Chaudhury (10%), Neena Tejpal (10%)

Source: Adapted from an *India Today* cover story (Pradhan and Jayaraman 2013, 34).

JOURNALISM, DEMOCRACY AND CIVIL SOCIETY IN INDIA

The NewsX Sale Case

The last and final example in this paper relates to the complicity of the 2G scam tainted corporate lobbyist, Nira Radia, in the sale of NewsX television channel (incorporated in India in December 2006). The case was exposed when the leading news magazine, *The Outlook,* uploaded transcripts of 140 taped conversations between Nira Radia and top politicians, journalists and corporates on its website[4] (as discussed in some detail in an earlier section), making the contents of the calls available in the public domain. As a result of a widespread public outrage and following public interest litigation, the case was monitored by the investigating wing of the income tax department. Investigators went through the transcriptions of the tapes, especially the tape dated 29 May 2009 relating to the conversation between Jehangir Pocha, a former journalist and ex-editor of *Business World,* and Radia, uncovering the connection, among other things, between Radia and the NewsX sale. Well-known media critic and scholar, Sevanti Ninan, in an article in *Live Mint*, terms the transaction relating to the sale of NewsX as a case of "surrogate media ownership" (Ninan 2013b). Referring to a detailed report by the Serious Fraud Investigation Office (SFIO) of the Ministry of Corporate Affairs Report in 2013, Ninan (2013b) points to the "complex web of investments" by India's largest corporation, RIL, in the companies that launched the media group 9X and the news channel NewsX. The SFIO report which was submitted to the Supreme Court of India on 11 November 2013 by the Centre for Public Interest Litigation (CPIL) makes apparent an "intricate cross holding where each shareholder had a vested interest in the financial transactions of the other entity" (SFIO 2013, 8). Further, using flow charts and diagrams, the report elaborates on how a bevy of frontline and second-rung companies were in a complex shareholding pattern, in which "the buyer and the seller were one and the same group, that is, Reliance. The maze of companies and web of fund movements was created only to hide the identity of the group" (25) as per a "premeditated plan" (25). Moreover, Ninan (2013b) points to "a foreign direct investment (FDI) angle to the surrogacy. Entertainment company 9X had multinational investment firm New Silk Route as an investor. To have 9X and *NewsX* as linked companies would have violated the FDI restriction on foreign investment in news channels" (Ninan 2013b).

Indeed, the trend of non-news businesses finding that investing in news and information businesses, in particular television, is a rewarding option shows that benefits that accrue out of controlling the news media space: the ability to lobby for issues, block out potentially any negative coverage of itself, gain political clout and visibility, and not least of all, social prestige and power. From the little known to the most fêted companies, even though inexperienced in the news business, they have all been vying to invest in media. This in turn, I have argued in this article, has severely disparaged the nature of journalism practice in the country while causing irreparable structural changes in the relationships inside the newsroom—among journalists and most significantly between the owners and marketing departments and the editorial. The editorial has essentially either towed the logic of the owners or has been heavily controlled. This "surrogate ownership", to use Ninan's phrase, has resulted in the rise of what this paper calls phantom journalism. In addition to the blunting of journalism's main purpose, concentration of media ownership has further complicated the situation beyond the dynamics of the newsroom, to the macro level of policymaking and regulation. The growing forays of big corporates into the media sector need to be read from such a perspective of ownership concentration and autonomy of the media. Independent journalist and academic Paranjoy Guha Thakurta, documenting the

RIL takeover of India's largest media conglomerate TV18 in 2014, points out that it must be understood against the backdrop of the earlier January 2012 deal in which RIL announced a "complex, multilayered financial arrangement that involved selling its interests in the Hyderabad, Andhra Pradesh-based Eenadu group founded by Ramoji Rao to the Network18 group … The two entities went on to raise approximately Rs 4,000 crore [US$740 million], including Rs 1,700 crore [US$315 million] from its promoters" (Thakurta 2014, 13). Not only was the RIL takeover of TV18 through the earlier bail-out of Eenadu TV done in a series of multifarious transactions (for a detailed discussion, see Thakurta [2014] and Thakurta and Chaturvedi [2012]), the motives of which became clear only much later, the repercussion that this RIL–TV18–Eenadu deal holds for the future of media diversity and independence in this country is too acute to ignore as it will only serve to concentrate the "country's already oligopolistic media markets" (Thakurta 2014, 12).

Concerns over growing media concentration and a corporate takeover of the press have intensified since the decade following the globalization of the economy in 1991. For instance, the 200-page draft report on *Study on Cross Media Ownership in India* by the Administrative Staff College of India (ASCI), Hyderabad in 2009 documented the extent and nature of vertical and horizontal integration and the existence of cross-media ownership in India across Hindi, Tamil, Telugu, Malayalam and English-language media markets. It recommended that before ascertaining rules for cross-media ownership regulation, the concerned authorities must conduct a market analysis factoring in the structure of the relevant markets and the competition concerns (ASCI 2009, 154). It further suggested that "disclosure norms that make cross media affiliations and ownership clear to the viewer need to be published" (155). It is noteworthy (ASCI [2009] points to this) that data on media ownership in India is scant, hard to procure and ill documented. Given such obfuscation of the information on the media by the media itself, critics like Ninan warn that in India, "as media ownership gets more varied and colourful, it has become the one governance issue crying out for more transparency. Token rules exist for both the print media and television" (Ninan 2013b).

While the corporate takeover of the press is not entirely new, one needs to be wary of the growing media concentration and subsequently its more direct influence on media content. It calls for a major debate on policy and regulatory practices in India to study the implications of local Murdochs and Berlusconis in our democracy that has for long prided itself on its free press.

Conclusion

The contemporary nature of news media ownership in India, as the foregoing discussion evinces, is conjectured with rising instances of fraudulent practices, sham transactions (primarily to evade taxes) and opaque funding structures. As the amount of financing to the news genre from non-media/news players increases, there is a need for greater transparency about ownership even as corporate media ensures that most of such information is withheld from the public. As proxy news ownership easily hedges accountability and transparency that the media owe to the public, its dangers are not hard to fathom. Not only does it lead to concentration of news business in the hands of a few, but in the wrong hands. This surrogate media ownership (Ninan 2013b), interferes with some central tenets of journalistic ethics—truth, transparency and accountability. It poses fresh challenges for the governance of an already hard-to-regulate media ecology rife with fraudulent transactions and corrupt practices. The latest Telecom Regulatory Authority of India (TRAI) report released in August 2014 points out that "the principal matters of concern relate to and derive from the political and corporate ownership of the media" (TRAI 2014, 69). It recommends a list of reporting requirements for media entities, including what it calls "transparency disclosures" that are to be placed in the public domain. These include the following documents to be submitted annually: shareholding pattern; foreign direct investment pattern; interests, direct and indirect, of the entity in other entities engaged in the media sector; interests of entities, direct and indirect, having shareholding beyond 5 per cent in the media entity under consideration, in other media entities/companies; and details of key executives and Board of Directors of the entity, among other documents (TRAI 2014, 82). However, this is not the first time the TRAI has enlisted a set of regulatory recommendations on media ownership. The ones that it laid earlier, in 2008 and 2012, have failed to curb "unhealthy media practices" (TRAI 2014, 85) which have only intensified in complex ways since then.

To begin with, any attempt at regulating such malaise in the media business must start with locating the beyond profit-making benefits that accrue out of investing in the news business. One of them is buying favourable public opinion for candidates during elections. This was the substance of the startling revelations made by the two-member sub-committee (comprising Kalimekolan Sreenivas Reddy and Paranjoy Guha Thakurta) instituted by the Press Council of India (PCI), in its report detailing what it calls paid news (PCI 2010). The PCI report explains the phenomenon of "paid news" succinctly:

> The entire operation is clandestine. This malpractice has become widespread and now cuts across newspapers and television channels, small and large, in different languages and located in various parts of the country. What is worse, these illegal operations have become "organized" and involve advertising agencies and public relations firms, besides journalists, managers and owners of media companies. Marketing executives use the services of journalists "willingly or otherwise" to gain access to political personalities. So-called "rate cards" or "packages" are distributed that often include "rates" for publication of "news" items that not merely praise particular candidates but also criticize their political opponents. Candidates who do not go along with such "extortionist" practices on the part of media organizations are denied coverage. (PCI 2010, 5)

It is significant that while there was ample evidence of paid news and, for the first time, it has been articulated by the Press Council in such unambiguous terms, action to curb such practices began only in the aftermath of the 2009 General Elections. Yet the 2014 General Elections only witnessed a rise in the phenomenon, not a decline. The media remains in denial, much as the propaganda model (Herman and Chomsky 1988) had pointed to this characteristic of the press as its dislike of "media flak" or avoiding of any critical scrutiny of itself. Moreover, it is able to influence policymaking in its favour through its powerful industry associations. That said, the recent arrest and denial of bail of two powerful media barons, Subrato Roy and Tarun Tejpal, for two very different reasons, should serve as a warning to media moguls who expect to evade law and regulation given their highly privileged position. In hindsight, the Zee extortion case traces its genetic material to such a media code that weighs its products as a set of rewards and punishments that can buy and sell public opinion instead of looking upon news and information as a public good. Unlike several other developed media markets around the world, including those in the United States, Canada and the United Kingdom, there are no clear policy strictures articulating restrictions on cross-media ownership of print, television and radio in India (with some provisions built into the FM radio segment), despite the fact that India is the 14th largest entertainment and media market in the world, with industry revenues contributing to 1 per cent of the country's gross domestic product. Beside the need for regulation that will reduce concentration in media ownership, the role and function of press councils and media watch groups need to be strengthened. They remain hazy and irrelevant to the overall media environment.

From chit fund media barons like the Saradha Group owner Sudipta Sen to the jail sentencing of Subrato Roy and Tarun Tejpal, it is clear that if journalism has to play a constructive role in a democracy it should not be reduced to becoming a trade, intensely impacting the self-reflective communicative spaces that are available in the public sphere for audiences. There is a deep cleavage between the public interest and social responsibility remit of the media, on the one hand, and profit-making that essentially requires media to sell news, on the other hand. Increasingly, attempts are being made to own the media by proxy, producing a kind of phantom journalism in which the real sponsors never stand up. In this sham media culture, the overriding importance of media to a democracy is lost. Therefore, the news business in the decades following liberalization of the Indian media has witnessed a bi-polar division of media ownership between either the big media corporations (the Rupert Murdoch-led Star TV network, Zee Television network, TV Today Group and TV18 Group all becoming major media conglomerates with mergers, acquisition and where cross-media ownership has become the *modus operandi* of such growth) or by influential politicos (as in the south by the Reddy and the Maran families). The situation has been complicated further as deregulation and privatization has meant clandestine firms with such entities involved in illegal collection of money and black money launderers investing in news business for multivariate interests.

It is evident that crony capitalism is transforming journalism in India. This redefinition is not to one of a conscience-keeper of society but to that of a business model that panders to vested interests in the name of journalism. It has, needless to say, a profound and telling impact on the news practice. Investigative journalism has vanished, as paid news and advertorials, where virtually everything is up for sale, much like its owners, has sabotaged the news media space. This breed of news that relies more on high-decibel visibility and devious sensationalism to earn profits impacts journalistic ethics negatively by its hegemonic, preposterous and ritualized subservience to the power structure, being a derivate of the same ilk; and it is only getting more entrenched and deeply embedded.

Therefore, a political economy of news production with crony capitalism structured into its institutional design augurs bad news for democracy as one set of fraudulent practices fails to question larger instances of corruption and poor governance. The market context of the production of news makes the profession susceptible to control and manipulation by powerful political and capitalist powers, creating a conflict of interest with its role of a public sentinel in modern democracies. The five cases discussed above substantiate the point that such *phantom journalism*, with a mysterious nature of pooling finances and clandestine money trails, is inconsistent with any assumed notions of journalism as key to building critical consciousness in society. It casts a doubt on the enabling role of contemporary journalism when its own principles and practices are ephemeral, secretive and transitional—much like a phantom, masquerading between spotlights and shadows.

DISCLOSURE STATEMENT

No potential conflict of interest was reported by the author.

NOTES

1. All currency conversions in this article are calculated at a US Dollar to Indian Rupee conversion rate of 60.97 as on 13 September 2014.
2. The 2G spectrum scam is considered to be among the biggest corruption rackets in the history of the country, reportedly resulting in a loss of up to INR 1.76 lakh crore (US$40 billion) to the national exchequer due to undercharging of frequency allocation licences to mobile telephony companies. Following public interest litigation, the Supreme Court of India in February 2012 quashed all 122 licences issued in 2008 by the then Communications and Information Technology minister A. Raja, declaring them illegal. An aftermath of this scam, along with the Commonwealth Games scam and the Coalgate scam, was the launch of the India Against Corruption campaign culminating in the formation of the Aam Admi Party.
3. A copy of the SEBI notice is available at http://www.sebi.gov.in/cms/sebi_data/attachdocs/1366731012533.pdf.
4. For the transcripts of the Radia tapes, visit the website of the news magazine *The Outlook* at http://www.outlookindia.com/article/The-Radia-Tapes/268214.

REFERENCES

ASCI (Administrative Staff College of India). 2009. *Study on Cross Media Ownership in India: Draft Report*. New Delhi: Ministry of Information and Broadcasting.

Anand, Utkarsh. 2013. "2G Case: SC Issues Contempt Notice against Sahara Chief Subrata Roy, Others." *The Indian Express*, December 9. http://archive.indianexpress.com/news/2g-case-sc-issues-contempt-notice-against-sahara-chief-subrata-roy-others/1205299/.

Bagdikian, Ben H. 2004. *The New Media Monopoly*. 7th ed. Boston, MA: Beacon Press.

Baker, Edwin C. 2002. *Media, Markets, and Democracy*. Cambridge: Cambridge University Press.

Baker, Edwin C. 2007. *Media Concentration and Democracy: Why Ownership Matters*. Cambridge: Cambridge University Press.

Bhushan, Bharat. 2013a. "Money Matters." In *The Hoot Reader: Media Practices in the Twenty-first Century*, edited by Sevanti Ninan and Subarno Chattarji, 332–334. New Delhi: Oxford University Press.

Bhushan, Sandeep. 2013b. "Manufacturing News." *Economic and Political Weekly* XLVIII (23): 12–15.

Business Standard. 2013. "Mamata Sets up Fund for Duped Saradha Investors." *Business Standard*, April 24.

Chakravartty, Paula, and Srirupa Roy. 2013. "Media Pluralism Redux: Towards New Frameworks of Comparative Media Studies 'Beyond the West.'" *Political Communication* 30 (3): 349–370.

Chowdhury, Subhanil. 2013. "The Political Economy of Shadow Finance in West Bengal." *Economic and Political Weekly* 48 (18).

Dalal, Sucheta. 2003. "Selling News or Buying Silence?" *Rediff.com*. March 5. http://www.rediff.com/money/2003/mar/05dalal.htm.

Doyle, Gillian. 2002. *Media Ownership*. London: Sage.

Dutta, Ananya, and Shiv Sahay Singh. 2013. "Chit Fund Scam Accused Blames Trinamool MPs." *The Hindu*, April 25.

FICCI (Federation of Indian Chambers of Commerce and Industry) KPMG International. 2013. *The Power of a Billion – Realizing the Indian Dream: FICCI-KPMG Indian Media and Entertainment Industry Report 2013*. New Delhi: KPMG International Cooperative.

Herman, Edward, and Noam Chomsky. 1988. *Manufacturing Consent: The Political Economy of the Mass Media*. New York: Pantheon Books.

Indian Express. 2012. "Naveen Jindal vs. Zee News: Two top TV Executives Held for 'Extortion.'" November 28. http://archive.indianexpress.com/news/naveen-jindal-vs-zee-news-two-top-tv-executives-held-for-extortion-/1037281/.

Jebaraj, Priscilla. 2012. "Jindal Plays CD, Claims Zee editors Demanded Rs. 100 Crore." *The Hindu*, October 25. http://www.thehindu.com/news/national/jindal-plays-cd-claims-zee-editors-demanded-rs-100-crore/article4031340.ece.

Jeffrey, Robin. 2000. *India's Newspaper Revolution*. 3rd ed. New Delhi: Oxford University Press.

McChesney, Robert Waterman. 1999. *Rich Media, Poor Democracy: Communication Politics in Dubious Times*. Urbana: University of Illinois Press.

McChesney, Robert Waterman. 2003. "Corporate Media, Global Capitalism." In *Media Organization and Production*, edited by Simon Cottle, 27–40. London: Sage.

McChesney, Robert Waterman. 2008. *The Political Economy of Media: Enduring Issues, Emerging Dilemmas*. Urbana, IL: Monthly Review Press.

Muralidharan, Sukumar. 2007. "Broadcast Regulation and Public Right to Know." *Economic and Political Weekly* 42 (9): 743–751.

Ninan, Sevanti. 2007. *Headlines from the Heartland*. New Delhi: Sage.

Ninan, Sevanti. 2013a. "Sun-shine in Tamil Nadu." In *The Hoot Reader: Media Practices in the Twenty-first Century*, edited by Sevanti Ninan and Subarno Chattarji, 322–323. New Delhi: Oxford University Press.

Ninan, Sevanti. 2013b. "A Surrogate Media Ownership." *Live Mint*, November 13. http://www.livemint.com/Opinion/FbTn976LbPqSWvs9RukmUN/A-surrogate-media-ownership.html.

Ninan, Sevanti, and Subarno Chattarji, eds. 2013. *The Hoot Reader: Media Practices in the Twenty-first Century*. New Delhi: Oxford University Press.

PCI (Press Council of India). 2010. *"Paid News": How Corruption in the Indian Media Undermines Democracy*. PCI Sub-Committee Report. http://www.outlookindia.com/article.aspx?266542.

Pradhan, Kunal, and Gayatri Jayaraman. 2013. "Disgrace: A Fabled Media Star Falls over Allegations of Rape." *India Today*, December 9.

Rajagopal, Arvind. 2001. *Politics after Television: Hindu Nationalism and the Reshaping of the Public in India*. Cambridge: Cambridge University Press.

Roy, Srirupa. 2011. "Television News and Democratic Change in India." *Media Culture Society* 33 (5): 761–777. doi:10.1177/0163443711404467.

Saeed, Saima. 2009. "Negotiating Power: Community Media, Democracy and the Public Sphere." *Development in Practice* 19 (4/5): 466–478.

Saeed, Saima. 2013. *Screening the Public Sphere: Media and Democracy in India*. New Delhi: Routledge.

Sasi, Anil, and Subhomoy Bhattacharjee. 2014. "Subrata Roy Arrest Row: The Not So Beautiful Story." *The Indian Express*, March 9.

Schiller, Herbert I. 1989. *Culture Inc.: The Corporate Takeover of Public Expression*. New York: Oxford University Press.

SFIO (Serious Fraud Investigation Office). 2013. *Serious Fraud Investigation Office Report*. New Delhi: Ministry of Corporate Affairs. http://www.thehoot.org/web/simages/2013/11/12/2013-11-12~2.pdf.

Singh, Gyanant. 2011. "Sahara Group Chief Subrata Roy in 2G Probe Tangle." *India Today*, May 7. http://indiatoday.intoday.in/story/sahara-group-chief-subrata-roy-in-2g-probe-tangle/1/137409.html.

Sinha, Nikhil. 1998. "Doordarshan, Public Service Broadcasting and the Impact of Globalization: A Short History." In *Broadcasting Reform in India: Media Law from a Global Perspective*, edited by Monroe E. Price and Stefaan G. Verhulst, 22–40. New Delhi: Oxford University Press.

Suresh, Appu Esthose. 2013. "Two Companies that Put Rs 28 Crore in Tehelka Linked to Jindal Firm Named in Coal Scam FIR." *Indian Express*, December 13.

Thakurta, Paranjoy Guha. 2011. "Manufacturing 'News.'" *Economic and Political Weekly* XLVI (14): 12–14.

Thakurta, Paranjoy Guha. 2014. "What Future for the Media in India? Reliance Takeover of Network 18." *Economic and Political Weekly* XLIX (25): 12–14.

Thakurta, Paranjoy Guha, and Subi Chaturvedi. 2012. "Corporatisation of the Media: Implications of the RIL-Network18-Eenadu Deal." *Economic and Political Weekly* XLVII (7): 10–13.

Thussu, Daya K. 1999 "Privatizing the Airwaves: The Impact of Globalization on Broadcasting in India." *Media, Culture and Society* 21 (1): 125–131. doi:10.1177/016344399021001007.

Thussu, Daya K. 2007. "The 'Murdochization' of News? The Case of Star TV in India." *Media, Culture and Society* 29 (4): 593–611. doi:10.1177/0163443707076191.

TRAI (Telecom Regulatory Authority of India). 2014. *Recommendations on Issues Relating to Media Ownership*. New Delhi: Mahanagar Doorsanchar Bhawan.

Venkatesan, J. 2011. "Contempt Proceedings against Sahara Chief Begin." *The Hindu*, May 6.

SHAMING THE NATION ON PUBLIC AFFAIRS TELEVISION
Barkha Dutt tackles colorism on *We the People*

Radhika Parameswaran

The commercial discourses of the skin-lightening cosmetics industry in globalizing India have propped up the ideological legitimacy of colorism or skin color discrimination whereby dark-skinned Indians are viewed as inferior to and less valued than light-skinned Indians. Two episodes of NDTV journalist Barkha Dutt's national public affairs television program We the People *(2008 and 2013) tackle the growing problem of commodity colorism in India. My textual analysis of these two episodes of* We the People *examines the ways in which Barkha Dutt takes up and creates a forum for debate on the incendiary issues of racism and colorism on her show. I consider the agents, institutions, and social structures she holds accountable in these programs, and I explore the perspectives on anti-colorism and anti-racism that gain visibility or get marginalized in* We the People's *televised terrain of democracy and civil society.*

Introduction

On Sunday, October 6, 2013, NDTV's well-known media personality and celebrity journalist, Barkha Dutt, looked directly at viewers of her weekly late evening national public affairs show *We the People*, as she greeted *and* interrogated them with a microphone in her hand, "Hello and welcome to *We the People*. Are we Indians deeply racist? Why are we so obsessed with fair skin?" This provocative 2013 episode of *We the People*, titled "An Un-fair Obsession," was a sequel to a previous episode "Not Just Skin-deep Prejudice," which aired on September 14, 2008, and on that earlier episode, Dutt makes a similar demand of NDTV's viewers in her trademark bold and confrontational style, "Good evening and welcome to *We the People*. Is India a country of closet racists? Even today, are we obsessed with fair skin and are we biased against those with dark complexions?" Staging a raucous and disruptive theater of "shaming the nation" on television, these two episodes of *We the People* contest the regressive epidermal politics of colorism and racism that has saturated public culture in the new global India, which has witnessed an unprecedented surge in the manufacture and sales of skin-lightening products over the last two decades. The proliferating commercial discourses of India's burgeoning skin-lightening beauty industry—billboards, commercials, advertisements, celebrity endorsements, and public relations events—peddle "gendered pedagogies" of the body replete with visual lessons that cast imperfect skin as "abject and as a social taboo" (Kenway and Bullen 2011, 285). Such commodity discourses of beauty products as agents of remedy, salvation, and upward mobility circulate within the context of an India that is caught up in the neoliberal rhetoric of its own transformation, from occupying marginal "third world" status to becoming a lucrative "emerging market" and "rising global power."

Sold widely in Asia, Africa, and the Middle East, skin-lightening products, one of the fastest growing sectors of the global skin-care industry, and their accompanying commercial skin stories coach consumers to endorse the troubling premises of colorism. Sociologist Glenn (2008, 281) defines colorism, a pervasive axis of inequality found in many societies worldwide, as a "social hierarchy based on gradations of skin tone within and between racial/ethnic groups." Black sociologists in the United States were among the first to shift the lens of inquiry in critical race studies from binary models of racism (White/non-White) to the more complex beliefs and practices of internalized racism based in skin tone—colorism—that perpetuate discrimination against dark-skinned black people within their own communities (Celious and Oyserman 2001; Falconer and Neville 2000). Black feminists, in particular, have argued that dark-skinned black women experience skin color discrimination to a far greater degree than black men, both in the public sphere of work and employment *and* in the private sphere of family, marriage, and romantic relations (Hill 2002; Hunter 2002). The global skin-lightening beauty industry's significations of the inferiority of dark skin, as anthropologist Saraswati (2012) notes, emerge from historical structures of pigmentocracy (hierarchy of pigmentation) that marginalize dark-skinned people of color living in western nations and natives of such non-western nations as India, China, Philippines, Indonesia, Vietnam, Singapore, Taiwan, Bolivia, Venezuela, Tanzania, Senegal, and Ghana. Commercial beauty discourses promoting skin codes of social distinction in postcolonial India sustain a pigmentocracy that draws its currency from casteism and classism, racism and colonial history, and disputed hegemonic mythologies of a superior light-skinned Aryan race's conquest of dark-skinned Dravidians.

Barkha Dutt's staging of two full-length episodes of *We the People* that tackle racism and colorism intervenes in the midst of the boom in sales of skin-lightening cosmetics in India to offer a lively and vigorous counter-discourse of resistance to the fetishization of light skin color in commodity culture. Following her welcome greeting in the 2008 episode, Dutt targets Hindustan Lever's Fair & Lovely for its global dissemination of colorism, "Why is it that Fair & Lovely is the largest selling fairness product in the world? Is the fairness industry really unfair and ugly?" Indeed, India's intensifying public love affair with the pigmentocracy of skin-lightening cosmetics has caught the attention of major media outlets in other parts of the world. A 2007 *New York Times* story describes the "unabated sales" of skin-lightening cosmetics in India: "Skin-lightening products are by far the most popular product in India's fast growing skin care market, so manufacturers say they ignore them at their peril. The $318 million market for skin care has grown by 42.7% since 2001, says Euromonitor International, a research firm" (Timmons 2007). Packed with quotes from business executives and data on sales of cosmetics, a BBC story titled "Unbearable Lightness of Being" describes the "snow white syndrome in India, a market where sales of whitening creams are far outstripping those of Coca Cola and tea" (Ray 2010). In 2006, Bollywood celebrity and global supermodel, Aishwarya Rai, whose face had testified to L'Oreal White Perfect cream's mastery over the science of melanin destruction, could not escape being grilled on the Oprah Winfrey show about why "Indians spend over a hundred million dollars on skin lightening cosmetics" ("Aishwarya Rai Interview with Oprah Winfrey" 2006). Classified as among the most light-skinned celebrities in India, Rai responds to Oprah in a bland and diplomatic fashion while carefully avoiding any mention of her earlier modeling work for L'Oreal White Perfect. She repudiates colorism, and playing the role of a dutiful cultural ambassador of her nation, calls for a tolerant and inclusive multi-cultural celebration of the diverse plurality of Indian men and women's bodies. Such well-intentioned, but, partially voyeuristic western media accounts that aim to "expose" the ugly underbelly of a primitive pigmentocracy that haunts a modernizing non-western nation rarely incorporate the voices or agency of opinion leaders, organizations, and individuals, who have fought against the strong currents of colorism that flow through the circuits of everyday culture in India.

What does a critique of the abject conditions of the dark-skinned Indian body look like when an iconic Indian woman journalist—Barkha Dutt—orchestrates discussions of colorism and racism on her award-winning show *We the People*? Barkha Dutt, the Group Editor for English News at NDTV, a leading television network in India, and a weekly columnist for the *Hindustan Times* and *Khaleej Times*, has become a household name among middle-class television audiences for her athletic performances as the host of her weekly current events show *We the People* (borrowed from the preamble to the Constitution of India), where the topics discussed range from electoral politics and political scandals to international news and controversial social issues (Parameswaran 2012). My textual analysis of these two episodes addresses the following questions: How does Barkha Dutt tackle these incendiary issues of racism and colorism in India? What agents and institutions and power hierarchies does she hold accountable in her critiques of colorism? Which are the voices of anti-colorism and anti-racism that gain visibility or get marginalized in *We the People*'s televised terrain of democracy and civil society? The first step in my methodological approach involved viewing each episode from start to finish twice for a holistic assessment of the program's format and Dutt's hosting style. I then watched each episode numerous times in a more choppy and repetitive fashion to unpack systematically the visual and performative aspects of *We the People*'s moving images; transcribe and transform the audio portion to text along with notations on the non-verbal body language of various actors; and complete an inventory of the topics that emerged, names and profiles of experts featured, and speaking times allocated to different experts. After verifying and correcting drafts of transcriptions with more repeat viewing, I then read closely and analyzed the transcribed audio text and notes for denotative and connotative meanings.

The Ugliness of Beauty Norms

Dutt divides her studio audience into two groups: experts, celebrities, and leaders who represent various sections of the Indian national body politic (corporate, political, media, and academic institutions, and non-governmental organizations (NGOs) and activist/social movements) and ordinary Indian citizens (often the middle-class English-speaking elite) from different socio-economic strata. In *We the People*'s stadium-style studio arena, participants are seated in a concentric, multi-level ascending circular formation with expert speakers typically seated in the lowest interior circle. Host Barkha Dutt performs the role of an agile interlocutor as she leaps quickly from person to person while shooting questions, fielding responses, expressing contrasting opinions, nudging shy participants, and interrupting dominating speakers' monologues. Notwithstanding this English-language television program's interpellation of an elite Indian national audience, the composition of the studio audience and the relatively intimate, informal, and unruly atmosphere of debate in the studio signal *We the People*'s attempt to simulate an ideal democratic public sphere that provides access to and registers a wide range of arguments and perspectives. In the two episodes under scrutiny in this article, Dutt supervises and sets the boundaries of debate among representatives of the beauty industry (models, magazine editors, owners of modeling agencies, and salon beauticians), television and film actors, advertising industry professionals, journalists, academics, lawyers, and medical professionals (psychiatrist and dermatologist). She typically spends the first half of the program quizzing these experts before she turns the show over to ordinary citizens.

One major theme that emerged across both episodes of *We the People* is a critique of the hegemonic and exclusionary ideals of light-skinned beauty that govern both the mediated realms of Indian advertising, film, and television representations and the social norms and practices of everyday life (Osuri 2008; Karan 2008). On the 2008 episode, model and Bollywood actress Deepal Shaw sets the tone for the heated discussion that follows with the outspoken observation that her skin tone, which was several shades darker than superstars Katrina Kaif or Aishwarya Rai, limited the roles she could play on screen because darkness and duskiness were associated with forbidden, primitive, and raw sexiness and "sensuousness" rather than with being wholesome, beautiful, and innocent, that is, a woman with light skin color signified a respectable potential life partner that a man might take home to his mother. A visibly outraged Deepal also questions the irony of light-skinned beauty's elevation in a country where a "majority of people are dark skinned." In the 2013 episode, Barkha Dutt invites well-known actress Nandita Das (also considered to be more dark-skinned than her counterparts), who has acted in such major international films as *Fire* and *Earth*, to lead the show with a critique of rampant colorism in society and in the Bollywood film industry. When Dutt addresses beautician Ambica Pillai openly as someone who is not "fair," Pillai laughs and declares her satisfaction with her own skin color, but also makes note of the demand for skin-lightening services from brides who beg her to make them "ten shades fairer" for their wedding ceremonies. After some hesitation, a small retail business owner echoes Das' concerns about the exclusion of dark-skinned Indians in the booming urban media and service sectors (airline, hospitality, and tourism) to admit hesitantly that all things being equal, he would hire a light-skinned candidate over a dark-skinned candidate for a sales or service position because good-looking employees have greater chances of gaining the trust and approval of customers. Presenting these different opinions and regulating the flow of emotional currents through her studio space, Dutt skillfully brings out the ways in which skin color discrimination permeates the different crevices of Indian society.

We the People's serious examination of colorism in the Indian modeling, acting, and service professions in these two episodes (2008 and 2013) builds on the momentum of earlier critiques of beauty and skin color discrimination in mainstream Indian popular culture. *Femina* magazine's September 1, 2000 issue's cover story "Dark is Beautiful: Why Are We Still Carrying the Dark Skin Prejudice," was among the first major stories in India's mainstream corporate media to challenge colorism (Bose 2000). This story interrupts the elevation of the lightness/fairness ideal in beauty norms, outlining historical explanations that point to "fairness as an impostor, introduced into India through the Western other" (Reddy 2006, 75). In this cover story, cosmetologists, fashion photographers, beauticians, and supermodels bemoan colorism and note that the fashion industry has slowly begun to recognize Indian models for personality and poise rather than complexion. Zee channel's evening serial *Saath Phere-Saloni Ka Safar*, launched in 2005 and broadcasted till 2009, chronicled female protagonist Saloni's struggles with overcoming prejudice against her dark skin color within her own family. Similarly, the Star Plus television drama *Sapna Babul ... Ka Bidaai* (2007–2010), featured a main female lead Ragini, a young woman with a dark complexion, who is rejected by suitors in the arranged marriage system and often compared unfairly to Sadhana, her lighter-skinned female cousin. Actress Parul Chauhan, who plays Ragini on *Bidaai*, is one of the featured guests on the 2008 episode of *We the People*, and she testifies during the show that her skin was darkened further for her role on *Bidaai*. Barkha Dutt's insertion of normative beauty's exclusionary ideologies into the more weighty "public affairs" terrain of *We the People* legitimizes the issue of sexism and colorism as topics that are worthy of serious national debate. She brings the Indian beauty industry's workers—models and actors—out, from behind the screens and pages of fictional television and glossy niche women's magazines, onto the stage of her journalistic program to lay bare the ugly underbelly of skin color prejudice in a burgeoning sector of India's capitalist economy.

Dutt leads her 2013 episode with an introduction of actress Nandita Das as the public face of the activist campaign "Dark is Beautiful," launched by the organization "Women of Worth." Dutt's decision to showcase Nandita Das as the leading voice on her talk show reflects the global spread of the "celebritization" of social and humanitarian causes, a trend in many mediatized societies whereby social movements, citizens' organizations, global governance institutions, and NGOs harness celebrity capital to brand and gain publicity for their causes (Duvall 2011; Wheeler 2011). Kavitha Emmanuel, the founder-director of the Chennai-based organization "Women of Worth" launched the "Dark is Beautiful" campaign to raise awareness about widespread skin color discrimination in Indian society, including in the media, beauty, and service industries, and to provide ordinary people with an outlet to express their sadness or frustration regarding discrimination based in skin color (Krupa 2013). Das' face adorns the 2013 campaign's posters headlined as "Stay Unfair, Stay Beautiful," and gazing directly at her audience, the actress laments the lack of public debate on skin color bias at a time when society is filled with "blatant and subtle reinforcements that only fair is lovely."

Standing in as a glamorous and recognizable alibi for founder Kavitha Emmanuel, actress Nandita Das imports popular psychology's therapeutic discourse of individual pain, internalized prejudice, and confession into the televised arena of *We the People* (Ilouz 2008; Peck 1995). When Barkha Dutt prods Das about her motivation to endorse the "Dark is Beautiful" campaign, the actress denounces the skin color discrimination that affects small children like her neighbor's dark-skinned daughter, who are taunted and teased for their dark skin in school because that "kills your self-esteem" and low self-esteem, she asserts, can cripple children emotionally, preventing them from pursuing even simple and normal activities in their daily life. Supermodel Nethra Raghuraman recounts the skin color bias she faced as a child, "Also, in my school life and college life, I was told I was ugly … you're so dark, you're so dark, you're so dark. My parents made me believe who I am and what I am … they made me confident." Dutt brings out this theme further on the show when she solicits the opinions and confessions of her carefully selected studio audience members. One distraught mother speaks with anger and frustration lacing her voice, "I would like to say that, when my daughter was born, she was dark. Everyone who came to the hospital was horrified to see her … but from the time, two years old to when she was a little older, I started telling her 'brown is your lovely chocolate color.'" Speaking in Hindi with an encouraging tone, Dutt interviews a young covered Muslim woman about her emotional and physical abuse at the hands of her in-laws and husband, who rejected her for her dark skin, eventually sending her back to her parents' home. These embodied and performative confessional testimonies, when narrated on television in conjunction with a well-known female talk show host's support, call upon *We the People*'s studio and national audiences to bear public witness to the trauma and pain that colorism inflicts on its victims.

In the process of orchestrating a debate on the epidermal politics of beauty and physical appearance in Indian society, Dutt's *We the People* does feature some discussion of the origins and implications of colorism in India, but these important sociological and historical perspectives on patriarchy, colonialism, caste, class, and race that fuel colorism receive only fleeting and superficial attention. The 2008 episode is practically silent on this topic, but the 2013 episode includes brief references from invited experts. At one point in the discussion, neuro-psychiatrist Dr. Rajesh Parikh cautions against making sweeping judgments of patients' light skin fetish as a mental disorder, but suggests that society needs to understand the historical reasons, "So, historically, races that are Caucasian have overpowered darker races. That is what happened on our continent. They brought with them their myths and their stories prevail today because they were the victors." Actress Nandita Das shares her frustrations with the class prejudices of the film industry where she experiences pressures to lighten her skin in order to signify distance from poverty and manual labor, "When I do a character, which is upper middle class or educated, that's when the make-up man or the director will say, 'I know you don't like to put make-up and all of that, but it will be really nice if you lighten your skin because this is an affluent character.'" Feminist lawyer Veena Gowda, who receives very little air time, pushes Dutt and the studio audience to unpack further the "racial, classist, and casteist" origins of colorism, arguing that in India we "believe that being fair is also upper caste and upper class," but Dutt quickly moves onto another expert. On the 2008 episode, a young man in the studio audience interjects passionately to point out the links between colorism and racism in Indian society, "I have an African friend, I'm a first-year college student … And let me tell you, he's been subjected to such appalling discrimination, such appalling racial discrimination by us, Indians." Dutt thanks him for his honesty, but shifts hastily to another topic, thus missing the opportunity to engage her national audience in introspection on the racist treatment of Black sojourners and students in India.

Putting the Advertising Industry on Trial

Both episodes of *We the People* offer a rare view of the advertising industry on trial, with Barkha Dutt grilling seasoned advertising professionals about their troubling endorsement of colorism when they hire only light-skinned models or when they create advertisements and commercials that project dark skin as a disease, as inferior to light skin, and as a deterrent to Indian women's achievement of happiness or professional success (Parameswaran and Cardoza 2009). Postcolonial feminist scholars have produced a sustained critique of the ways in which the advertising industry in globalizing India has reinforced and exacerbated hegemonic feminine ideals of beauty and domesticity (Chaudhuri 2001; Munshi 1998; Reddy 2006), but Dutt takes these criticisms one step further by interrogating and holding advertising professionals accountable on television for advertising's culpability in spreading and legitimating colorism. Alyque Padamsee—former

CEO of Lintas advertising agency, well-known English theater director, winner of the Padmashree award, and Mumbai Advertising Club's "Advertising Man of the Century"—appears on the show in 2008 *and* 2013 in his capacity as the creative director of advertising for Hindustan Lever's Fair & Lovely skin-lightening products. Dutt also features Prahlad Kakar, leading Indian advertising film director and founder and director of Genesis Film productions, on the show. Kakar's and Padamsee's willingness to appear on *We the People*, given the show's reputation for taking on controversial topics, testifies to Barkha Dutt's star power as a media celebrity in her own right.

If Dutt's persona tilted toward being a sympathetic and therapeutic mediator with some of the women studio participants referenced in the earlier section, in contrast, she cultivates a far more oppositional and adversarial persona in her conversations with elite advertising experts. Viewers see shades of the feisty Barkha Dutt, the hard-nosed investigative journalist and one of the few Indian women to report from the frontlines of war, emerge in her assertive interactions with Padamsee and Kakar. In her opening verbal exchange with Padamsee in the 2008 episode, Dutt does not hold back, "Alyque Padamsee, as somebody who is the architect of Fair & Lovely in India and then Fair & Handsome ... Alyque, aren't you embarrassed? Aren't you embarrassed? How can you stand up as a liberal of Bombay and endorse nonsense like fairness is a virtue?" When Alyque, an expert on theater production, responds to say that "fairness is not a virtue," but just an aesthetic property that helps light reflect off people's bodies, Barkha Dutt fires back impatiently while vigorously shaking her head to indicate disagreement, "Isn't that racist, isn't that racist?"

On the 2013 program, she first hails Padmasee as "the granddaddy of fairness cream advertising," and then, violating professional journalistic tenets of objectivity and the commitment to produce a "balanced treatment" of the topic, Dutt proceeds to declare, "Alyque, I agree with you on so many things, but on this, I have got to say I am so much in disagreement. I have to declare my bias on this program." When Alyque tries to interrupt and cut her off, she stops him and inserts herself as a "dark-skinned woman" into the narrative arc of the program, "No, you listen to me first, No, You listen to me first, No, you listen to me first ... I'm not sad, but I'm not under-confident, and I have a huge problem with how many ads link confidence to fair skin." Later in the conversation, Dutt also challenges Padamsee to judge whether he thought she herself was unattractive, and when Padamsee insists that Dutt is good-looking because she wears make-up for her television role, she retorts immediately with another personal question, "You're saying to me that if you rub this war paint off, then I'd be an ugly duckling?" Dutt also subjects Prahlad Kakar to her critical scrutiny at the beginning of the 2008 program, calling him out for racism and sexism when he admits that he has to succumb to many corporate clients' demands for light-skinned female models because they want their products to be associated with high status and respectability. Kakar redeems himself later in the show though when he takes the position that he would not advertise fairness creams on principle, thus distancing himself from Padamsee as a more progressive advertising professional.

Deploying her skills as a seasoned moderator, Dutt allocates a fair share of time on *We the People* to other invited experts who openly share their frustration with the Indian advertising industry's complicity in promoting light skin as a valued form of bodily capital. Mumbai's well-known freelance journalist, poet, and children's book author, Jerry Pinto, denounces angrily the flood of Fair & Lovely commercials that produce the dark-skinned woman as an abject person: "everything about her spells loser, her hair is bad, her clothes are bad ... and then she puts on this cream that claims to do things by attacking the pigment God gave you, and therefore attacking your selfhood." A few minutes later, in response to Dutt's query about the source to blame for society's collective biases, Pinto unequivocally lays the blame on advertising professionals, even as he directs his contempt first at Padamsee and then at Kakar, "I'm saying these people get together in rooms, yeah, these sinister advertising types ... and they actually work out in a clinical and completely horrible manner that we can play on neuroses, we can play on fear." When prompted by Dutt, sociologist Shiv Vishwanathan agrees with Pinto, offering his academic opinion that advertising is a "fake science" that capitalizes on and fuels folk fears on colorism that circulate on the ground.

Padamsee, who is given far more air-time than any other experts on the 2008 *and* 2013 episodes of *We the People*, blends a discursive cocktail of postmodernism and neoliberal conceptions of choice to rationalize his production of Fair & Lovely commercials. He insists defensively on the 2008 episode that the desire for light skin is no different than consumers' dissatisfaction with a spectrum of bodily imperfections and deprivations, "What's wrong with having a long nose? What's wrong with being cock-eyed? What's wrong with wearing torn clothes? What's wrong with not having a bath for three days?" Parroting a similar view on the 2013 show, he argues that skin-lightening products fulfill the same aspirations for beauty as lipsticks, *kaajal* [eyeliner], smooth pimple-free skin, and padded bras. Padamsee blames Dutt for not posing more fundamental questions about "beauty and ugliness" and about why even educated Indians, who indicate preferences for brides or grooms in matrimonial advertisements, never embrace ugliness. He defends Indian consumers' right to choose beauty products that promise them advantages in a trendy and competitive marketplace. On the 2013 show, actress Nandita Das gently tries to counter Padamsee's vision of ahistorical and apolitical consumer choice, but her brief and quietly delivered argument that there is a difference between "personal choice and societal prejudice" in the context of widespread skin color discrimination in India does not match Padamsee's vigorous, loud, and lengthy monologues.

Whether intended or not, these open and direct discussions with advertising professionals on commodity colorism transform *We the People*'s television arena into a pedagogic space for broader reflection on the relationship between advertising and hegemonic social norms and practices. Although Prahlad Kakar expresses a more liberal point of view regarding skin-lightening commercials than Padamsee does, he too joins the corporate bandwagon of accusing society rather than advertising for the exclusionary practices that some have to endure, "All advertising, at the end of the day, is actually a mirror that society looks into, and wants to see what they want to see ... if society doesn't see in it what they want to see, it never works." Journalist Jerry Pinto contests Kakar's views that shift all the blame for prejudice onto society, "There is a neurosis, there is a problem with color that exists ... it has been exacerbated by advertising. Another example, dandruff ... when I was growing up, dandruff was not a social issue and now it is." Pinto's opinions echo scholarly work on advertising's tutelary and generative functions, particularly in the context of globalizing India where large segments of the population have been experiencing their active interpellation into mediated forms of consumer citizenship (Rajagopal 1998). On the 2013 episode, Mahesh Mathai, cinematographer, argues that as a communication professional, he would not want to participate in the production of any messages that cement prejudice, lead to discrimination, or lead to segregation of a group, thus clarifying his perspective that advertising is capable of solidifying *and* generating hegemonic norms with society sometimes leading the charge and sometimes following behind advertising.

After inviting comments from Padamsee, Kakar, Mathai, and Pinto on these two episodes, Barkha Dutt makes the bold move of asking her studio audience and other experts whether fairness products and advertisements promoting them should be banned. On the 2013 episode, she moderates discussion on the topic, inviting a range of different opinions, but is careful not to express her own stance, unlike a few other moments on the program where she volunteers her opinions freely. She is also vigilant about not presenting herself as an anti-corporate activist—she does not encourage a campaign to boycott these products nor does she push those who say they would support a ban to speak at length about their feelings or their plans to implement a boycott. Indeed, toward the end of the program, she becomes far less adversarial with Padamsee, and in her closing summary, she also avoids all reference to any bans and simply notes that "beauty is not in the eyes of the beholder, beauty derives from your sense of self and nothing is worth losing that, we leave it there." On the 2008 episode, she poses the question of banning advertisements for skin-lightening products and invites model Deepal Shaw to offer final comments in the concluding portion of the program. Backtracking from her initial displays of outrage and anger, Shaw volunteers the opinion that these products have "a right to exist because it's a person's personal choice ... we are not against fairness creams, you know against fair skin, but we are trying to say that don't be against dusky skin." Letting Padamsee have the last word, she allows him time to present the closing argument that the best route to solving the problem of commodity colorism in India would be to market these products using such euphemisms as "brightening" instead of hitching the branding process to lightening or fairness. Adopting a conciliatory tone, Dutt agrees with him that "we can live with that much better ... and yes, Alyque, it would be a start to have Fair & Lovely go with Bright & Lovely ... it begins with us, with our parents and what we tell our children." Dutt's compromised finale to both episodes blunts the more radical path she appeared to take half-way through these programs; in the end, she places the burden of reducing and eliminating colorism and racism in India on adult individuals (who should develop a strong sense of self) and on parents (who should help their children overcome racism and colorism).

Conclusion: The Possibilities and Limits of *We the People*'s Counter-discourse on Colorism

When pitted against the commercial discourses of commodity colorism that have invaded India's public semio-sphere of the last two decades, Barkha Dutt's *We the People* offers a robust and significant counter-discourse of critique that seeks to undermine the ideology of pigmentocracy. Ordinary Indian citizens, academics, and activists have registered their opposition to the aggressive promotion of light skin as the ticket to romance, marriage, fulfillment, and professional success (Parameswaran 2013), but these forms of contestation emerging from civil society on the ground gain further legitimacy when they enter the circuits of mainstream national media. Alexander and Jacobs (1998) urge scholars to view the media as a central, not merely supplementary, mechanism for facilitating the "communicative space" of civil society in mediatized environments, "What this means is that civil society must be conceived not only as a world of voluntary associations, elections, or even legal rights, but also and very significantly, as a realm of symbolic communication" (24). As they note, if civil society is considered a "sphere of influence and commitment, mediated through public opinion," media become a crucial tool for non-state and grassroots actors to gain support for their causes and to put pressure on elite power brokers in society (26). News media, even more than expressive or fictional media, have the power to act as a "symbolic forum for different individuals and groups, all battling for interpretive authority" over social, economic, and political concerns (30). Selecting members of different constituencies on her public affairs show, journalist Barkha Dutt creates a viable alternative "communicative space" for the staging of a symbolic civil society that interrupts the hegemonic commercial and cultural narratives that reinforce skin color discrimination in India. Unlike ordinary individuals, Dutt, as an insider of NDTV's upper-management and a celebrity journalist, is also able to invite and question elite representatives of the Indian advertising and media industries in the televised public arena of her show for their perpetuation of colorism.

Yet, *We the People*'s production of a symbolic civil society also has some serious limits. Celebrity voices from the film and beauty industries dominate the program's field of discourse, and Dutt's interrogation of advertising professionals starts off as a fierce attack, but meanders toward a conclusive rhetoric of compromise and accommodation that fails to produce a serious indictment of commodity colorism. Dutt could have also channeled the streams of conversation flowing through *We the People*'s studio toward a more serious discussion of the ways in which rampant inequalities of gender, class, caste, region, and tribe intersect with and structure the regressive epidermal politics of media representations in globalizing India. Her roster of experts assembled for these shows could have easily featured leading Indian scholars in feminist studies and sociology to educate properly a national viewing public on the social and historical dimensions of colorism. She gives short shrift to related concerns on the social construction of race and racism, thus ignoring colorism's damaging influences on the treatment of African and African-American tourists, students, and visitors in India.

Although Dutt's episodes of *We the People* seek to push the boundaries of debate on commodity colorism and racism, we cannot forget that her interventions, staged on NDTV's platform, have to operate within the constraints of the political economy of commercial television and mainstream journalism in India. As critics have noted, the capitalist business models that India's rapidly growing news media of the post-liberalization era have adopted—dependence on advertising and sponsorships, driven by ratings and other measures of market share, and nourished by a diet of abundant public relations and paid content—has had serious implications for the voices that get heard and the concerns that earn visibility in the public sphere (Sonwalker 2002; Thussu 2007). Claiming the largest segment of India's market share for cosmetics from 2000 to 2005 and an expanding menu of creams, soaps, and lotions since the early 1990s, skin-lightening products are advertised widely in print, electronic, and outdoor media, with Hindustan Lever's cheaply priced cosmetics dominating Indian television's advertising space (Parameswaran and Cardoza 2009). On the 2013 episode of *We the People* studied here, Dutt herself draws attention to the ways in which the political economy of NDTV could undermine the progressive intent of her critiques of advertising's complicity with colorism. She makes a tongue-in-cheek comment that she would "not at all be surprised" if NDTV chose to air a Fair & Lovely commercial "right there" during a break in her show. In the end, despite these limits, I argue that *We the People*'s programs on colorism do stage a credible and robust simulation of an anti-hegemonic, civil society counter-discourse on television that shames the modernizing nation (India)—with its claims to inclusivity and tolerance—for its silence on the problem of colorism.

ACKNOWLEDGEMENTS

The author thanks MA Journalism student (Indiana University, Bloomington), Shang Yune-Hsu, for her meticulous transcription of online episodes of *We the People*. This research was made possible by the support of a 2013 Summer Faculty Fellowship from the Department of Journalism, Media School, Indiana University, Bloomington.

DISCLOSURE STATEMENT

No potential conflict of interest was reported by the author.

REFERENCES

"Aishwarya Rai Interview with Oprah Winfrey." 2006. http://video.google.com/videoplay?docid=-2278044500626117388.

Alexander, Jeffrey C., and Ronald N. Jacobs. 1998. "Mass Communication, Ritual and Civil Society." In *Media, Ritual and Identity*, edited by Tamar Liebes and James Curran, 23–40. London: Routledge.

"An Un-fair Obsession." 2013. *We the People*. NDTV, October 6. http://www.ndtv.com/video/player/we-the-people/we-the-people-an-un-fair-obsession/293403.

Bose, Rahul. 2000. "Dark Is Beautiful: Chocolate Cream." *Femina*, September 1, 13–18.

Celious, Aaron, and Daphna Oyserman. 2001. "Race from the Inside: An Emerging Heterogeneous Race Model." *Journal of Social Issues* 57 (1): 149–165. doi:10.1111/0022-4537.00206.

Chaudhuri, Maitrayee. 2001. "Gender and Advertisements: Advertisements: the Rhetoric of Globalization." *Women's Studies International Forum* 24 (3): 373–385.

Duvall, Spring-Serenity. 2011. "Celebrity Travels: Media Spectacles and the Construction of Transnational Politics of Care." In *Circuits of Visibility: Gender and Transnational Media Cultures*, edited by Radha S. Hedge, 140–158. New York: New York University Press.

Falconer, Jameca, and Helen Neville. 2000. "African-American College Women's Body Image: An Examination of Body Mass, African Self-consciousness, and Skin Color Satisfaction." *Psychology of Women Quarterly* 24 (3): 236–243. doi:10.1111/j.1471-6402.2000.tb00205.x.

Glenn, Evelyn N. 2008. "Yearning for Lightness: Transnational Circuits in the Marketing and Consumption of Skin Lighteners." *Gender & Society* 22 (3): 281–302. doi:10.1177/0891243208316089.

Hill, Mark E. 2002. "Skin Color and the Perception of Attractiveness among African-Americans: Does Gender Make a Difference?" *Social Psychology Quarterly* 65 (1): 77–91. doi:10.2307/3090169.

Hunter, Margaret L. 2002. "If You're Light, You're Alright: Light Skin Color as Social Capital for Women of Color." *Gender & Society* 16 (2): 175–193.

Ilouz, Eva. 2008. *Saving the Modern Soul*. Berkeley: University of California Press.

Karan, Kavita. 2008. "Obsession with Fair Skin: Color Discourses in Indian Advertising." *Advertising & Society Review* 9 (2): 1–19. http://theshadeofbeauty.files.wordpress.com/2012/11/advertising-society-review-obsessions-with-fair-skin-color-discourses-in-indian-advertisinge2809d.pdf.

Kenway, Jane, and Elizabeth Bullen. 2011. "Skin Pedagogies and Abject Bodies." *Sport, Education, and Society* 16 (3): 279–294. doi:10.1080/13573322.2011.565961.

Krupa, Lakshmi. 2013. "Dark Is Beautiful." *The Hindu*, September 8. http://www.thehindu.com/features/the-yin-thing/dark-is-beautiful/article5104215.ece.

Munshi, Shoma. 1998. "Wife/Mother/Daughter-in-law: Multiple Avatars of Homemaker in 1990s Indian Advertising." *Media, Culture & Society* 20 (4): 573–591. doi:10.1177/016344398020004004.

"Not Just Skin-Deep Prejudice." 2008. *We the People. NDTV*, September 14. http://www.ndtv.com/video/player/we-the-people/not-just-skin-deep-prejudice/96434.

Osuri, Goldie. 2008. "Ash-coloured Whiteness: The Transfiguration of Aishwarya Rai." *South Asian Popular Culture* 6 (2): 109–123. doi:10.1080/14746680802365212.

Parameswaran, Radhika, and Kavitha Cardoza. 2009. "Melanin on the Margins: Advertising and the Cultural Politics of Fair/Light/White Beauty in India." *Journalism & Communication Monographs* 11 (3): 213–274.

Parameswaran, Radhika. 2012. "Watching Barkha Dutt: Turning on the News in Television Studies." *South Asian History & Culture* 3 (4): 626–635.

Parameswaran. Radhika. 2013. "Exfoliating Colorism: Contestations, Comedy, and Critique in a Transnational Field." Paper presented at the annual meeting of the International Communication Association, London, June 17–21.

Peck, Janice. 1995. "TV Talk Shows as Therapeutic Discourse: The Ideological Labor of the Televised Talking Cure." *Communication Theory* 5 (1): 58–81. doi:10.1111/j.1468-2885.1995.tb00098.x.

Rajagopal, Arvind. 1998. "Advertising, Politics, and the Sentimental Education of the Indian Consumer." *Visual Anthropology Review* 14 (2): 14–31. doi:10.1525/var.1998.14.2.14.

Ray, Guha Shantanu. 2010. "India's Unbearable Lightness of Being." *BBC*, March 23. http://news.bbc.co.uk/2/hi/8546183.stm.

Reddy, Vanita. 2006. "The Nationalization of the Global Indian Woman: Geographies of Beauty in *Femina*." *South Asian Popular Culture* 4 (1): 61–85. doi:10.1080/14746680600555691.

Saraswati, Ayu. 2012. "'Malu': Coloring Shame and Shaming the Color of Beauty in Transnational Indonesia." *Feminist Studies* 38 (1): 113–139.

Sonwalker, Prasun. 2002. "'Murdochization' of the Indian Press: From By-line to Bottom-line." *Media, Culture & Society* 24 (6): 821–834. doi:10.1177/016344370202400605.

Thussu, Daya. 2007. "The Murdochization of News: The Case of Star TV in India." *Media, Culture & Society* 29 (4): 593–611.

Timmons, Heather. 2007. "Telling India's Modern Women They Have Power, Even over Their Skin Tone." *New York Times*, May 30. http://www.nytimes.com/2007/05/30/business/media/30adco.html?_r=2&.

Wheeler, Mark. 2011. "Celebrity Diplomacy: United Nations' Goodwill Ambassadors and Messengers of Peace." *Celebrity Studies* 2 (1): 6–18. doi:10.1080/19392397.2011.543267.

PLAYING REPORTER
Small-town women journalists in north India

Disha Mullick

This article presents the findings of a study on women reporters in mofussil *(small towns), in semi-rural or newly urban India. Through in-depth face-to-face interviews with women reporters in four north Indian states, the study documented and analysed the experiences of women reporters outside the metro cities, including a small numbers of women from marginalised castes, of their work environments and policies that inhibit women from entering or staying in the profession. Even in an environment where media was seen to be highly commercial, partisan, political and a dirty business, women were knowledgeable about how to navigate this sphere, how to challenge its norms and how to make their place in it. Findings show that by engaging in media production—knowing fully well the deeply embedded class, caste and gender conventions of this institution—they placed themselves in a position to challenge the status quo, in the private and public spheres, and play out the notion of lived, engaged citizenship.*

Introduction

Three things that happened with me when I became a reporter: first, people made fun of me thinking it was crazy for a woman to be a journalist. Then, they opposed me when they saw I was rising and, finally, they had to accept me for what I was. Even now, people will look at me incredulously and ask me how come I'm a journalist. (Interview with a reporter in central Madhya Pradesh, November 2013)

In 2013, I was part of a research team that travelled through four states of north India and interviewed women reporters in small towns about their experiences of journalism. Since the late 1990s, the landscape of media in India has changed substantially. Rural readership has increased, newspapers are reaching deeper into the hinterland; more pages and stories are dedicated to news from small towns even in mainstream broadsheets; more networks for news exist (Ninan 2007). There has been a boom in electronic news media—national and local channels have launched, moved into 24/7 cycles, with a pressure to produce stories at high speed. With media liberalisation and subsequent corporatisation, the ideal model was one that involved low (editorial) investment and resources, but high revenues and profits: it made sense to tap vast rural markets to boost readership/audience figures. Even more recently, newspapers have gone online: news now reaches new audiences even in smaller cities through the internet, through mobile phones and through video (Priyadarshan 2013). Although over the past decade, women have become visible to some extent in metropolitan and especially English-language media, they are a rare phenomenon in the dusty, teeming public sphere of small-town India. The simultaneous bravado and struggle of entering journalism in small-town India as a woman echoes through many reporters' life stories and many of those who I interviewed for this paper.

The study on which this paper is based was conducted by a team of urban and rural media practitioners who work with *Khabar Lahariya*—a rural newspaper that is produced by rural women journalists in six districts of Uttar Pradesh and Bihar. As practitioners in the field of grassroots media in Uttar Pradesh for close to 12 years, my colleagues and I have first-hand experience of the exclusion of women from rural areas of Uttar Pradesh, especially from marginalised communities, in mainstream journalism. In this period, many changes had occurred, even in relatively underdeveloped areas of north India. The study was designed to understand how these changes were impacting on the media in smaller towns in Hindi-speaking regions, both in Uttar Pradesh and in other large states of north India. More specifically, were there more women in the media, outside the big cities? And if so, how were they negotiating the contemporary media field?

The present paper draws on the findings of this study on women reporters in small towns (WMNT 2014). It attempts to complement the existing literature on women in the media, internationally and in India, which largely focuses on the participation of urban women journalists, with the voices of women reporters working in small towns and semi-rural areas of north India. The experiences of these reporters throw into relief the prevalent notion of law and order being a major cause for the negligible participation of women in rural reporting. Women navigate male publics, that is, spheres governed by policies and norms framed by men, within a patriarchal society—a notion that we, on the heels of Pateman (1989) and others, poke and prod at—in their role as journalists. The women we interviewed constantly challenge and are challenged by the gender identities they inhabit, and exist between performance of these identities and subversion of them. In the end, on a micro stage, they demonstrate what it entails for women to engage with democratic processes: making visible the very patriarchal nature of the democratic public. The process of setting themselves up, and inhabiting the public sphere as a reporter, was experienced and articulated as an active engagement with power, and lived citizenship. I found Mouffe's "radical democratic" ideas of citizenship useful as a lens to analyse the narratives of the reporters, who struggled with what may be defined as their entitlements as citizens —mobility, access to information, freedom of expression of opinion; "citizenship is not a status granted on the basis of some essential characteristic. Citizens have to enact their citizenship on a day-to-day basis through their participation in everyday political practices" (Mouffe 1992, cited in Rodríguez 2001, 18).

The first section of the article details and reviews literature on the participation of women in the media, the second section describes the methodology of the study, while the final section moves into the stories of women reporters, drawing heavily from these narratives to present the messy, but dynamic nature of involvement of women in media in small towns.

Women in Media: Context Setting

The research, studies and surveys on women in media, internationally and within India, mostly focus on their low participation, and presence in management and decision-making roles. Whereas the international data show a participation of 33.3 per cent of women in news media (across all media forms), in India the situation is more disappointing: in India only 25 per cent of the journalists in media organisations were women. A report by the

Global Media Monitoring Project (Sarah, O'Connor, and Ndangam 2010) said that there were 24 per cent of women in news media, globally. The content and coverage of news was steeped in gender stereotypes: in only 13 per cent of news focused on women or women's issues did the reporting and writing show some depth and understanding. In India, the participation of women in the media was a mere 12 per cent, and the numbers of women in decision-making roles and management are very low compared to men. Work over the last decade in India in this area has shown similar statistics about participation and roles of women in the media; also, that the structure and work environment is created assuming the presence of men, while women journalists are constantly made to confront the need to balance work and home (Joseph 2005). Studies have shown that over 60 per cent of women journalists have faced some sort of harassment at the workplace, most often by senior employees, and this includes written, oral as well as character assassination of women journalists—which is common within media organisations (Franks 2013). The situation was slightly better in the English press. Women are kept away from serious and high-risk reporting, for instance the coverage of riots, and women are not allotted night shifts. More opportunities are provided to women in soft beats or features (Joshi, Pahad, and Maniar 2006). While more women were to be seen as news anchors, in the context of political reporting, or at the time of elections, for instance, it was male reporters who were more often seen and heard airing their opinions (Priyadarshan 2013), or with male bylines in newspapers—almost five times as many!

The study reported in this paper aimed to fill the gap that exists in terms of documentation of the experiences of women in media outside the big cities. Many of these mirror the situation of women in media outlined above, but some women's life stories demonstrate very different strategies of negotiation and survival necessitated in small towns and cities. Recent work has explored the rapid proliferation of regional and Hindi newspapers, a greater proportion of rural news with an increase in rural newspapers and stringers and distribution, and the strong links between them (Ninan 2007). In electronic and print media, and within and outside the cities, a predominance of journalists and management from upper castes, and a negligible proportion of other castes and communities, both reflected and was the reason for an elite hold over the media. Data that exist on the district level too show a shockingly low, a mere 2.7 per cent, presence of accredited women journalists, with some states showing no presence of women at all at the district level (Chamaria, Kumar, and Yogendra 2006). However, little literature exists that qualitatively explores and analyses the participation of women in media outside the metros.

Methodology

The study of women reporters was conducted in four states of north India, Uttar Pradesh, Madhya Pradesh, Rajasthan and Bihar, between August and December 2013. Given our resources and time, the focus was on Hindi or regional media. In order to gauge the participation of women in media in the state, in each of the four state capitals—Lucknow, Jaipur, Patna and Bhopal—the data collection included a combination of qualitative and quantitative tools—interviews, group discussions and questionnaires. Once the states for study had been identified, the Registrar of Newspapers in India website was used to source a list of registered publications in each state. A sample of 10 media organisations was selected to analyse their editorial staff profiles—focusing on the socio-economic, education and job profiles of women employees. All media forms were included: print, broadcast, electronic;

mainstream and alternative media; and private and state-owned media. The selection of media organisations was purposive, so that the 10 organisations selected had at least one woman employee on the editorial staff. These quantitative data, substantiated by interviews and focus group discussions with media experts in the state, provided a context to the qualitative interviews which form the primary data sample, which included interviews with five women in each of the four states, located in small towns and non-metropolitan cities of these states. It is through the experiences of these 20 women working in the largest states in north India that the study aimed to explore the life worlds of women reporters—their challenges, concerns and their specific contributions to the media world.

Findings

Journalism through the Lens of Small-town (Women) Reporters

The narratives of women reporters located in small towns necessitates an understanding of the larger canvas of media in India, and how changes over the last few decades have impacted on the way media works, as you travel deeper into the country. Srirupa Roy's exploration of the world of contemporary news media production in India's small towns provides apt context to some of my own observations. "India's news revolution has brought to the fore not just new texts, audiences, and viewing practices, but also a new sector of employment; new structures, cultures, and practices of work; new aspirations; and new configurations of class and status relations and mobilities", writes Roy (2011, 764). Despite the importance of a wide network of news sources in the large and deregulated media market (stringers), the structure and economics of liberalised media in India meant that no newspaper is willing or able to pay full-time reporters to report from villages and districts. At the small-town level, your job (in a loose sense) and your reputation as a journalist or a media person depends on your ability to maintain and increase circulation, and source revenue for your publication or news channel. Reporting or newsgathering is secondary—except to the extent that it facilitates circulation and advertisements. What is also of primary importance is the social capital that you can generate, by networking and relationship-building *vis-à-vis* the powers that be—politicians, administration, land owners and developers, local mafia. At each geographical tier, media in India occupies a powerfully generative role in the body politic, making it, "a site where in fact new patterns of dominance and power are being forged, and new kinds of entrepreneurial subjects are amassing economic, social, and political power" (Chakravartty and Roy 2013, 356).

Even if, as Chakravartty and Roy (2013, 356) hold, there were more possibilities for "entrepreneurial subjects" to access power, these were not people on the margins of society. Women and anyone outside an educated, elite caste and class were not often found to be journalists in this business of power brokering, soliciting revenues, and social and political favours (Naqvi 2008; Ninan 2007; Joseph 2005; Padgaonkar and Singh 2012). But this too required a deeper exploration: how did gender identity intersect with the requirements and possibilities of a wider-spread, liberalised media in India? These are the questions and presumptions which framed the in-depth conversations with women reporters, and in which their experiences were located.

This section is divided into two parts: the first locates the women reporters who were interviewed in the sphere of small-town media, as outlined above, and part observes, part analyses the physical and social labour involved in establishing themselves. The second part takes a step back from these observations, and looks at the negotiation of gender norms involved in the becoming and being a woman reporter. The hypothesis that runs through and ties together these stories and observations of women reporters at work is informed by Pateman's critique of the separation of the public–private sphere in political theory, and the assertion that women's inclusion in the public sphere hinges specifically on their sexual difference from men. Pateman writes, "Women have been included as 'women'; that is, as beings whose sexual embodiment prevents them enjoying the same political standing as men. Women's political position … is full of paradoxes, contradictions and ironies" (Pateman 1989, 4). This fact reflects in women's navigation of the profession of journalism in a patriarchal context. Watching women journalists at work in small-town India shows the constant bleeding in of patriarchal norms and roles that delimit women's lives, to their personas as successful journalists in a political, public sphere, defined and inhabited by men. The reporters' existence struggles between these terms of inclusion and exclusion, as women, journalists and citizens.

"Setting" Up to Be a Local Reporter

A prominent woman journalist, with two decades of experience in reporting at the district and state level, who I spoke with to build an understanding of women becoming reporters in small towns, told me dramatically that "It's like jumping into a fire. It's a business of blackmailing and commerce. Chasing people for money due. There's no system of support—not moral, not economic" (interview in central Uttar Pradesh, August 2013). By and large the women interviewed were middle class, upper caste, from service—mostly government service—families, educated up to high school, and then pushing for further education entirely under their own steam. Some had families with financial problems; a few were married happily (to journalists), some unhappily, but most faced financial pressures after marriage as well. Entering journalism was most often about a need to be independent (economically); more often than not, this necessitated entering the public sphere, and this introduced them to both the opportunities and thrills of negotiating the "male" public. Once out and about, meeting people, having ears and eyes open to possibilities and opportunities, once a certain crucial inhibition and inertia to stay within normative professions had been challenged, media was a difficult profession to leave. It afforded almost instant access to space and people, a notion of lived citizenship, that one has the right and power to information that can change your circumstances in a democracy. Even if the reporters mentioned the issue of low or unpredictable pay in media, it did not seem to deter them. Opportunities and contacts were made on their own, even if a few women did mention knowing journalists while they grew up. Being located in small towns provided advantages and disadvantages in this journey. Doing things successfully seemed to depend on two things: setting yourself up in the district/establishing an identity and making it work financially. This meant setting up contacts at different levels, transactions and barters, monetary and otherwise. Almost all the reporters acknowledged both the power that came with being a reporter in a small town, as well as the hard work in establishing yourself. The juxtaposition was often between the glamorous world of television news that we see, and the constant mining for contacts and exclusive stories that reporting actually entailed. The reporters expressed extreme pride in the nature of networks they had managed to set up, as well as discomfort with what they saw as male prerogative over networking and its techniques in journalism: drinking with and chatting up various officers of power. Each reporter's description of setting themselves up reiterated that networking was not a male skill; that they were as well networked as any other journalist in the district; and in fact their methods of newsgathering and weaving a web of contacts was more rigorous than other male journalists.

> I've been working for eight years, I have a network. Everyone knows me. There are stringers from all the papers—we co-ordinate with each other. I give them some news, they give me some, especially with crime stories, etc. ... I don't exclusively do only reporting or only business for anyone. I can't manage my finances or my status with only reporting, so I also do business, it's necessary. (Interview with a reporter in western Uttar Pradesh, December 2013)

> See, the people who say men have better sources of information, they don't know much about journalism. You don't get stories from spending four hours with a politician or in a police station. You get stories out of your own wherewithal. I have sources in the police, with politicians, and they know me too. But your real sources are people. Spending time with them, staying in touch with them, you find out all the happenings in the villages and cities—even things that don't get reported in the police station. (Interview with a reporter in eastern Bihar, November 2013)

Challenging the notion that being known and knowing in the public sphere was a male prerogative often went hand-in-hand with an assertion that perhaps theirs was a more ethical and righteous form of journalism, not involving sycophancy and obsequiousness, but a concern only with the matter at hand, and not with the payoff of what they wrote. The attempt seemed to be to shrug off their gender identities, while also marking their exceptionalism—even if they were doing something socially unacceptable for women to do (circulate in the public domain, keep relationships with all and sundry), they did it as good, sincere reporters. Whether or not this was true, their form of networking and newsgathering definitely involved hard, hard work, and awareness of themselves and their sources in a critical, insightful way. In explaining how she had managed to set herself up, the reporter below, young and confident, demonstrated a shrewd understanding of how her male peers related to their sources, and quite a melodramatic bravado in her own practice of journalism:

> When a person is honest, people want to be associated with that person. My relationship with the people for whom I have written news is what matters more than my equations with the powerful. Everyone knows Jyotiraditya Scindia [a minister of parliament, and member of a royal family] and most journalists address him as *Maharaj Saab*. I was the first one to tell him that I won't call him that because it's unconstitutional and we are journalists ... There was a set structure of sucking up to political leaders and writing accordingly that I broke and worked with honesty. So many journalists are into paid news these days. I have never done that. I have never given in an incorrect news story. And if ever anyone threatened me so some news is not carried, I never backed down. If something or someone is wrong, I made it a point to write about it. (Interview with a reporter in central Madhya Pradesh, November 2013)

However, more experienced reporters were more cynical about the "exceptionalism" they were afforded by virtue of being women, and in fact reiterated the labour involved in challenging this, in being allowed a space in this profession. The irony, of course, is that in a profession that depends so heavily on political and economic networking, gender norms cause women to be far more persecuted for their work than their male counterparts. The reporter below emphasised her good relationship with the district administration many times, describing how she would often be picked up by the District Magistrate's car when covering stories in the district. Only later in the interview, and just as a matter of course, did she speak about the public perception that came with this "advantage":

> People in the media would say that I got the opportunity to go with the [District Magistrate] because I was a girl. Then they said I got advertisements also because I was a girl. Media people don't have a very good perspective. Even my parents opposed what I did—they said, did I not have enough to feed myself, that I was doing this kind of work? When I went out with my camera, people would crowd around me. Everyone wanted to know who I was. To make myself known, I first got my visiting cards typed. I would give away almost 200 cards every week. Wherever I went, I'd give cards to each person I saw, even children. Till today, I haven't changed my number, this is why even today, I get news very easily. (Interview with a reporter in central Bihar, November 2013)

The reporters who were interviewed had varying relationships with the economic reality of their profession, involving the business of soliciting advertisements and recovering money due. Some took it in their stride and excelled at it—these were often the older reporters, for whom economics had played an important role in drawing them into media. Some disassociated themselves from this part of the work, either because their post or their situations allowed them to, but took the high moral ground about why they would not, or could not, do this. Again, this reiteration of ethics seemed gendered in our conversations, that whatever the general practice in media, there were some things that, as women, they would not do. The line of persuasion seemed to be that their reputation as good journalists was built on this difference of work ethic; this was also their response to a wider public that slandered them as women of bad character.

> The economic situation is very bad in district-level media. Local newspapers give no salary, there's no money except for advertisements. I won't [solicit advertisements]. I've never done this. I feel embarrassed. So this could also be a reason why fewer girls come into this profession. You know what journalists do here, right? Brokering. You see them in the [Superintendent of Police] office in the morning. They'll bring a case, talk to all the people concerned—what they should be covering for free, they will charge for it. What kind of an image are they making of journalists? For the district administration? No image at all. Today, I can talk to any of these officials on the phone, tell them that they need to take some action, help such and such person. And they listen to me. This is the impact an image makes. (Interview with a reporter in western Uttar Pradesh, December 2013)

Hard, Soft and Everything Else: The Possibilities of Small-town Reporting

Given the nature and structure of small-town reporting, and the fairly brazen lack of objectivity involved therein, based as it was on economic, political and social favours, the possibilities of rigorous journalism were compromised from the start. It was revealing to analyse the notions of the inability of women (expressed by almost all male state-level editors we interviewed) to cover crime and politics, when this was actually shorthand for selling one's journalistic integrity to the highest bidder. In small towns, where publications and channels were only represented by a single (almost always male) stringer, and with the industry awareness that a "proper journalist was someone who wrote stories about the 'big issues', which meant the political power game" (Stahlberg 2006, 58), the presence of a woman stringer/reporter added an interesting dimension. If a reporter—male or female—missed a story, because they would not or could not cover it, they would lose their per-story revenue, and maybe even their job. Being a reporter meant covering politics, crime, business and the rest of it. But the reality was that repercussions of writing about crime and politics catapult back sooner and with greater force in small towns where webs of relationships—the nexus between money, class, caste, commercial and personal interests—are smaller and tighter, and power can be exerted quickly to silence. Given this, the stories covered by the reporters we met—of mafia and politicians, police encounters, smuggling, trafficking—showed both courage and an understanding of local politics and power that came from their engagement in the public sphere, and continuously challenged the presumption that women journalists had limited understanding or ability to be political beings.

> There was a case that I investigated, involving a [member of the state legislative assembly (MLA), elected from the party in majority at the time]. The case involved a girl who had run away with someone, and the person she ran away with had taken refuge in the house of this MLA. I did full investigation on this case, against the MLA, when he was in power ... Today, I think, it was a big risk, and whoever I tell the story to tells me that. But journalism isn't just about reading and writing. It's about a passion. It's not about earning money. If you don't feel strongly about it, if there isn't risk involved, then there's no pleasure in it. (Interview with a reporter from central Uttar Pradesh, August 2013)

Whether and how women reporters, in positions of double vulnerability, wrote about institutions and individuals in power was an area of interest, and so the interviews with reporters dwelt on these examples. Here there were stories of courage and of risk taken, of strategies learnt along the way. One young interviewee from Rajasthan explained,

> There are ways to get stories which challenge the system printed. Keep this off record! If your paper is not ready to publish your story then you say your rival paper will print it and we won't and then you will blame the reporter that I missed the story—they will have to print it then! We create pressure on management just like they create pressure on us. From your training you know this is how it works.

There was, however, an honesty about how power structures—whether external or internal management—worked to control these reporters, and in which situations a gendered threat was felt, as women working in the field. It became clear that these were situations in which the reporters also felt isolated, and lacking in both social and professional support to defend them against those they were challenging. Again, there was the same dilemma outlined above—to be appreciated as courageous and an exception because these were women taking risks that not many men did; as well as to mark themselves as good journalists, gender notwithstanding.

> I've been reporting on illegal development [private urban development projects not authorised by the state/city council]. There's a big development project here, and I went and took photos. So they came to me. I said, why can't you get this authorised? They've sent me 5000 rupees—just yesterday. I sent it back. I said I will print the story, and I won't take money. But now I'm thinking, they're powerful people, maybe it's better to just take the money. You have to do this sometimes! So I'll print the news, but write it differently. In the past, I've printed stories with names of officials, politicians. Now I've started faxing

stories to the Chief Minister, Commissioner of Police, the Information Department. I want a reaction to the news as well as action. I wrote something about a prominent political leader here, about an incident in one of their public meetings. It got printed, and then I got threats, my editor got threats. So I got discouraged—I have a family, I have kids, I can't afford this. The organisation told me not to worry, but I'm local here, if something were to happen, I'd bear the brunt of it, not them. (Interview with a reporter in western Uttar Pradesh)

Tackling Gender Head On: The "Woman Reporter" in a Big Bad Male World

Before interviewing women reporters in smaller towns, conversations with experts, editors and women journalists in the capital cities created a narrative of the contemporary situation *vis-à-vis* women in media, a profile of urban, educated, middle-class and upper-caste women, and a set of fairly grim numbers regarding their proportion to men in the profession. The backdrop finally drawn, against which the interviews with women reporters themselves were done, was one in which, despite the growth of print and electronic media over the past 15 years, deep-rooted stereotypes existed, which saw media as a profession unsuitable for women. The interviews were conducted when there was a churning in the public perception of sexual assault in the media: the Shakti Mills case in Mumbai (in August 2013) of the gang rape of a woman journalist, and the allegations of rape against the influential editor-in-chief of a weekly news magazine (November 2013) had raised hackles. Despite (or because of) this, senior management spoke loud and unashamedly about the responsibility, burden and liability involved in hiring women reporters, especially in areas or in beats that were "risky" ("Sometimes they need to be controlled too, some girls have too much passion/enthusiasm. The management is fearful to make them crime reporters", interview with an editor in Uttar Pradesh, August 2013); the high investment and low returns, into staff that "would marry and leave"; the need to either provide protection or safety, else keep them from situations which could put them (and the organisation) at risk. Women entered for "glamour" and then left, when hard work was what was on offer. With these presumptions in mind, the existence and nuances of the lives of women working as reporters in small districts provided a sharp contrast.

Barely any part of the interviews, whether around their history, location, content, working practices and so on, did not reference in some way that these were women in a male sphere. Being women reporters was also a label they tried to dissociate themselves from, when it tied them down, or determined how people saw them and their work. Moving and interacting in the public sphere—meeting, seeking information and accountability, feeling the confidence and wherewithal to see beneath the surface of current events, to raise critical questions—these made them very visible in their local contexts. Being women in this role, and most often the only women journalists in the area—their gender and sexual embodiment informed all their interactions: how they walked, talked, dressed and with whom they interacted. Our discussions about reporting, and reporting as women, provoked contradictory responses across and even within each interview. The reporters had a pragmatic and also an analytical understanding of gender norms—what they were expected to do, wear, where they could be, how they should speak—and how they challenged them by being in this profession. They also read the responses of people they interacted with, family, colleagues, sources of information, and spaces that they moved within, through an awareness of their own gender location: there was an awareness of how and why people looked and responded to them in the ways they did—paternalistic, protective, dismissive and leering. In our conversations, as in their lives and work, the reporters played multiple and contradictory roles: good journalists, good women, holding tight and then distancing themselves from their gender identity.

The world outside the micro-patriarchal environment—the newspaper office, in particular—provided challenges, risks and dangers based on gender and sexual norms, of what women could and should do. To a certain extent, working in the larger public, outside a structured office environment, provided greater flexibility and opportunity. Our conversations and observations of the reporters' lives and work revealed that, firstly, they were conscious—both implicitly and explicitly—of a (male) gaze that followed them around and impacted on their work, and how they presented and saw themselves. This consciousness—of being experienced, weighed down because of their gender, despite any other identity they performed—was expressed sometimes as hard work, sometimes with anger or cynicism, and sometimes as a philosophical acceptance of gender difference which did not deserve struggle or resistance. But to be a good, rigorous, on-the-ball reporter, you have to let go of any norm that restricts where you move around, and who you talk to. In other words, you let go of the aspiration (collective, social and, therefore, individual too) to be a good woman, who stays within a prescribed space and does not speak unless it is absolutely required. However, as discussed earlier, it was also convenient to play on the gendering of certain qualities to their advantage, building the case for women reporters having greater integrity and honesty than their male counterparts—so taking on gender stereotypes associated with women in the profession and using it in their own defence. The reporters we spoke to understood this in some depth, and articulated it in complex ways. As in other instances of women finding their ways through gender, the reporters performed—both with us and with others in their worlds—multiple roles. The narratives about their professional lives drew on repeated references to language, dress, information and hyper-awareness of the public gaze to define each of these roles.

> I'm a reporter. [Yet] If I go and see any official, I'm first seen as a woman. I feel this when I go—I see other journalists hanging around, chatting with them. If I told an official I wanted to speak to him in private, he'd get scared—and refuse! This has happened with me. So I say, why are you looking at me as a woman? I'm a reporter—why can't you see me as that? If I can look you in the eye, why can't you? If I need to speak to them about a story, is it necessary to have to do that in front of other reporters? But when they refuse, they make you feel like a woman, you begin to feel guilty for asking. If you ask for their number, they'll say, no, no, don't call me at home—what if my wife picks up? Now, if your conscience is clear, why should you be worried if anyone calls you anywhere? I'm Shehnaz, the editor of a weekly paper. But no, when I enter the gate—they look at you as a woman, and think, how is she looking, she's dressed up well today. However I present myself, I will always be seen as a woman and nothing else. (Interview with a reporter in western Uttar Pradesh, December 2013)

When the conversation focused on being women out in the field, the gloves came on: each step the reporters had taken was contested, by gender, class, caste conventions. No amount of success in their profession or social sophistication would work in their favour: what was required was a deep knowledge of social convention, and the political ability to subvert it. Or as this reporter from one of the regions with the highest crime record in the country puts it, "shamelessness"—indeed, turning the gender norm of "shame" on its head, key to keeping women in their place—is what you need to employ:

> In my village—it's a Rajput village, and you know historically how Rajputs have treated women, how they have misbehaved. I'm saying this and I'm from the same community. I leave the house with my *ghunghat* [veil] over my head normally—and I'm a district-level journalist! My father-in-law will call me to say, this incident has happened, make a call and find out. Even so, I still have to leave the house with my head covered! The Pradhan [village head] of the village calls me—he is my husband's uncle—and says, call the Sub Divisional Magistrate (SDM) for such and such work. I cover my head and make the call! I can't say I won't—*bawaal ho jayega* [there will be an uproar]! I've got used to it with much difficulty. I was riding my bike once in a sari, and I fell off—saved my life with much difficulty! I told my husband, and he said, come let's go get some *salwar kameezes* [a long shirt and pants, commonly worn by women, but often not allowed after marriage or in the marital home]. In this line, you have to be shameless, *besharam*, you have to have courage and honesty—and then you can work. (Interview with a reporter in western Uttar Pradesh, December 2013)

Clearly, the onus was on the woman reporter to manage and control her language, body, behaviour, personal and public life—whether by offence or defence. If setting up a network and reporting in small towns required hard work, confronting a patriarchal gaze that questioned your ability and credibility every moment was even harder. It required drawing on different kinds of support, playing different roles in public and private life, cultivating a cynical bravado as well as cultivating pride about the nature of their work. The reporter below, for instance, nursed a deep bitterness, while having a shrewd understanding of how her profession challenged the society she lived in:

> You know what people think of women journalists, don't you? Women journalists are considered half call girls. And half the things you hear are true, that they will go to bed with people for stories and favours … No, I don't know anyone like this, but this is what you hear, these are the stories. You haven't asked me the disadvantages of being a woman reporter. Let me tell you. I'm unmarried. Single. No one will marry me. Our society isn't sensitive to women journalists. They will be singled out, pointed at when they walk down the road. "The girl is very bold…" Let me tell you that there are three or four professions—women police, lawyers, reporters, and now, in big cities, air hostesses—these are not considered good for women, and they make society very uncomfortable. How can you have a family when your hours are uncertain, you are going anywhere at any time? (Interview with a reporter in Rajasthan, September 2013)

Newspaper offices, where they existed in the towns we visited, seemed to be a common space where the reporters were made very aware—mostly uncomfortably so—of their gender. It became quite clear that the more structured the work environment, the more it chafed against the women reporters. The reporters themselves responded sometimes frankly and critically to the atmosphere in offices—admitting an inability to deal with the taunts, the sexualised atmosphere, the discriminatory editorial and administrative policies. As mentioned before, the views of the interviewees were not consistent, even within a single conversation they would both shrug off discrimination and reveal deep scars from it. A common response, like the young reporter below, was that your self-training to work as a reporter involves a disciplining and a creation of personal space, which it is your responsibility to maintain:

> As women we have to be very careful. There are no trainings and there is no time to make any mistakes. Half the time, it is this pressure of being flawless that gets to the young people who have just joined. I maintain a very strict disposition in the office here. As you can see, I am the only woman journalist in the entire office here. People don't set boundaries for me, I set boundaries for them. I will decide what and how many words you use to speak to me. This boundary and this distance one has to create and maintain to be able to work peacefully. (Interview with a reporter in central/eastern Uttar Pradesh, August 2013)

Although the study was not focused on sexual harassment and most interviews did not directly broach the issue of sexual harassment in the workplace, almost every interview with a woman reporter touched upon this issue. The harassment was seen as a part of the job, part of the negotiation of the media workplace; an extension of the way women journalists were viewed in towns and cities—mobile, forward and worldly-wise. It took the form of innuendo or direct sexual banter, assault, or in discriminatory practices, like dropping stories, or not providing opportunities for women to share their stories and views in editorial meetings. By and large, this harassment went without complaint or redress, for fear of losing face or their jobs. However, perhaps more often than their big-city counterparts, these lone reporters had made decisions about what kind of workplaces they would tolerate, and had made their stands patently clear, both within and outside their offices. They had gained considerable respect because of this.

> I once hit the Bureau Chief of a well-known Hindi daily. He had a very disgusting talking style and attitude. The file would be sent off [to press] at 7 pm but ... he would insist that I stay till 10 to attend phone calls. He would sit upstairs in his office and I'd be doing nothing and everyone else would have left the office by then. I didn't like this. Girls have a very good sixth sense and I could tell he didn't mean well. So I objected. Then he started harassing me by criticising my stories and not putting them in the newspaper. I brought up the matter again. He got angry and told me in a very condescending way, "What do you think of yourself? Girls are easy to come by". I got very angry, took off my sandal and hit him with it. (Interview with reporter in central Madhya Pradesh, November 2013)

Conclusion

This study on the experiences of women working as reporters at the district level is by no means comprehensive or all-encompassing of regional difference. However, the study does reveal patterns of entry, experience and survival in the world of small-town north India as a woman reporter. The space between, and the play of roles of good woman (honourable) and good journalist (*besharam* or shameless)—with all the contradictions and agency this involves—was very revealing for the kinds of limits and possibilities for women in a field like journalism. What emerged was generative as well as oppressive aspects of the power play in a democratic sphere. Recording the experiences of women reporters working over years in small towns made visible in a very real and situated way the discriminatory structure and functioning of media, and how it works to mitigate the entry of marginalised voices—and here we specifically look at women's voices, rural women or women outside big cities. The profiles of the women interviewed were, by and large, of women pushed into the public domain by economic necessity, but once drawn into the access to power that media afforded, have not seen their professions as merely livelihoods, but crucial aspects of their identities in the world. For them, journalism was a way of being live, engaged citizens in their world, a role which once inhabited, was difficult to let go of. This despite the fact that their work and lives involve a constant negotiation, and in multiple ways, the restrictions of gender on the job—what they can report on, where they can go, what they should or should not wear, how and how much they should speak, and to whom. These are both limiting factors, and involve holding themselves above the normal levels or expectations—of knowledge, of morality, of decorum—both within and outside their workplaces. Their position in the public sphere, their articulation about the way they are watched, engaged with, dismissed, how their stories are treated by their editors—these all provide a critical understanding of how gender norms get played out in the public sphere. Their presence shakes and shifts the landscape of a male political public sphere—this can be read in male responses to and discomfort of them, both within and outside the office space, the desire to keep them either outside the field, outside "hard" or serious reporting, like that of politics, economics or crime, or in a box labelled "woman reporter". The onus lies with the reporters themselves to create a work environment for themselves, both to counter and ease the discomfort that their transgression causes.

In the manner in which the reporters critically observed and articulated their necessary subversion of gender norms and challenges to the socio-economics of the media market—in their stands, their presence, their stories—a curtain is drawn to reveal the patriarchal nature of the public sphere. There is clearly a need for media in the current context to take into account these voices in the way it hires, reports, functions, manages itself, for it to be a stronger, more critical, more robust tool.

DISCLOSURE STATEMENT

No potential conflict of interest was reported by the author.

FUNDING

This study on which this article is based was supported by the United Nations Democracy and Equity Fund [grant number UDF-IND-10-382].

REFERENCES

Chakravartty, P. Aula, and Srirupa Roy. 2013. "Media Pluralism Redux: Towards New Frameworks of Comparative Media Studies 'Beyond the West.'" *Political Communication* 30: 349–370.

Chamaria, Anil, Jitendra Kumar, and Yadav Yogendra. 2006. "Survey of the Social Profile of Key Decision Makers in the National Media." Media Studies Group. Accessed February 24, 2014. http://mediastudiesgroup.org.in/research/survey/survey_detail.aspx?TID=1.

Franks, Suzanne. 2013. *Women and Journalism*. London: I.B. Tauris.

Joseph, Ammu. 2005. *Making News*. New Delhi: Penguin Books India.

Joshi, Uma, Anjali Pahad, and Avani Maniar. 2006. "Images of Women in Print Media – A Research Inquiry." *India Media Studies Journal* 1 (1): 39–51.

Macharia, Sarah, Dermot O'Connor, and Lilian Ndangam. 2010. *Who Makes the News?* Global Media Monitoring Project Report. Accessed July 15 2015. http://cdn.agilitycms.com/who-makes-the-news/Imported/reports_2010/global/gmmp_global_report_en.pdf.

Mouffe, Chantal. 1992. *Dimensions of Radical Democracy: Pluralism, Citizenship, Community*. New York: Verso.

Naqvi, Farah. 2008. *Waves in the Hinterland: The Journey of a Newspaper*. First paperback ed. New Delhi: Zubaan Books.

Ninan, Sevanti. 2007. *Headlines from the Heartland*. Los Angeles, CA: Sage.

Padgaonkar, Lalita, and Shubha Singh, eds. 2012. *Making News, Breaking News, Her Own Way*. New Delhi: Tranquebar.

Pateman, Carole. 1989. *The Disorder of Women: Democracy, Feminism, and Political Theory*. Stanford: Stanford University Press.

Priyadarshan. 2013. *Khabar bekhabar*. New Delhi: Samayik Prakashan.

Rodríguez, Clemencia. 2001. *Fissures in the Mediascape. An International Study of Citizens' Media*. Cresskill, NJ: Hampton Press.

Roy, Srirupa. 2011. "Television News and Democratic Change in India." *Media, Culture & Society* 33 (5): 761–777.

Stahlberg, Peter. 2006. "On the Journalist Beat in India: Encounters with the Near Familiar." *Ethnography* 7 (47): 47–67.

WMNT (Women Media and News Trust). 2014. *Zile ki Hulchul: Conversation with Women Reporters in Small-town India*. New Delhi: Women Media News Trust.

THE POTENTIAL AND LIMITATIONS OF CITIZEN JOURNALISM INITIATIVES
Chhattisgarh's CGNet Swara

Kalyani Chadha and **Linda Steiner**

The challenges faced by rural communities in India in both access to mainstream media and coverage by it have major implications for democracy and civic participation. CGNet Swara, a citizen journalism initiative, attempts to address this problem by enabling rural or tribal communities to obtain and report news, and, to facilitate coverage of their concerns, by acting as "a bridge" between those communities and professional news outlets. Our research on the project's relationship with mainstream news outlets in central India finds that while at least some professional journalists endorse the ideals of citizen journalism, they reject the idea that CGNet Swara can assist them. These findings lead us to re-evaluate the potential of citizen journalism as a transformative and democratizing force.

Introduction

Several experiments that turn on the participation of non-professionals in collecting, reporting, analyzing, and disseminating news are provoking enormous ferment in journalism around the world. New technologies and applications such as blogging, social networking, and streaming help citizens challenge journalists' monopoly to define, produce, and disseminate news. Especially as the relevant technologies become cheaper and easier to learn and adapt, citizens without training or experience in journalism now have many ways to work with (or potentially sidestep) professionals, operating "outside, through and within" mainstream news media (Cottle 2009, xi). Our research analyzes one such citizen journalism experiment, CGNet Swara, in Chhattisgarh, in central India; our particular focus is its relationship with professional news outlets operating in the region.

CGNet Swara is accessed via mobile phones, which were introduced in India in 1995–96 and are becoming a dominant medium throughout Asia for accessing information.[1] What is distinctive about this free, voice-based service is that even people with low levels of writing literacy can contribute and share information: with its design and development team handling the complicated technology, anyone with a phone can call CGNet to report local issues. Stories verified and approved by moderators are available for playback online (cgnetswara.org) as well as over the phone.

Enabling the largely oral communities of central India to share news is significant: these tribal peoples—predominantly rural and impoverished—cannot access news in their own languages (Saha 2012). Mainstream print and broadcast media available in the region publish exclusively in Hindi or English. India's highest circulation English and Hindi dailies devote only 2 percent of their space to rural issues, and most rural coverage focuses on violence, crime, disasters, suicides, and malnutrition (Mudgal 2011). Moreover, Chhattisgarh, which became a state in 2000, has long seen violent clashes between Maoist (Naxal) insurgents and state forces, making the hinterland unsafe for reporters. The result is a significant news deficit for most of the state's population. CGNet founder Shubhranshu Choudhary, who has both BBC and print journalism experience, summarizes the problems of the region's 100 million, largely uneducated tribal peoples: "No journalists understand their languages or belong to their communities ... so their views are not represented. The 95 percent are ignored."[2] He says local journalists overlook tribal issues due to structural problems and financial problems; national journalists cannot speak tribal/local languages or hire fixers who do. Thus, CGNet potentially enables tribal communities to share news they find particularly relevant and that may deserve a broader hearing. However, journalists' objections to citizen participation, objections that may reflect globally inflected claims about their professional authority and role in democracy, appear to keep news organizations from cultivating effective relationships with CGNet and from developing or using their stories.

CGNet Swara

CGNet began in 2004 as a website and listserv for discussing local issues. It was hampered, however, by both the oral tradition of rural communities and the low rate of internet penetration. Development of India's internet infrastructure has been highly uneven; like other components of the market-based system that emerged as a result of liberalizing India's economy, new media technologies are primarily limited to English-speaking urban audiences. In Chhattisgarh, where internet penetration is a dismal 0.5 percent (Internet and Mobile Association 2012), villages could not benefit from the online project's opportunities. In 2010, Choudhary decided instead to exploit mobile telephony in India's rural areas, where increased competition and deregulation brought down costs such that mobile penetration rates dramatically rose to 35 percent (Black 2012). With the benefit of a Knight International Journalism Fellowship, Choudhary launched CGNet Swara, or Voice. The service allows villagers to send and receive cell phone messages through an interactive voice response (IVR) technology. Audio and text versions of recordings, about three minutes long, are also available on CGNet's website (a moderation bottleneck remains unresolved). Approximately 30 students, community leaders, and activists learned the technology during a two-day training program.

One staff analysis found that since its inception, CGNet Swara has logged close to 100,000 calls; 98 percent of callers listen; only 2 percent call in to report (Saha 2012). According to the development team (Mudliar, Donner, and Thies, 2013), during its first 20 months, the largest proportion of the messages offered news, followed by grievances and opinions. Finding that women had called in 31 percent of the messages—all from rural and poor backgrounds—in 2013 Choudhary trained some 90 women to report more effectively (Segran 2013). Indeed, after one woman reported that three men had raped a tribal woman in her village, local police arrested the alleged rapists. In another village, a woman said that officials heard her reports about employment, subsidized food and healthcare and not only got back to her directly but also resolved issues she had raised. She said: "I can raise issues related to my village in my own language without any fear of reprisal" (Segran 2013).

Staffers occasionally try to spur action on the reports by sharing them with mainstream journalists or government officials, a sharing that presumes CGNet will be properly credited. CGNet's founder claims that professional journalists use Swara stories without acknowledgment. He explains the problem this way:

> Their relationship has become more antagonistic ... It is very unfortunate, local media see us as a competitor—which we cannot be and never intended to be. Every platform has its problems and strengths. We understand the structural problems of mainstream media and we want to fill in the gaps.

Professional outlets seem unlikely to regard CGNet as "competition." What, then, is the source of conflict? After briefly discussing professional journalism and citizen journalism experiments in India, we discuss responses to CGNet and to citizen journalism from 10 professional journalists working in the area to figure out the basis of the antagonism and to explain professionals' reluctance to use CGNet Swara more often.

Indian News Media

Colonialists and missionaries introduced newspapers to India primarily as a vehicle for supporting British rule. Indigenous newspapers soon followed, first launched mainly to promote social, religious, educational, and political reforms; political figures launched many newspapers to advance anti-colonial philosophies. By 1947, when India achieved independence, the print press had developed a strong tradition of advocacy and political partisanship. In subsequent decades, press freedom was constitutionally protected; but Indian newspapers were increasingly controlled by industrial or business groups who used their news outlets to lobby for their own economic interests. Following the economic liberalization of the 1990s, India's media landscape expanded dramatically. Rapid liberalization and deregulation opened the door to expansion and investment by multinational companies, including international satellite-distributed television. Despite the sheer number of media outlets, however, many worry that the Indian news industry is becoming increasingly consolidated, with a few players controlling specific market segments (Administrative Staff College of India 2009). India's private radio stations cannot yet produce independent news shows, although they can re-broadcast news from All India Radio, the government radio channel; of the 4000 community radio stations that the government claimed would be operating by 2011, only 300 are functioning (PK 2013).

The emergence of Indian news organizations either allied with political parties or owning non-media enterprises has led to a pronounced shift away from public-service news, among other worries. Commodification, the quest for ratings, and the "Murdochization of the Indian press" have led to, among other problems, a dumbed-down focus on entertainment, and breaches of ethics and professional ideals (Sonwalkar 2009). The nexus in India between media, business, and politics—and the corresponding ethical challenges—was recently exposed when prominent national journalists were heard on tape advising a major lobbyist; journalists acted as intermediaries for the lobbyist and provided her clients with scripted interviews and favorable columns (Chadha 2012). A related and notorious form of corruption involves "paid news." Several parliamentary candidates have admitted paying news organizations, including the three largest circulation dailies, to run favorable coverage. The Press Council of India's (2011) report on paid news complained of pervasive corruption involving journalists and media organizations. Media companies continue to resist judicial attempts to introduce enforceable codes of conduct. The founder of The Hoot.org, a South Asian media watch website, explains why journalists rarely report on media scandals, even incidents involving other media houses: "Tomorrow it could be our turn" (Ninan 2010).

Journalism education is developing in India through both degree and certificate programs, including for rural correspondents and stringers. But some training programs were established by large media conglomerates or other private enterprises merely to suit their organizational needs; and several private schools offering journalism courses charge tuition 20 times more than university equivalents (Karan 2001). Relatedly, neither classrooms nor mainstream newsrooms emphasize ethics. Rao (2009) finds that journalists assert that borrowing Western formats did not undermine their reporting about social [in]justice. But, Indian journalists are ill-equipped to address the serious ethical pressures and conflicts of interest they face (Rao and Johal 2006).

The history, the problems, the challenges, and even the successes of the news industry in India might suggest that citizen efforts offer great potential. Widespread—and substantiated—accusations of corruption in mainstream journalism in India would seem to open up opportunities for non-profit, non-monetized projects. Is that the case?

Citizen Journalism Globally and in India

Citizen journalism is a somewhat fuzzy term used in different ways by different people at different times. Originally "public" journalism was conceptualized as a way for mainstream news organizations to engage and work with local audiences, to cure the cynicism then alienating citizens, and to heal the professional–public divide that appeared to undermine democracy. The goal of public journalism was to re-engage citizens in civic life, even if journalists ultimately produced most of the finished "products." Now, a range of practices stand firmly under the "citizen" banner, from collaborative projects initiated and run by citizens (almost never in this context does "citizen" refer to legal or voting status) to crowd-sourcing by professionals, to full-fledged partnerships of professionals and "amateur" news hounds. Reinvigorating democracy also remains a goal of citizen journalism.

Online citizen journalism began in India in 2005, when the news website Rediff.com posted local residents' eyewitness accounts of crippling rains in Mumbai (Sonwalkar 2009). Founded in 2006, Merinews.com spurred the creation of several Indian citizen journalism websites; its MyNews.in is one of the few citizen journalism sites to insist that participants adhere to its ethics code (Roberts and Steiner 2012). Consistent with Indian citizen journalists' emphasis on episodic crises, Mumbai-based citizens blogged and posted Twitter and Flickr news about the 2008 terrorist attacks, again beating mainstream organizations (Sonwalkar 2009). By 2009, according to Sonwalkar, albeit applying a low threshold for success, citizen journalism was generating hope that it could enrich the public sphere; enable expression of a wide range of opinions, including those of the marginalized; and expose corruption, human rights violations, and sexual harassment. While typically citizen journalism initiatives focus on urban areas, a few initiatives focus on rural areas. Prominent here are voice-activated community platforms like GramVaani, accessed by phone, in rural India. Co-founded by a computer science professor and a former McKinsey consultant, GramVaani gets over 2000 calls a day in the Jharkhand area and hopes to grow a hundred-fold (PK 2013). The service campaigns for water conservation and HIV/AIDS prevention, besides airing regular programs; all that content comes from "expert" sources. In addition, local groups can call a toll-free number to tell stories, which are validated and edited. Other experiments taking hold involve mobile-phone dissemination of blogs in tribal languages, and SMS services. CGNet Swara, however, is the only IVR initiative focused on citizen-provided news.

Method

To explore CGNet Swara's relationship with, and reputation among, professional news organizations, we interviewed CGNet's founder as well as journalists working in the area on behalf of leading local, regional, and national news organizations. We used purposive snowball sampling to locate journalists; our familiarity with Indian journalism helped us to identify a couple of journalists willing to talk; they helped us find others. This non-probabilistic sampling was appropriate, given our interest in understanding how journalists perceive citizen journalism, particularly CGNet. Following Holstein and Gubrium (1995), we see interviews as relying on the active selection of "persons" rather than "population." Between November 2012 and March 2013, we interviewed 10 journalists, evenly drawn between national and local news outlets. For interview-based research, 10 participants is sufficient to go beyond the anecdotal and "investigate in detail the relationship between the individual and the situation" (Kvale 1996, 102–103).[3]

The eight men and two women interviewed included veterans with 25–30 years of journalism experience as well as younger ones with 10–15 years of experience. Conducted by telephone in English or Hindi, the interviews lasted 30–60 minutes; our semi-structured questions centered on their perceptions of citizen journalism and of CGNet. Journalists were allowed to speak anonymously. A native speaker translated the Hindi interviews into English. Once transcribed, the transcripts were analyzed to identify recurring ideas and categories, and later considered collectively for thematic patterns.

Journalists' Understandings of Citizen Journalism

All the journalists expressed their impressions of citizen journalism in adamant, vivid language. They typically defined citizen journalism as involving "ordinary" people without formal journalism training who focus on important local issues. They largely agreed that citizen journalism can bring news from rural areas, where mainstream media do not reach and have no reporters. Having begun with a reasonably supportive definition, however, most of them soon became more negative; as elaborated below, they challenged citizen journalism for its activist agenda and lack of fact checking or verification.

Among those most positive about citizen journalism and CGNet was the bureau chief for the *Central Chronicle* who had worked for many different news outlets including NDTV. His small paper, published from Bhopal, did not cover development issues and marginalized people, he said, since the mainstream press has little interest in these issues and since (conventional) journalists are pressured to pander to audiences. At least ideally, he said, citizen journalism can help connect mainstream media to important issues that are difficult for them to cover, especially in the interior. Having categorized everyone in states like Chhattisgarh as either rulers or the ruled, he said that mainstream journalists ignore the "ruled" (tribal people) and their "pitiable" situation.

The strongest condemnation of citizen journalism came from a journalism professor who edits the *Daily Chhattisgarh*, a Hindi daily with a circulation of 54,000 published from

Raipur, the region's main city. Citizen journalism could never help journalists, he said, since it is "too one-sided" and "lacks any balance." This editor apparently tells students that citizen journalists are agenda-driven activists who actually damage journalism: "They wear the mask of journalism but push an agenda. They are unfamiliar with the parameters of journalism." Another citizen journalism skeptic had worked for several dailies, including the *Indian Express* and the *Financial Express*, and now edits the Raipur edition of the *Dainik Bhaskar*, the region's largest circulation Hindi daily. He conceded that his paper occasionally—but not often—asked people for photos, comments on stories, and tips. While he acknowledged that citizen journalism might help reveal local public opinion, he justified its unpopularity. He argued, "It comes with problems too, mainly, how do we know the information is accurate, who's behind it and why? This can be hard to determine and I think that's a problem."

Indeed, every journalist mentioned the difficulty, if not impossibility, of verifying information from citizen journalists, thus causing concerns about accuracy and truth. One NDTV reporter directly accused citizen journalists of ignoring standard journalistic procedures. As a result, in her view, citizen journalism's "novelty factor" is unsustainable. On principle, she said, NDTV does not invite ideas from citizens.[4] Even the *Central Chronicle* bureau chief expressed multiple concerns about citizen journalism, including that untrained citizens are motivated by an "agenda," as well as problems with verification and credibility. "We cannot work without evidence," he said.

Ironically, national journalists saw citizen journalism's greatest potential in helping regional news organizations, while regional journalists highlighted its potential to help national organizations that lacked local and especially tribal contacts or access. The *Central Chronicle* journalist said national media looked at CGNet Swara, but not local or regional media. On the other hand, a NDTV journalist conceded that national media cover Chhattisgarh mainly in the context of Maoist unrest. She added, "The people who can really use [CGNet] stuff are the more local journalists." Likewise, a woman working for the Asian News International, which provides multi-media news to bureaus throughout Asia, said Asian News International does nothing with citizen journalism. Having previously worked for two national news channels, she described local journalists in the central tribal region as potentially benefiting from citizen journalism, since they are very poorly paid and they develop overly comfortable relationships with local police and government officials. That is, the local media avoid stories putting authorities in a negative light. In her view, larger national outlets will do those stories precisely because they are not dependent on local authorities or economic interests. Another theory came from the *Daily Chhattisgarh* editor, who claimed his reporters and stringers in rural areas could find their own sources and stories. At best, he said, citizen journalism's audience was activists and non-governmental organizations (NGOs).

Asked for examples of citizen journalism, several broadcast journalists recalled a CNN-IBN effort about disadvantaged communities in cities. The editor of *Hari Bhoomi*, a Hindi daily that publishes two editions in the region, acknowledged that in 2009 his paper started to let readers submit photos and information. But he had seen no independently produced citizen journalism projects, nor would he ever ask readers for story ideas. After all, he said, very few people will do this every day. The chief editor of *Deshbandu*, a broadsheet with a circulation of 500,000, noted that his paper's main edition *once* undertook a UNESCO-funded educational project in 100 villages. Otherwise, in his view, citizen journalism was essentially inactive in India. For example, he dismissed an NDTV experiment as merely "giving a few people mics and some minimal training." "I think they do it like a ritual, something that's fashionable," he added.

A NDTV reporter described herself as "particularly interested" in rural development and health/literacy; she had covered Chhattisgarh as well as other regions with tribal populations with similar problems and issues. On the other hand, "nothing much has come from it." Echoing the *Deshbandu* editor she added:

> You can't give people minimal training with a camera and expect them to produce journalism. I think citizen journalism is very reactive; you have an incident and maybe for a time people are interested but not on a day-to-day level. It just takes too much work.

Positions on CGNet Swara

Journalists' evaluations of citizen journalism strongly tracked with their evaluations of CGNet Swara. All but one of the journalists had heard about CGNet directly from Subhranshu Choudhary, its founder. Some had known Choudhary when he was a BBC journalist and had followed his work. A few had checked out the website, either because they were curious, or, less often, wanted information on some project.

The *Central Chronicle* editor, the journalist who was the most positive about citizen journalism, was also the most positive about CGNet as a form of citizen journalism. He described CGNet's purpose as highlighting issues of tribal peoples and local communities who otherwise have no voice. On the other hand, he said few people know about CGNet: "It has not really taken off in a big way. They raise issues, which is good, but what about action?" He essentially described a double bind: mainstream journalists "are very reluctant" to cover the issues that CGNet addresses as these do not interest urban audiences, yet only mainstream journalists can effectively disseminate stories and bring about action. Although he rarely looks at its website, he said his paper used a CGNet story about a government rural employment program. Apparently the *Central Chronicle* had investigated further and verified CGNet's information about people who were never paid. The *Central Chronicle* picked up a second story about people denied ration cards because they were either unwilling or unable to pay bribes to local authorities.

The *Hari Bhoomi* editor had seen CGNet's website and occasionally read its listserv. But he dismissed it as a source, and doubted it had much reach or impact. In his opinion, journalists do not pursue local stories of the type highlighted by CGNet, partly because their main audience is not interested in these stories. He also attributed the dismissal of CGNet to significant conflicts with political and economic interests in the region, where media owners often also own other types of businesses. "It's a very complicated situation here for journalists, especially low-level stringers who cover the rural areas," he said. Ultimately, he saw CGNet as an information source that can help professionals, albeit not full-fledged journalism. Journalism involves more than information, he insisted; it requires ethics and ethics training. Having challenged the ethical basis of citizen journalism, he said: "It is not clear how exactly CGNet operates. They say they verify but we don't know how or to what extent."

The editor of *Deshbandhu*, a central India newspaper with a New Delhi edition, conceded CGNet's conceptual potential. Yet, he said, "It is too unstructured and raw. There is no moderation of the content, no verification; it's like a free-for-all. Can we just believe what someone who has a mobile phone and says something?" The *Deshbandhu* editor said he occasionally looked at it out of curiosity but his reporters did not: "There's too much irrelevant stuff. There is no way to determine if the information is accurate. Who are the sources? Who is checking their stories?" The most damning part of his attack came in his claim that CGNet remained unconnected to mainstream media: "There is no real follow up, no dialogue with the government to see what they are doing." He was adamant that much of CGNet "has nothing to do with journalism." According to him, while CGNet wants to give voice to marginalized/tribal people, it fails to do so; even regionally it is ineffective.

The NDTV journalist said CGNet shared citizen journalism's problems, that is, not operating within professional parameters. She conceded that CGNet may highlight issues important to local communities but doubted its impact. "Ultimately, problematic as it is, it is the mainstream media which has the potential to raise awareness on a meaningful scale that might lead to some action or change." She called the initiative "interesting" but unworkable, at best it is an unverifiable form of data collection focused on "very, very local" problems. "Personal testimony alone cannot be the mainstay of the whole thing," she insisted. "No matter how powerful a story is, in the end you have to verify ... So you can't just report on something because someone called it in."

The Asian News International reporter was somewhat more positive about CGNet, saying it could highlight local issues "that larger media don't focus on at all." She did look at it occasionally, finding it a useful starting point for leads and sources. But even she rejected it as journalism, because it doesn't show "both sides of an issue" and is "90% activism." She repeated her reasoning: "They are too agenda based. Also, they only focus on the negative. They only emphasize the problems and there is no follow up."

The *Dainik Bhaskar* editor was familiar with CGNet, which he called a way for "activists" to publicize their issues. *Dainik Bhaskar* would not use the website, given its "very narrow" focus, its association with "activist types" disinclined to cover Maoism, and its lack of verifiability. "How do we know it's true?," he asked rhetorically. In his view, "Not many people or journalists are aware of it ...The average tribal is not really involved in this. So if the goal is to get ordinary people involved I don't think that's been very successful."

Again showing how disdain for citizen journalism mapped onto disdain for CGNet, several reporters who opposed citizen journalism dismissed CGNet as completely one-sided activism with little significance or relevance. The *Daily Chhattisgarh* editor, who had worked for many years for *Deshbandhu* (as had Choudhary), mentioned a report on local mining produced by a progressive think tank. According to him, CGNet covered the story exclusively from the think tank's environmental perspective, ignoring the government's detailed rebuttal.

Can CGNet Help Journalism?

In several speeches over the last decade, former Press Council of India Chairman G. N. Ray has criticized Indian journalism and journalists for a commercialized, corporatized, market ideology. Speaking on National Press Day in 2010, he blamed post- Independence globalization for opening the floodgates to cut-throat competition and "market dominated corporate capitalism" in journalism, thereby trivializing news. Given that both CGNet and professional journalists acknowledged that mainstream media have little presence or interest in India's interior, partly because of language, and partly because of the profit basis of increasingly corporatized media, citizens might seem to help address the shortage of qualified professionals and CGNet would appear to be an accessible, cheap source of local news.

But critics saw using the website as potentially more work for them, given their anxieties about ethics and professionalism. Given the deadline pressures on journalists, one editor said, they have no time to monitor something whose information is raw and unverified. As far as we know, CGNet Swara has never been accused of corruption and bribery. No claims about inaccuracy have been substantiated. That said, one major problem is its casualness regarding ethics training—albeit a casualness common to citizen journalism initiatives (Roberts and Steiner 2012). Its founder says:

> We tell them basic things, the things that are not negotiable like not using bad language, telling lies, making things up, abusing the platform … Other ethical decisions are up to them. We feel the people can make ethical decisions based on their community.

Merely training participants to distinguish facts from opinions and to provide both sides of the story does not seem sufficient. More importantly, professionals—not despite but apparently because of their defensiveness about the ethical reputation of mainstream news organizations—are unwilling to chance citizens' integrity. The mainstream reporters interviewed here understood the problems and challenges of their profession. Newspapers in particular rely on underpaid (and sometimes never paid) contract workers. One interviewee admitted that most rural reporters are poorly paid stringers, who face real threats if they challenge established interests. "So they are also much more susceptible to being paid off by local authorities and business interests." Others acknowledged that local newspapers are often allied to particular political or corporate interests, so avoid confronting them. A couple of reporters had personally witnessed reporters accepting money from local politicians, businessmen, and police. One such witness to stringers receiving holiday "gifts" said, "No wonder journalists don't cover mining, deforestation, and industrialists' land grabbing." No professional we interviewed mentioned CGNet's report on how, during a rigged public hearing, the owner of the largest circulating newspaper in Chhattisgarh received approval to buy a coal mine.

The NDTV reporter was one of several to concede that national media have become "more corporate"; meanwhile, regional media face enormous control by owners and direct pressure from politicians. Among other potential punishments, the state government can withhold advertising, "the lifeblood of most local media." She even mentioned the very real danger facing journalists of being attacked or killed, referring to three journalists supposedly killed in recent car accidents.

In the context of such acknowledgment of mainstream news organizations' problems, the repudiation of CGNet offers multiple ironies. First, calls for additional regulation of journalism are increasing (Press Council of India 2011), given journalists' ethical lapses. Meanwhile, the press–government relationship is already cozy, including in Chhattisgarh, where the government paid several leading private television channels for positive pieces about its efforts. Apparently, the government's public relations department haggled over the pricing schedule with the Hindi TV channel Sahara Samay before approving Samay's proposals (Bhardwaj 2012). Defending this approach to showcasing government successes as "advertising," one Chhattisgarh public relations officer said funding anti-Naxal coverage was necessary to counter Naxal propaganda: "Everything is in white, duly recorded and accounted" (Bhardwaj 2012). Meanwhile, even CGNet's fiercest critics do not accuse it of pandering to the government.

A second irony is the dismissal of CGNet as activist, given the legacy in India, both pre- and post-Independence, of a reform-minded journalism aiming to serve a public agenda. It might be noted that Choudhary explicitly distances himself from Maoism, but does not reject the "activist" label, noting how the project increasingly links rural and urban activists. But an agenda has become something "bad." The *Daily Chhattisgarh* editor insisted:

> Journalism and this so-called citizen journalism are completely different from each other. Citizen journalism is almost entirely activism, no balance, no neutrality. When we write against someone, we give them the opportunity to respond to the criticism but that's not true of citizen journalism. Also, we verify, cross-check, they don't. They operate without the problems of professional standards and practices and do whatever they want.

Meanwhile, others argued that the project was activist, but ineffectively so. A couple of editors insisted that CGNet raises issues but these must be amplified, which occurs only if the information is picked up by other (real) media. One editor said CGNet needs to get its activism "into the mainstream media because without it, they are not likely to reach the people who make decisions … Raising issues is fine but it's not enough especially if you don't pursue them further."

A third irony cuts in the opposite direction: professional journalists regularly credited CGNet with using local languages, yet Choudhary concedes that most of CGNet's messages are in Hindi; far fewer are in Kurukh or Gondi. CGNet hopes to improve the audio portal to automatically process content, especially in Indic languages (Saha 2012). In any case, according to a moderator, while nearly all of CGNet's most-active posters are journalists or NGO activists, the top 21 posters include five Adivasis, two Dalits, and six from "backward castes." This seems to be an admirable record. Meanwhile, Choudhary's growing awareness of CGNet's limitations and its potential for achieving status among journalists may be indicated by the fact that the similar voice-based platforms he wants to launch in Indonesia and Afghanistan would promote health, education, and agriculture, not news. In 2013, CGNet began Sangeet Swara, a citizen channel for songs, poems, jokes, and entertainment; every recording is posted immediately and callers can vote on which content is best.

Conclusion

Citizen journalism around the world seems buffeted, and not to its benefit, by extreme, unsubstantiated assessments. Professional journalists claim, without systematic evidence, that citizen journalism is subjective, amateurish, and haphazard in quality (Roberts and Steiner 2012). Conversely, advocates celebrate citizen journalism by exaggerating unusual one-time cases, usually disasters. CGNet's self-assessment is likewise overly glowing, claiming to score well "on the triple matrix of social desirability, economic sustainability and technological feasibility" (Saha 2012, 25). Even-handed evaluations of CGNet Swara must note both its potential and limitations.

That professional journalists would be skeptical of a formation often directly challenging its status and authority is hardly surprising. Professional journalists have long tried to maintain their authority and jurisdiction by claiming particular practices and forms of news as their own, and by implication, excluding others. They engage in boundary-work (Gieryn 1999), which involves attributing certain methods, forms of knowledge, and values to an institution in order to distinguish and demarcate what its practitioners do from what non-professionals do. In India, journalism occupies a conflicted space, given challenges to its independence, ethical standards, and quality. Precisely because of the resulting status anxieties, mainstream news organizations seek to underscore their status as "professionals" *vis-à-vis* potential challengers. Although in practice their monopoly over objectivity and facticity, their autonomy, and ethical purity are debatable, these key values have become part of journalists' occupational ideology. Given the problematic absence of verification procedures and explicit ethical guidelines, even those willing to view citizen journalism and CGNet as supplementing mainstream media assumed that neither could be "counted" as journalism. The uniform emphasis on these issues from the journalists suggests that the less confident that professionals are about their status, the less willing they are to tolerate unprofessionalism, even from a "supplement."

With many alternative and activist projects, including in public and citizen journalism, the major satisfaction for participants is the participation itself. Legacy news organizations may even launch partnerships with citizens less to get news (ideas or sources) and more to offer citizens the feeling of participation, to let them enjoy the sense of involvement in meaningful activity that fundamentally connects to democracy. This may explain the satisfaction of engaging in news projects using Twitter and other social networking platforms. It may explain why tribal peoples, albeit few, call up CGNet to report news. Choudhary says: "Our mission is to democratize journalism so that it is not limited to journalists." This, too, suggests that CGNet's "democratizing" refers to a broadened, shared sensibility of participation. That is, the point is participation in (not production of) journalism, making the institution of journalism more horizontal, less top down. If the goal were to produce or enhance direct participation in democracy *per se*, however, the initiative's impact would seem far smaller. Rao (2008) underscores the paradoxical implications of globalization for Indian broadcasting: market pressures undermine its commitment to public service journalism, yet journalists also demand political accountability and giving voice to otherwise marginalized people, thus strengthening the democracy. When democracy is understood in terms of a sensibility for justice, CGNet enhances democracy. Nonetheless, with professionals still largely the agents for holding governments (and police) accountable, it does not directly expand citizen participation, even in the way it intends.

As *Deshbandhu*'s editor said, journalism mediates between people and the government, but CGNet remains unconnected to civil society. Even "the bridge between these communities and the media" that Choudhary hoped to build has not developed. Moreover, these findings raise deeper questions about contemporary journalism in India, which, as we show, is negotiated in the context of several interacting factors ranging from globally pervasive but nonetheless fragile professional ideologies to localized economic and political pressures. Such interactions, we argue, have major consequences for journalism and democratic processes. CGNet Swara's failure to "bridge" the citizen–professional divide and to position the experiment in terms of the larger public sphere suggests continuing challenges for citizen journalism, potentially undercutting confidence that it currently operates a transformative force for democracy.

DISCLOSURE STATEMENT

No potential conflict of interest was reported by the authors.

NOTES

1. Henceforth referred to as CGNet.
2. Information and quotes attributed to Shubhranshu Choudhary are from an interview on June 27, 2012.
3. We also interviewed (but did not quote here) several other journalists and media observers who do not work in the area but who offered insight into professionals' views of citizen journalism and of rural coverage in India.
4. Sonwalkar (2009) "counts" as citizen journalism NDTV letting audiences respond to stories, dictate the order of items on one bulletin, and submit story ideas.

REFERENCES

Administrative Staff College of India. 2009. *Cross Media Ownership in India*. Hyderabad: ASCI Research and Consultancy.

Bhardwaj, Arun. 2012. "Chhattisgarh Govt Pays for All TV News That Is Fit to Buy." *Indian Express*, December 7. http://expressindia.indianexpress.com/story_print.php?storyId=1041594.

Black, George. 2012. "India Calling." *Onearth*, February 21. http://www.onearth.org/article/india-calling.

Chadha, Kalyani. 2012. "Twitter as Media Watch-dog? Lessons from India's Radia Tapes Scandal." *Global Media and Communication* 8 (2): 171–176. doi:10.1177/1742766512444347.

Cottle, Simon. 2009. "Preface." In *Citizen Journalism: Global Perspectives*, edited by Stuart Allan and Einar Thorsen, ix–xii. New York: Peter Lang.

Gieryn, Thomas F. 1999. *Cultural Boundaries of Science: Credibility on the Line*. Chicago, IL: University of Chicago Press.

Holstein, James A., and Jaber F. Gubrium. 1995. *The Active Interview*. Thousand Oaks, CA: Sage.

Internet and Mobile Association. 2012. "Internet in Rural India." http://www.iamai.in/reports1.aspx.

Karan, Kavita. 2001. "Journalism Education in India." *Journalism Studies* 2 (2): 293–300.

Kvale, Steinar. 1996. *InterViews: An Introduction to Qualitative Research Interviewing*. Thousand Oaks, CA: Sage.

Mudgal, Vipul. 2011. "Rural Coverage in the Hindi and English Dailies." *Economic & Political Weekly*, August 27.

Mudliar, Preeti, Jonathan Donner, and William Thies. 2013. "Emergent Practices around CGNet Swara." *Information Technology and International Development* 9 (2): 65–79.

Ninan, Sevanti. 2010. "Oh What a Lovely Blackout." *The Hoot*, November 26. http://thehoot.org/web/home/story.php?storyid=4959&mod=1&pg=1&sectionId=1&valid=true.

PK, Jayadevan. 2013. "Doers: Bringing Change at the Grassroots with Technology." http://www.nextbigwhat.com/aaditeshwar-seth-gramvaani-297/.

Press Council of India. 2011. "Report on Paid News." http://www.presscouncil.nic.in/home.htm.

Rao, Shakuntala. 2008. "Accountability, Democracy, and Globalization: A Study of Broadcast Journalism in India." *Asian Journal of Communication* 18 (3): 193–206.

Rao, Shakuntala. 2009. "Glocalization of Indian Journalism." *Journalism Studies* 10 (4): 474–488.

Rao, Shakuntala, and Navjit S. Johal. 2006. "Ethics and News Making in the Changing Indian Mediascape." *Journal of Mass Media Ethics* 21 (4): 286–303.

Roberts, Jessica, and Linda Steiner. 2012. "The Ethics of Citizen Journalism." In *Digital Ethics Research & Practice*, edited by Don Heider and Adrienne Massanari, 80–98. New York: Peter Lang.

Saha, Anoop. 2012. "Cellphones as a Tool for Democracy: The Example of CGNet Swara." *Economic & Political Weekly* XLVII (15): 23–26.

Segran, Elizabeth. 2013. Innovators Enlist Citizen Journalists to Combat India's Rape Crisis. Global post blog, November 26, http://www.globalpost.com/dispatches/globalpost-blogs/rights/india-rape-crisis-citizen-journalism.

Sonwalkar, Prasun. 2009. "Citizen Journalism in India." In *Citizen Journalism: Global Perspectives*, edited by Stuart Allan and Einar Thorsen, 75–84. New York: Peter Lang.

CONNECTING ACTIVISTS AND JOURNALISTS
Twitter communication in the aftermath of the 2012 Delhi rape

Thomas Poell and **Sudha Rajagopalan**

This article examines how feminist activists, women's organizations, and journalists in India connected with each other through Twitter following the gang rape incident in New Delhi in December 2012. First, the investigation draws on a set of +15 million tweets specifically focused on rape and gang rape. These tweets, which appeared between 16 January 2013 and 16 January 2014, were collected and analysed with the DMI Twitter Capture and Analysis Toolset. Second, to gain further insight into how Twitter enables and shapes civil society connections, the article builds on 15 semi-structured interviews with Indian feminist activists and journalists, who actively participated in Twitter communication on the gang rape incident. The analysis of the Twitter and interview data reveals how the platform allows these actors to make ad hoc connections around particular protest issues and events. These connections alter both activist and journalist practices, and ultimately facilitate the current transformation of public discourse on gender violence. Twitter helps to keep this issue consistently on the front burner. In this sense, a significant shift from the past has occurred, when media coverage typically died out after an incident ceased to be news. Yet, our study also suggests that connectivity is tempered by Twitter's limited Indian user base, and users' focus on the "crime of the day."

Introduction

The 2012 New Delhi gang rape of Jyoti Singh Pandey, called Nirbhaya or Damini before her family agreed to make her name public, sparked mass protests and attracted worldwide media coverage. More fundamentally, in the following year, it triggered pivotal changes in public attention for the problem of gender violence in India. Historically, Indian mainstream news reporting on sexual assault and harassment has been quite rare, bearing a regrettable resemblance to banal crime briefs or sensational stories rather than demonstrating a deep engagement with the subject of violence as an enduring social feature (Joseph 2006, 2014). Landmark cases like the 1974 Mathura rape and the 1987 Shah Bano verdict have led to spikes in media coverage, but have not changed the character of media discourses (Katzenstein 1989, 62; Phadke 2003, 4567; Mody 1987, 939). The Delhi rape in December 2012 and the agitations it occasioned are similarly marked by unprecedented mediatization. After the incident, major news outlets began to devote attention to gender violence as a social problem. This time traditional media have been complemented by a hotbed of protest and outrage on social media platforms. This largely middle-class wave of protest, involving a turn to digital media to sustain and channel public anger, has been noted by scholars (Rao 2013; Sen 2013). The purpose of this article is to examine this recent discursive shift and to unpack the ways in which Twitter communications may have fostered new connections and altered the nature and longevity of public conversation on violence against women. In doing this, the article will address the transformations in activism and journalism and the significance of these changes for civil society relations in India.

Twitter and other social media have been considered central to the current changes in public discourse, as they have provided the rising middle class with the opportunity to voice its concerns and grievances about institutional corruption and the failure of the judicial system to act against gender violence. Over the past years, the number of internet users in India has grown to 213 million, of which about 93 million use Facebook and 33 million Twitter (Patel 2014). While only a relatively small section of the Indian population uses social media, they are nonetheless very voluble and seen as influential in shaping debates and conversations in other media outlets (Belair-Gagnon, Mishra, and Agur 2014; Ahmed and Jaidka 2013). Among the most active social media users are many journalists, feminist activists, students, and more generally young middle-class women and men. Thus, social media potentially constitute vital points of connection between these different actors (Rao 2012; Shah 2012; Chattopadhyay 2011, 2012; Belair-Gagnon, Mishra, and Agur 2014).

This article focuses on Twitter, which is regarded as a particularly important platform for "public" communication. Recent research has especially devoted attention to the impact of Twitter on public communication during the December protests in the direct aftermath of the Delhi gang rape. Ahmed and Jaidka (2013, 125) found that "the common man and activists unleashed a wave of citizen journalism through their posts and retweets." In turn, Belair-Gagnon, Mishra, and Agur (2014, 1068) show us that Indian and foreign journalists used Twitter to "monitor updates and get immediate responses from activists at events." Building on these studies, the present investigation adopts a longer-term perspective to gain insight into the more durable connections and day-to-day exchanges between journalists, feminist activists, bloggers, and women's organizations on the platform around the issue of gender violence. This approach can provide deeper understanding of the enduring impact of Twitter on public communication and enhance our understanding of how this platform and other social media promote connections between key actors in Indian civil society.

Mobilizing Around Women's Issues

To understand how Indian women's organizations and feminist activists use social media today, it is important to note that the "movement" for women's rights in India has not been homogeneous or centrally organized in previous decades. This plurality is one of issues and positions, but also one of styles. By the 1980s, strategies of connecting with other actors and publics became particularly diverse. "Demonstrations, street plays, seminars, symposia, group meetings, and mass parades were resorted to. Postcards, letters, telegrams, etc., were sent to the judiciary and the government" (Krishnaraj 2012, 330). This means that the current spectrum of groups and voices speaking up on issues related to gender violence, on a variety of online and offline platforms, is not a "new splintering" of an otherwise "cohesive" movement, but very much in keeping with the historical, plural nature of the movement and its methods. As Tharu (1986, 122) clarifies, the movement has never had card-carrying members, no centralized organization, and "even an intra-group consensus is often not assumed or demanded."

While some women's groups have had party affiliations and sought change through legislations, others have focused on "empowerment" through grassroots work to enable communities of women to become full participants in society and in the political process (Calman 1989, 945–946). Further, women's groups have fought on other fronts such as issues of the environment and displacement (Krishnaraj 2012, 331). They have also evolved along axes of caste and regional identities, given how gender discrimination works closely with these other pervasive forms of social exclusion. Various activists and scholars have rightly pointed out that this multiplicity of groups, perspectives, issues, and strategies should not be understood as "fragmentation," but appreciated as a form of "diversification," or in the words of Calman (1989, 942) as competing "tendencies."

Digital media have led to a further fanning out of activist positions and strategies within this spectrum of groups. For instance, the women's organizations whose Twitter activity we have investigated in this project and whose representatives we have interviewed vary enormously in their methods and goals. In many of these cases, the term "organization" can only be used loosely. Often an organization has less than a handful of people steering its activity both offline and online. For these projects, the support bases are ephemeral publics that modulate the frequency and nature of their involvement. Some members of these publics only post blogs and tweets, while others are also or only present during offline activities. Their use of new technologies is a common feature, as they all have successfully integrated digital platforms into their activism; they maintain active websites, blogs, Facebook pages, and Twitter handles.

This embrace of new technologies for activism must be framed within the context of the rise of a new generation of middle-class activists, an important force behind the recent protests against poor governance, as well as against gender violence. This emergent wave of middle-class activism has been referred to as the "India Shining" variety—those that are persuaded of the necessity of neo-liberal policies and garner sympathy from corporate and technocratic India (Sitapati 2011, 41–42). Their activism is exemplified by the India Against Corruption campaign, which also relied heavily on social media to build its support base. This new strand of activism is attributed to the growing estrangement between the state and new confident publics that have risen in the post-liberalization decades, a process that appears to them to be bogged down by a seemingly out-dated mode of politics and governance. These activists hate the political class and claim to speak for all (42). Critics have complained that such movements have a pronounced neo-liberal, urban middle-class vocabulary and bias, ignoring the greater culture of violence and other groups' long on-going protests in the country (Shah 2012; Mani 2014). Cultural critic Mani recently argued that feminist discourse in India today is not engaged with systemic gender violence, but tied up with neo-liberal public sentiment and its accompanying emphasis on sexual freedom as a single barometer of women's rights (Mani 2014, 28). The use of digital media by many in this new activism also lends itself for critique, as it appears to indicate a disconnect from "ground realities" rather than committed engagement with activism. Roy (2012) emphasizes that the new generation of activists "must decide whether to go the glossy Twitterati way or take the road to Tahrir," suggesting that being vocal on social media alone is an intrinsically non-radical act. The "road to Tahrir" represents a mode of street agitation, where the "Twitterati way" is inadequate when not accompanied by such action. From this point of view, the digital platform is far removed from the "street" or "public square."

In light of these new forms of mobilization and activism, as well as the critique with which they have been met, it is of interest to see how Twitter communication gives shape to an evolving public discourse on gender violence. To what extent does it facilitate new connections between the wide variety of feminist activist groups, as well as between activists and journalists? And, how do such connections shape public discourse on gender violence? This, in turn, helps us address the larger question of social media's role in shaping new civil society alliances and networks.

Method

The starting point of this analysis is a dataset of approximately 15 million tweets containing the words "rape" or "gangrape," sent by more than 5 million unique users over the period of a year, from 16 January 2013 until 16 January 2014. These tweets have been collected and analysed with the Twitter Capture and Analysis Toolset of the Digital Methods Initiative (Borra and Rieder 2014). Subsequently, from this dataset, the 10 keywords most frequently included in tweets pertaining to the Delhi gang rape case have been selected: "India," "Delhi," "Nirbhaya," "Damini," "Delhigangrape." "Delhirape," "MumbaiGangRape," "Asaram," "Suryanelli," and "Tejpal." Querying the full dataset on the basis of the 10 keywords generated a subset of 1,008,460 tweets, specifically focused on the Delhi gang rape case and related issues. These tweets were sent by 311,611 unique users.

To identify the key mainstream journalists, women's organizations, and feminist activists and bloggers in this large set of users, we have coded the top 100 most "mentioned" and most "mentioning" users for occupational background, and whether they are connected with an Indian or international organization. Note that news organizations were left out of the analysis, as most of these organizations primarily use Twitter to disseminate and promote their own news content (Hermida 2013). To trace the Twitter network in which the identified journalists, women's organizations, and feminists were entangled, we coded all of the users mentioned by these actors. Taken together, the two rounds of coding produced a list of 24 mainstream journalists, 16 feminist activists, bloggers, and writers, and 19 women's organizations.

To examine how journalists, women's organizations, and feminists associated with each other, we have analysed four important ways in which users connect with each other on Twitter: by "following," "mentioning," "retweeting," and by using a common "hashtag." First, we investigated, for each selected user, which of the other identified users followed this user.[1] This analytical step provides insights into how content circulated between users. Second, the mentioning patterns have been reconstructed by querying the dataset for the mentioning activity of each selected user. Third, we have explored the retweeting activity of the users to determine how they reinforced each other's tweets and potentially produced collective accounts. Finally, the investigation traces the use of hashtags by the key users to determine whether they organized their Twitter communication in a shared manner.

To gain insight into what was exactly exchanged between the central users, we categorized the tweets that were disseminated through mentions, retweets, and organized by particular hashtags. In the case of the mentions, we collected a sample by scraping for the tweets in which one of the selected users was @mentioned at the start of the tweet. For the retweets, we, subsequently, focused on sets of the 100 most frequently shared tweets. Not to impose any preconceived categories on this material, two coders independently labelled the collected tweets through emergent coding (Stemler 2001). We first assembled categories by examining the material, and, subsequently, consolidated a checklist of keywords and phrases in a coding manual (see Appendix A). In addition to coding the tweets for the discussed issues, we also coded them for their apparent "purpose," distinguishing between tweets that appeared to aim for "conversation," "information exchange," "proclaiming a point of view," or "promoting an event or publication."

To contextualize the analysis of the Twitter data, we conducted, between February and April 2014, 15 semi-structured interviews via Skype with eight feminist activists and seven journalists and bloggers. The eight activists are:

- Jasmeen Patheja of Blank Noise, an organization committed to ending street sexual harassment.
- Rita Banerji of 50 Million Missing, an organization that creates awareness about female gendercide.
- Anja Kovacs of the Internet Democracy Project and Genderlog, which is a curated online platform for gender issues.
- Sakshi Kumar of Justice for Women, a Twitter-based organization set up in the aftermath of the Delhi rape with the specific purpose of spreading information about the crime.
- Meghana Rao of Breakthrough, a human rights organization with campaigns against domestic violence.
- Bina Nepram of the Manipur Gun Survivors Network, concerned with gender and violence in conflict areas in north-east India.
- Bhavana Upadhyaya, a social worker.
- Swarna Rajagopalan of Prajnya Trust, a non-governmental organization (NGO) for advocacy and research on gender and security.

The seven bloggers and journalists included both independent writers as well as those working with news organizations:

- Nilanjana Roy is a freelance writer and literary critic who has written on gender issues for *Business Standard*, *Telegraph* (Kolkata), and the *International New York Times*.
- Harini Calamur is a jounalist and Head of Digital Content at Zee Media.
- Nirupama Subramanian is a journalist with *The Hindu*.
- Rohini Mohan is a journalist whose work has appeared in *Tehelka*, the *Caravan*, *The Hindu*, and also on Al Jazeera and CNN-IBN.
- Natasha Badhwar is a freelance writer and columnist for *Mint*, co-curator of Genderlog, and a teacher of journalism.
- Deepika Bhardwaj is a journalist and film-maker.
- Anindita Sengupta is a writer, poet, and founder-editor of Ultra Violet, a site on contemporary feminism, whose articles on gender have appeared in *The Hindu*, *Deccan Herald*, and *The Guardian*.

These interviewees have been selected from the reconstructed Twitter communication networks, and by using word of mouth in the Indian activist and journalistic communities. All of them agreed to be named in this article. The interview sessions lasted an average of 60 minutes. The semi-structured interview approach was most suitable for exploring the largely uncharted terrain of Indian social media practices, as it allowed the interviewees to answer our open-ended questions from their own particular perspectives. Using the Delhi gang rape as a prism, our questions for interviewees centred around their use of Twitter in the aftermath of the rape, the role of Twitter in occasioning new connections with other concerned actors, and their observations about connections and exchanges on Twitter around the subject of gender violence. Once the interviews had been transcribed, we read them several times and tagged segments of interest, and identified central themes (Corbin and Strauss 2008). Analysing the interview data, we took into account that the interviews took place 14 months after the Delhi gang rape. Interviewees' observations combined specific recollections of Twitter activity after the incident with deeper reflections on their own Twitter experiences and on the vocabulary and tone of Twitter discourse in the subsequent year.

Connecting Activists and Journalists

Examining the connections between the identified journalists, women's organizations, and feminists, the fundamentally transnational character of this core Twitter network around the issue of gender violence in India becomes immediately evident. While most of these key users were located in India, many of them were linked to transnational news organizations, such as CNN, the BBC, and Reuters, or international women's organizations, such as Women Under Siege, Half, UN Women, and The Pixel Project. Of the 59 selected users, 37 (63 per cent) could be identified as "international." Probing the follower lists of these "international" users, it becomes clear that they were strongly connected with the selected Indian journalists of mainstream news outlets such as the *Hindustan Times*, NDTV (New Delhi Television), and *India Today*, as well as with Indian feminists and women's organizations, including 50 Million Missing, Genderlog, Justice for Women, and M for Change. Thus, Twitter seems to very much open up Indian public discourse on rape to the world at large.

Looking more specifically at the extent to which different types of users "followed" each other, it becomes clear that there are many interconnections as well. Numerous links can especially be observed between mainstream journalists and feminist activists, bloggers, and writers. Of the 24 identified journalists, no less than 21 (88 per cent) followed one or, in many cases, more of the feminists from our list. Vice versa, of the 16 feminist activists, bloggers, and writers, 14 (88 per cent) followed one or more mainstream journalists. Thus, the set of key users does not fall apart in different clusters, and these users appear to be highly aware of each other's points of view and issues of concern. This corresponds with the research by Belair-Gagnon, Mishra, and Agur (2014, 1065), who found that journalists' use of social media reflected the ideas and interests of "city-based women's groups, activists, university students and intellectuals." Of course, it should be observed that follower lists are rather static entities. To understand how users in practice interacted and connected with each other around the issue of gender violence, we need to examine how they employed "@mentions," "retweets," and "hashtags."

Starting with @mentions, one of the more personal and potentially "conversational" methods of connection, it is striking how many users employed this technique. Over two-thirds of all users tweeting on gender violence in India, 216,241 out of 311,611, included one or more @mentions in their tweets. Looking more specifically at the @mentioning activity of the selected users, the connections especially between the journalists and the feminist activists, bloggers, and writers become evident: 15 of the 24 selected journalists were @mentioned two or more times in the feminist tweets, while 10 out of the 16 key feminists were mentioned at various times by the journalists. Hence, these users not only "followed" but also actively engaged with each other on the platform.

A similar impression of an interconnected set of users emerges when we examine the retweet activity of the users. About 30 per cent of all users, 92,613, retweeted at least one tweet, with the most active retweeters sharing hundreds of tweets. While the percentage of retweets in the overall set is still not as high as during protest events or disasters, when often more than two-thirds of the tweets are retweets, retweeting nevertheless provided a (lightweight) means through which users connected with each other, and produced collective accounts (Poell and Borra 2012). Focusing more specifically on the retweet activity of the selected users, it is especially notable that a substantial part of the tweets that were retweeted came from within the group of key users. No clustering appeared to be taking place here either. Journalists, particularly, frequently shared tweets of women's organizations, feminist activists, bloggers, and writers. Taken together, having examined some of the key ways in which users connect on Twitter, the overall impression is that the platform greatly facilitated connections between different types of actors throughout the year following the gang rape case.

This is not to say, however, that these actors constituted or tried to constitute a community. Rather, they appeared to consider Twitter as a platform for general public communication. This is suggested by how these users organized their tweets through hashtags. Instead of primarily tagging their messages through issue-specific hashtags, such as #Damini and #Nirbhaya, they chose to use general hashtags, such as #India and #Delhi. Over the past years, it has become common practice among activists during major protests to disseminate their messages through particular hashtags. #g20report, #sidibouzid, #25jan, and #occupywallstreet are prominent examples of such hashtags, which effectively established temporary, issue-specific communication spaces. The users in our dataset clearly did not make such an effort. Of the selected users only 9 out of 59 employed the hashtag #Nirbhaya a few times, while none of them took up #Damini. They did occasionally use these pseudonyms for the Delhi gang rape victim in their tweets, but not as hashtags. By contrast, #India was used by 52 (88 per cent) of the selected 59 users, with some of them tagging hundreds of tweets with this hashtag. All this indicates that Twitter was very much treated as an open communication space for general public debate.

The image of an open communication platform, through which users can easily connect, was also put forward by the interviewees. Most of them agreed that Twitter has been important in bringing women's organizations and activists together, who may otherwise not have found each other in a country as vast as India. For example, Binalakshmi Nepram, the founder of the Manipur Women Gun Survivors Network, stresses that Twitter has been enormously valuable for her. As 90 per cent of her followers are located in other parts of India, Twitter significantly counteracts the north-east's isolation from the rest of India.[2] Moreover, as Rita Banerji, founder of the women's organization 50 Million Missing, makes clear, the platform not only allows Indian feminists to overcome geographical distances, but it also allows them to address a variety of societal actors: ranging from other activists, journalists, and NGOs to academics, public servants, politicians, governments, and international organizations.[3] Confirming this observation, Nirupama Subramanian, journalist with *The Hindu*, and activist and film-maker Deepika

Bhardwaj maintain that Twitter allowed them to raise issues related to gender violence with policy makers and politicians.[4]

An especially important theme in the interviews, which corresponds with the findings of Ahmed and Jaidka (2013), was that Twitter appears to substantially lower the barrier for people in India to become involved in activism and to be drawn into activist communication. For example, Jasmeen Patheja from Blank Noise, a community public art project that seeks to confront street harassment, told us about a tweetathon she ran after the Delhi gang rape, in which people from different professions were invited to make a pledge to keep the streets safe for women. Many of these people had never been involved in activism; for them Twitter provided an easy entry into the campaign for public safety.[5] Social media connectivity, however, not only lowers the barrier to entry into activism, but also lowers the cost of setting up an activist project or organization. Many of the key feminist projects and campaigns in the public discourse on gender violence in India, including 50 Million Missing, Blank Noise, and Justice for Women, mainly take shape through social media, requiring relatively few organizational resources to reach larger publics. A prominent example, in this regard is Justice for Women, which started as a Twitter hashtag. Its founder, Sakshi Kumar, remembers how she began to use the hashtag #justiceforwomen in the summer of 2012 after a young woman from north-east India was assaulted by a group of 20–25 men. The hashtag #justiceforwomen was meant to raise awareness and to function as an open call to ask people what could be done against gender violence. As the assault case triggered a lot of media attention and public anger, the hashtag quickly began to trend in India and, subsequently, worldwide. Encouraged by the massive support she received, Kumar developed the idea to set up a Twitter-based network to organize self-defence workshops for women in cities across India.[6]

Taken together, social media connectivity boosts the enduring pluralism of India's women's groups, but more importantly, it also facilitates connections, hitherto difficult to establish, between journalists and a wide variety of activist and civil society groups, projects, and campaigns.

Exchanges Between Activists and Journalists

While connectivity emerged as the guiding principle in tweets about the Delhi gang rape and gender violence, journalists and activists find indications of conversation and exchange on Twitter to be less promising. Swarna Rajagopalan, director of Prajnya, an advocacy and research group for women, peace, and security, says: "I think, too many people coming into Twitter, use it primarily to broadcast. And that's a waste."[7] Other interviewees echoed this view of Twitter. As Harini Calamur, responsible for digital content at Zee Media explains: "It's not primarily a content medium. It's a great place for instant reactions, it's a great place for publicizing your work, and it's a great place for forming connections."[8]

These observations are confirmed by the content analysis of the @mentions. Examining a sample of tweets in which the selected users address each other at the beginning of the tweet, it becomes clear that only some of these users actually treated Twitter as a tool to converse. While the sample contains tweets most likely to aim for conversation, only 35 per cent of the @mention tweets, as Figure 1 shows, could be coded as "conversational." In the sets of top retweets, "conversational" tweets were even less present. The following message by feminist blogger Vidyut, sent on 7 December 2013, is a

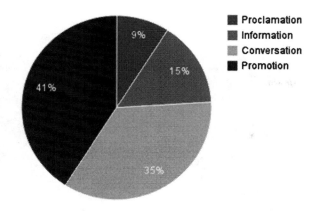

FIGURE 1
Purpose @mentions

good example of a conversational tweet from the @mentions-set: "@kavita_krishnan so what you are saying is that mass criticism in Tejpal case was right and Delhi Gang Rape was wrong? @AListRap @Charakan." Here Vidyut, a feminist blogger, is involved in a direct dialogue with activist Kavita Krishnan with the purpose of understanding her publicly expressed views on public reactions to widely publicized rape cases. However, most of the tweets that mention other users are promotional (45 per cent). Consider a typical promotional tweet from journalist Paloma Sharma to feminist blogger Rita Banerji, who runs 50 Million Missing: "@Rita_Banerji 'If you can't prevent rape enjoy it'—Why I am outraged by the CBI [Central Bureau of Investigation] Director's remarks: http://t.co/jJeW0bVu4i #rape #India" (14 November 2013). This tweet is addressed to Rita Banerji, but it is not conversational. Instead @mentioning is used to spread the word about an article that she has published.

In terms of discussed issues, clear differences can be observed between the different sets of top retweets. The top 100 retweets for all users, based on the 10 selected terms, are especially focused on new rape cases: 56 per cent of these retweets consist of rape reports (see Figure 2a). Mainstream news sources and also Indian and international celebrities figure prominently in this larger dataset. The mass of users appears especially interested in headlines about rape and celebrity proclamations of support or dissent. In turn, the top retweets of the selected feminists, women's organizations, and journalists are more varied (see Figure 2b). Besides reports of new rape cases (23 per cent), there is also attention for governance (14 per cent), the legal system (25 per cent), and public safety (14 per cent). Hence, for the key actors in public debate, Twitter functions as a space for articulating opinions and exchanging information on a range of topics related to gender violence.

This also becomes evident in the analysis of the top retweets of these actors featuring the widely used hashtag #India. In these retweets, there is also attention for other issues, including the effort to understand the cultural context in which rape occurs (9 per cent), statistics about rape (8 per cent), as well as protests against gender violence (9 per cent) (see Figure 2c). Particularly striking is that a small number of retweets in this set also focus on questions of caste and religion (1 per cent), which are otherwise not discussed in the top retweets. The general absence of this issue in the most shared retweets is another indication of the overall urban middle-class character of Twitter communication on gender violence.

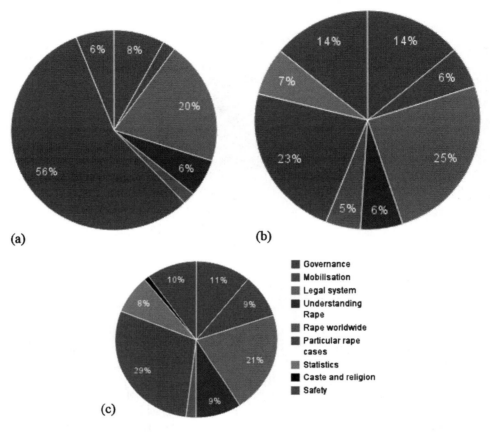

FIGURE 2
(a) Top retweets all users; (b) top retweets selected users; (c) top retweets #India selected users

The interviews helped to further contextualize these findings. Reflecting on the limited accommodation of substantive conversation or dialogue, all interviewees underscored that Twitter should be used in combination with other blogging platforms that allow more reflection and depth. Rohini Mohan, who writes for *Tehelka* and *The Hindu*, finds disquieting the "bestiality" and "voyeurism" on Twitter,[9] while journalist Anindita Sengupta finds Twitter discourse very polarized. Corroborating our Twitter findings, Sengupta recalls that most people on Twitter were mainly exercised by the question of suitable punishment and retribution.[10] They also appeared to be more interested in the "crime of the day" rather than enduring systemic violence, a tendency shared by other forms of media coverage of gender violence (Joseph 2014). Natasha Badhwar, columnist and film-maker who co-curates Genderlog, a crowdsourced group website on gender violence in India, found she first needed to reflect and write a considered piece and so chose to write columns on the rape in print media rather than respond on Twitter, where reactions tended to be impulsive and near-sighted.[11] Furthermore, print and television continue to be influential. Many of those interviewed noted that Twitter is mostly reactive to mainstream reports, which corresponds with our analysis of the general set of retweets, as discussed above. Connectivity is further circumscribed by the fact that Twitter is primarily used by a new generation of activists. Traditional women's organizations and activists have not yet embraced the platform, a fact also borne out by work on digital media cultures in India (Kovacs 2010).

More fundamentally, our interviewees critically reflected on the pronounced middle-class base of activist Twitter communication, which was also highlighted by the journalists interviewed by Belair-Gagnon, Mishra, and Agur (2014). Twitter's middle-class exclusivity was suggested in a number of indirect ways. Anja Kovacs of the Internet Democracy Project, who also curates @genderlogindia, reminds us that Twitter is used only by a small segment of India's vast population and therefore activism through other channels of communication continues to be essential.[12] Some interviewees suggested that Twitter communication and exchange are circumscribed due to the headline-centred interests of the general users. This resonates with the critique of middle-class movements like India Against Corruption that focus disproportionately on the question of accountability and appear less interested in addressing systemic injustice and exclusion. The interviewees suggested that most users who tweet on gender violence want to know what the system is capable of delivering, and do not engage with long-enduring forms of violence and everyday sexism. The analysis of the retweets from the general set of users confirms this: most of these retweets inform about new rape incidents and court verdicts, and call for suitable forms of punishment. Few of these tweets address the broader subject of patriarchy and common misconceptions about rape.

Finally, the near-absence of tweets on the interplay of gender, caste, and ethnic biases in violence against women suggest that Twitter exchanges on gender violence exclude vital issues and voices. Among the coded tweets, a small percentage of tweets focused on rape in disputed territories of India, at the time of the partition, after the recent communal riots in Uttar Pradesh, and the rape of Adivasi and Dalit women. Nilanjana Roy's observations underscore the exclusivist nature of the Twitter community:

> It [Twitter] has great potential. But it's good to be aware of the demographics of Indian Net usage, which is still predominantly male, and which has vast skews towards urban, affluent, English-accented India ... There's a major problem with language dominance—if Indian social media end up being ruled by a handful of dominant regional languages at the expense of a variety of local dialects, we'll exclude far too many communities and groups. There's an even bigger problem with gender skews and caste skews: Indian Twitter is an actively hostile environment for women seen as "outspoken" and often for people from lower castes, and this is very, very problematic. Women in particular often end up either censoring themselves, or wading through streams of abuse, if they voice controversial opinions.

In sum, both the coded retweets and observations of the interviewees suggest that Twitter's potential as a platform that facilitates civil society networks is undermined by its exclusion of vital voices in India's civil society, and its proclivity for information dissemination rather than dialogue.

Conclusion

Social media provide essential connections between journalists and a wide variety of feminist activist groups concerned about pressing social issues in India. The Indian women's movement, with its multiplicity of groups, perspectives, issues, and strategies, and lack of centralizing organizations, profits from social media connectivity, which raises its activist profile and facilitates connections with mainstream media. This connectivity strengthens Indian civil society and the democratic process by allowing these groups and other social actors to collaborate in common action around particular issues, as well as by helping journalists report about such action and issues. The data and interviews indicate that social platforms allow Indian feminist activists and journalists to make *ad hoc* associations around issues of common concern. While activism has become more diffuse and personalized, news reporting around the subject of gender violence has become open to a more fluid inflow of information and opinions, operating as it does in an "ambient media system" where news is ubiquitous and sources are many (Hermida 2010). Journalists, activists, and interested users participate in this ambient environment, collectively generating and sustaining attention for issues related to gender violence.

Twitter specifically helps to keep the problem of gender violence consistently on the front burner and in that sense marks a significant shift from the past, when media coverage has died out after an incident has ceased to be news. The sustained interaction around this issue builds a solid foundation for activism because it endures even when there are no agitations or other intermittent forms of activism around which to coalesce. Coupled with the connections with journalists who work both freelance and for large media organizations, these sustained conversations and engagement on Twitter about gender discrimination and violence are a vital form of political engagement.

Yet, our study also shows the limits of this kind of connectivity. While news of gender violence is "everywhere" on Twitter, our findings indicate that the platform's limited user base erodes its potential for dialogue. Less than 20 per cent of the Indian population has internet access, and only a small percentage of these users is on Twitter. This is reflected in the dominance of male, urban, middle-class, English-speaking users on the platform, and the absence of local languages, and representatives of rural communities and lower castes. Moreover, the potential for dialogue is further weakened by the inherent features of micro-blogging, which lends itself more to real-time information sharing around the event or crime of the day, rather than to substantive debate about enduring systemic violence. Consequently, our journalist and activist interviewees do not rely on Twitter alone, but also use a variety of other online and offline media platforms for networking and building civil society relations. It is in combination with these other efforts that social media communication has a fundamental impact on India's civil society relations and its democratic political culture.

DISCLOSURE STATEMENT

No potential conflict of interest was reported by the authors.

NOTES

1. Data collection took place on 20 January 2014.
2. Binalakshmi Nepram, Skype interview by Sudha Rajagopalan, 2 April 2014.
3. Rita Banerji, Skype interview by Sudha Rajagopalan, 13 March 2014.
4. Nirupama Subramanian, Skype interview by Sudha Rajagopalan, 26 March 2014; Deepika Bhardwaj, Skype interview by Sudha Rajagopalan, 21 March 2014.
5. Jasmeen Patheja, Skype interview by Sudha Rajagopalan, 29 March 2014.

6. Sakshi Kumar, Skype interview by Sudha Rajagopalan, 11 March 2014.
7. Swarna Rajagopalan, Skype interview by Sudha Rajagopalan, 19 February 2014.
8. Harini Calamur, Skype interview by Sudha Rajagopalan, 23 February 2014.
9. Rohini Mohan, Skype interview by Sudha Rajagopalan, 2 April 2014.
10. Anindita Sengupta, Skype interview by Sudha Rajagopalan, 4 April 2014.
11. Natasha Badhwar, Skype interview by Sudha Rajagopalan, 21 March 2014.
12. Anja Kovacs, Skype interview by Sudha Rajagopalan, 19 March 2014.

REFERENCES

Ahmed, Saifuddin, and Kokil Jaidka. 2013. "The Common Man: An Examination of Content Creation and Information Dissemination on Twitter during the 2012 New Delhi Gang-rape Protest." Digital Libraries: Social Media and Community Networks. *Lecture Notes in Computer Science* 8279: 117–126.

Belair-Gagnon, Valerie, Smeeta Mishra, and Colin Agur. 2014. "Reconstructing the Indian Public Sphere: Newswork and Social Media in the Delhi Gang Rape Case." *Journalism* 15 (8): 1059–1075. doi:10.1177/1464884913513430.

Borra, Erik, and Bernhard Rieder. 2014. "Programmed Method. Developing a Toolset for Capturing and Analyzing Tweets." *Aslib Journal of Information Management* 66 (3): 262–278.

Calman, Leslie J. 1989. "Women and Movement Politics in India." *Asian Survey* 29 (10): 940–958. doi:10.2307/2644790.

Chattopadhyay, Saayan. 2011. "'Online Activism for a Heterogeneous Time' the Pink Chaddi Campaign and the Social Media in India." *Proteus* 27 (1): 63–68.

Chattopadhyay, Saayan. 2012. "Online Journalism and Election Reporting in India." *Journalism Practice* 6 (3): 337–348. doi:10.1080/17512786.2012.663596.

Corbin, Juliet, and Anselm Strauss, eds. 2008. *Basics of Qualitative Research: Techniques and Procedures for Developing Grounded Theory*. Los Angeles, CA: Sage.

Hermida, Alfred. 2010. "From TV to Twitterati." *M/C Journal* 13 (2). http://www.journal.media-culture.org.au/index.php/mcjournal/article/viewArticle/220.

Hermida, Alfred. 2013. "#Journalism: Reconfiguring Journalism Research about Twitter, One Tweet at a Time." *Digital Journalism* 1 (3): 295–313. doi:10.1080/21670811.2013.808456.

Joseph, Ammu. 2006. "Editing Them Out." *Hindustan Times*, February 16.

Joseph, Ammu. 2014. "Reporting Rape." *LiveMint*; The *Wall Street Journal*, March 8. http://www.livemint.com/Leisure/jmh7bFAk1HNVwk5HpDSTbP/Essay–Reporting-rape.html.

Katzenstein, Mary Fainsod. 1989. "Organizing against Violence: Strategies of the Indian Women's Movement." *Pacific Affairs* 62 (1): 53–71. doi:10.2307/2760264.

Krishnaraj, Maithreyi. 2012. "The Women's Movement in India: A Hundred Year History." *Social Change* 42 (3): 325–333. doi:10.1177/0049085712454052.

Kovacs, Anja. 2010. "What's in a Name? Or Why Clicktivism May Not Be Ruining Left Activism in India, At Least for Now." *Centre for Internet and Society* blog, September 10. http://cis-india.org/raw/histories-of-the-internet/blogs/revolution-2.0/whats-in-a-name-or-why-clicktivism-may-not-be-ruining-left-activism-in-india-at-least-for-now.

Mani, Lata. 2014. "Sex and the Signal-free Corridor: Towards a New Feminist Imaginary." *Economic and Political Weekly* XLIX (6): 26–29.

Mody, Nawaz B. 1987. "The Press in India: The Shah Bano Judgment and Its Aftermath." *Asian Survey* 27 (8): 935–953. doi:10.2307/2644865.

Phadke, Shilpa. 2003. "Thirty Years On: Women's Studies Reflects on the Women's Movement." *Economic and Political Weekly* 38 (43): 4567–4576.

Patel, Atish. 2014. "India's Social Media Election Battle." *BBC News India*, March 31. http://www.bbc.com/news/world-asia-india-26762391.

Poell, Thomas, and Erik Borra. 2012. "Twitter, YouTube, and Flickr as Platforms of Alternative Journalism: The Social Media Account of the 2010 Toronto G20 Protests." *Journalism* 13 (6): 695–713. doi:10.1177/1464884911431533.

Rao, Anuradha. 2012. "'Sister-groups' and Online-offline Linkages in Networked Collective Action: A Case Study of the Right to Information Movement in India." *The Electronic Journal on Information Systems in Developing Countries* 52 (7): 1–17.

Rao, Shakuntala. 2013. "Covering Rape: The Changing Nature of Society and Indian Journalism." *Center for Journalism Ethics*. https://ethics.journalism.wisc.edu/2013/03/19/covering-rape-the-changing-nature-of-society-and-indian-journalism.

Roy, Siddhartha Swapan. 2012. "Tahrir Not Twitterati: The Future of Middle-class Movements in India." *OpenDemocracy*, March 14. http://www.opendemocracy.net/siddharthya-swapan-roy/tahrir-not-twitterati-future-of-middle-class-movements-in-india.

Sen, Amartya. 2013. "India's Women: The Mixed Truth'—An Exchange Replies." *New York Review of Books*, October 10. http://www.nybooks.com/articles/archives/2013/oct/10/indias-women-mixed-truth/.

Shah, Nishant. 2012. "Resisting Revolutions: Questioning the Radical Potential of Citizen Action." *Development* 55 (2): 173–180. doi:10.1057/dev.2012.3.

Sitapati, Vinay. 2011. "What Anna Hazare's Movement and India's New Middle Classes Say about Each Other." *Economic and Political Weekly* XLVI (30): 39–44.

Stemler, Steve. 2001. "An Overview of Content Analysis." *Practical Assessment, Research & Evaluation* 7 (17): 137–146.

Tharu, Susie. 1986. "Engendering Political Processes- or, What the Women's Movement Is Doing and What It Might Amount to, Some Day." In *What's Happening to India? The Last Ten Years*, 122–136. Melbourne: La Trobe University.

Appendix A
Coding Manual

Category	Example sentences
Governance	#police in #India won't file #rape cases. Some have raped victims!; @pmoindia: why aren't you accepting #verma suggestion to remove politicians accused of #rape.
Mobilization	The biggest movement against worldwide rape culture is now taking place in #India; Prosecution angry Indian citizenry urge court to "hang 'em high" in Delhi gang rape case.
Legal system	Have all our systems collapsed?; "No shortcuts on rape: make the legal system work"; Ordinance on rape law #India signed today on a Sunday by president; No #justice for the #suryanelli gang #rape victim is injustice to the #women.
Understanding rape	Consensual rape: understanding the (oxy)moron; Blame Victim RT @highheelswaali: Of course; "If girls look sexy boys will rape." Is this what Indian men really believe?
Rape worldwide	You thought India was dismissive of rape? Indonesian judge suggests rape victims enjoy the sex; #India makes to the top 10 global news items for #Rape!; yet 1 in 5 women are sexually assaulted in US.
Particular rape cases	This is one of the worst gang #rape / #sextrafficking cases in #India!; 16-yr-old raped by 40 men over 40 days; Brutal rape and murder of 3 young sisters sparks outrage in India.
Statistics	India has seen an increase of 336% of child #rape cases from 2113 cases in 2001 to 7112 cases; 143% spurt in #rape by #juveniles in #India in 10 years!
Caste and religion	Rape victims suffer in silence after Hindu–Muslim riots in India; Sexual assault and gang rape during September communal violence in Uttar Pradesh.
Safety	India asks what has changed since the #delhigangrape. Women don't feel safer but the urban conversation has changed; Women in new Delhi are signing up for self-defence courses in droves following a brutal gang rape last month.

HOW WELL DO INDIA'S MULTIPLE LANGUAGE DAILIES PROVIDE POLITICAL KNOWLEDGE TO CITIZENS OF THIS ELECTORAL DEMOCRACY?

Bella Mody

This article investigates journalism's supply of political knowledge to citizens in India's democracy. The contribution of newspapers to informed citizenship is measured by content analysis measuring the quantity, quality, and regional equality of political knowledge distribution. The content area selected for analysis of newspaper representations is the indigenous armed struggle modeled on China's Maoist revolution, the alternative to electoral democracy that both the Manmohan Singh and Narendra Modi administrations consider India's greatest internal security threat. All coverage from 2011 to 2012 in the highest circulation daily in each of five languages (Hindi, Telegu, Bengali, Urdu, and English) was selected for analysis. Findings in this article focus on the differences in the amount of coverage, topics that set the public agenda, how they were framed, and how the stories performed on a specially prepared news comprehensiveness index. Concerns are raised about significant regional inequalities in political knowledge supply to distinct linguistic electoral constituencies that are pulling at the seams of this young multiple-nation democracy. The article closes with a question relevant to all democracies: can for-profit news organizations be relied on as the only pillar of public citizenship education essential to democratic functioning?

Introduction

The Election Commission of the world's largest democracy has been rightly praised for how well it conducted the 2014 16th general election where 66 percent of over 800 million eligible voters cast their ballots. More than 10 million polling officials and security personnel staffed around 930,000 polling stations. Results were announced as scheduled on May 16, 2014.

Banerjee et al. (2010) found informed voters made better choices in an experiment in Delhi's slums—they found greater electoral gains for better performing candidates and also a reduction in the incidence of cash-based vote buying. The quality and quantity of disinterested political knowledge was a major influence on voters. The equitable distribution of disinterested political knowledge across electoral constituencies could potentially effect a major change in the money–muscle–media mix of political forces that shape national election outcomes. Given the context of India's electoral democracy with multiple sub-national constituencies and a single federal parliament, this study seeks to compare journalism as voter education across five languages in India.

This investigation focuses on India's newspapers and compares how comprehensively they presented a topic considered the country's greatest internal security threat by the previous Manmohan Singh government and the current Modi administration, namely the ongoing Maoist armed struggle alternative to electoral democracy. It is important to recall that the first amendment to India's Constitution that limited freedom of the press was also prompted by an unsuccessful Communist uprising that called for immediate armed revolt.

Home to the world's highest circulation English-language paper (*The Times of India*), India had over 12,000 registered dailies in 2012–2013, 85 percent of which were printed in one of India's regional languages. As circulation declines in the mature printed press industries of North America and Western Europe, it is expected that the younger newspaper industries of China and India will be similarly impacted but it is not clear when or whether smaller cities, towns, and villages under-served by newspapers could be a new frontier for expansion, given that advertisers will be looking for localized print editions in Hindi and regional vernacular languages (Patel 2014). The most recent Indian Readership Survey of 2013 (Scroll Staff 2014) shows regional-language newspapers are read most. Given around 10 percent internet penetration in mostly big metropolitan cities, market researchers estimate that regional market potential includes 545 million literates who do not buy a newspaper presently and approximately 20 million who are expected to enter the market annually until the current 25 percent national illiteracy is eradicated (FICCI-KPMG 2012–14). Market size apart, however, there is little empirical data on how the regional-language printed press performs in terms of informing democracy.

The article starts with an introduction to the political context of India, a young state of multiple nations. The next section introduces the Maoist movement as the topic that is analyzed in five of the highest circulation dailies in the country that potentially reach 70 percent of the population. The third section addresses the theoretical framework, followed by sections on research design and findings. The closing section is a summary and discussion.

The Context: India's "Multi-national" Electoral Democracy

The political reality of India in 2015 is that of a 67-year-young democratic federation of many culturally distinct one-time independent nations. These former nations were integrated and made part of the British (and also French, Dutch, and Portuguese) empires to supply raw materials and markets for the colonizers. The ancient Greek idea of democracy was adapted for a sub-continent-sized landmass with 22 languages, 29 states (presently), and regionally concentrated ethnic differences that Stefan, Linz, and Yadav (2011) categorize as a state consisting of multiple nations or "state-nation." Responsibility for different aspects of governance was divided between the regional governments and the federal government, e.g. domestic law and order was the responsibility of individual states while foreign policy and defense were federal responsibility.

Given this adaptation, governance in twenty-first-century India has been inevitably characterized by federal–regional tussles over power. Other challenges include growing inequality between an expanding new middle class and groups who have been bypassed (namely aboriginal native tribals, many Muslims, and most lower-caste Hindus), and huge growth in private business wanting access to land, minerals, and forest wealth in the homelands of indigenous groups.

The Topic Under Study: Armed Revolution as an Alternative to Parliamentary Democracy

As indicated in a previous work (Mody 2010), post-World War II former colonial states in Africa and South Asia are not unlike young Western European states of the mid-1600s in terms of struggles between contiguous but diverse ethnic and linguistic groups who find themselves lumped together incoherently in a new state. Resistance to these couplings is seen in 67-year-young India's separatist uprisings in the states of Punjab and Kashmir in the north and in Nagaland, Mizoram, and Assam in the north-east. In the north-east, many states have cultural identities that are linguistically and religiously distinct from the rest of India—Naga and Mizo are their first languages, Christianity is the majority religion.

Original Residents of India

One-time indigenous nations (called "adivasis" or aboriginals in India, "first peoples" in Canada, "natives" and "tribes" or ethnic groups in some scholarly literature) in central and eastern India are protesting the exploitation of their mineral and forest wealth by profit-making companies and economic growth-driven federal and regional governments. Enforcement of legal provisions under the 1996 Panchayat Extension to Scheduled Areas Act[1] and the 2006 Forest Areas Act[2] that would have improved their livelihood conditions has been irregular. The documentary video *Mine: Story of a Sacred Mountain* (Survival International 2010) produced by an international non-governmental organization concerned with land ownership rights of indigenous communities illustrates one phase of an ongoing struggle by Dongriya Konds in Odisha India.

Dalits

Another group left behind by India's development policies are members of occupational groups outside the fourfold Hindu *Varna* system (hereditary Brahmin, Kshatriya, Vaishya, and Shudra formalized under the laws of Manu in 3 AD) who were traditionally limited to menial work considered "unclean," such as the skinning of dead animals, production of leather goods, street cleaning, and manual "scavenging" (digging village graves, disposing of dead animals, and cleaning human excreta). Freedom fighter Mohandas Gandhi hoped that their status would improve by calling them "harijans" or children of God in the 1930s, but 70 years later, the 2001 census found that half of the 167 million still lived below the official poverty line and more than half of them could not write their name in any language. They now refer to themselves as "dalit" (from the Sanskrit which means downtrodden, or oppressed) despite the efforts of the chief designer of independent India's constitution lawyer and economist B. R. Ambedkar[3] (himself a dalit) who created a special list or "schedule" for affirmative action of dalits. Incidents such as the gang rape of two dalit teenage girls by upper-caste men (two of whom were police) in May 2014 (Harris and Kumar 2014) are daily occurrences. Despite discrimination being outlawed in independent India, Gandhi's "children of God" are often constrained to live in residential areas segregated from the homes of caste Hindus.

Inequality in the distribution of wealth, income, and human rights is widespread in old and new democracies. Do electoral democracies address grievances fast enough before aggrieved classes and ethnic groups see no alternative but armed struggle or secession? Scotland just voted on separating from the United Kingdom. Catalan in Spain is expected to follow. The Veneto region of northern Italy would like to split from Rome. Examples of armed struggle in new democracies may be seen in South Sudan, Ukraine, and the Boko Haram movement in Nigeria in 2014. India's Maoists (one of the country's three communist parties) have taken up the cause of indigenous communities and dalits exploited by both semi-feudal landlords and land-expropriating government agencies. In 2010, writer Arundhati Roy (IBNLive 2010) told a television channel that 99 percent of India's Maoists were tribals (but acknowledged that 99 percent of all tribals were not Maoists).

The birth of this Maoist party can be traced to a 1967 protest by landless peasants in Naxalbari in North Bengal bordering Nepal. Founded by a merger between Andhra Pradesh and Bihar's Marxist factions, the Maoist party's focus is displacement of tribals from their ancestral homelands due to mining, infrastructure development, special economic zones, and wildlife conservation activities.

In 2006, the Maoists were first declared India's "greatest internal security threat" by the Manmohan Singh administration. The federal government Home Ministry website (http://mha.nic.in/naxal_new) shows state government reports of 8498 deaths in incidents involving Maoists between 2003 and 2012. Banned in 2009 as a terrorist group of extreme left-wing members, 83 districts in nine central and eastern states in which they operate have been classified as "Naxal-hit" and are often called the "Red Corridor" in the press. The pro-business current Bharatiya Janata Party (BJP) ruling party led by Narendra Modi is expected to increase extraction of natural resources, especially forests, coal, minerals, and rivers. The Modi administration has declared it also considers the Maoist movement to be India's greatest internal security threat. Historians have pointed out that Marxist-inspired insurgencies have provoked reactions in India disproportionate to the potential threat they actually present (Jeffrey 2010).

Theoretical Framework

This comparison of newspaper contributions to informed citizenship in India is situated theoretically and empirically in the research tradition that investigates the provision of political knowledge in democracies. Previous scholarship includes the work of Michael Delli Carpini (1996), C. Edwin Baker (2002), James Curran (2009), Shanto Iyengar (1991), and Aalberg Toril and James Curran (2012) among others. Content analysis categories used to classify and compare the supply of political knowledge draw from Bennett's (1990) work on the use of sources, McCombs (2004) and Ghanam (1997) on agenda-setting topics and attributes such as location and characters, and frames that identify responsibility for remedial action (Iyengar 1991; Entman 1991).

Research Design

The study presents a slice of the data generated by a large comparative quantitative content analysis study of political knowledge supply by newspapers. The highest circulation daily newspaper was selected from regional markets in Bengali, Telegu, and Urdu, the Hindi-language (one of India's two official languages) market, and the English-language (the other official language) market. Regional newspapers were selected from those states that had recent experience of the Maoist struggle, namely *Eenadu* published in Hyderabad, Andhra Pradesh for 7 percent of India's Telegu speakers, *Anand Bazaar Patrika* published in Kolkata, West Bengal for 8 percent of India's Bengali speakers, and *Munsif* also published in Hyderabad, Andhra Pradesh for the 5 percent of India's Urdu speakers. The supply of political knowledge on this issue in Hindi (spoken by 41 percent of India according to the 2001 Census) was analyzed through inclusion of the Delhi city edition of *Dainik Jagran*, the world's highest circulation paper. Also included was *The Times of India*'s main edition published from Mumbai for the 8 percent of India who reported that they could speak English in the Census of 2001.[4]

The population of *all* articles published on the Maoist armed struggle was compared across five dailies to ensure capture of reporting on episodes that got press attention for only brief time periods, e.g. Salwa Judum, a state-created private militia consisting of tribals trained to fight against their fellow tribals working with the Maoists. The July 2011 to June 2012 time period was chosen for comparison because of availability and access to issues of five different newspapers in the same time period. This 12-month period featured the Supreme Court ruling abolishing the Chhatisgarh state government-created anti-Maoist militia Salwa Judum in July, the killing of Maoist leader Kishanji in November, the Maoist kidnapping of a tribal state legislator in Odisha in April followed by the release of a kidnapped Italian tourist, and the kidnapping and negotiated release of a respected district administrator Alex Menon.

The keywords "Mao" and "Naxal" were used to identify and save PDFs of articles from the selected dailies. Manual page-by-page searches through 12 months of newspapers were conducted for *Dainik Jagran* by this author and paid assistants in *Dainik Jagran*'s NOIDA library outside Delhi. Paid assistants at the University of Colorado conducted keyword searches of the online archive of *The Times of India*'s main edition edited in Mumbai. Paid graduate students at Osmania University, Hyderabad, identified articles through manual searches of *Eenadu* and *Munsif*. A paid assistant in Kolkata identified articles in the *Anand Bazar Patrika*, scanned them, and emailed them to the author.

Coding was conducted at the author's home institution by paid graduate student assistants whose native languages were Urdu, Hindi, Telegu, and English, following a week-long training course that enabled many revisions of draft content categorization schemes (code books) and plenty of practice runs. Inter-coder reliability was calculated by having all coders (English, Hindi, Telegu, Urdu, and Bengali) code the identical random subsample of 10 percent of English-language newspaper articles. After revisions and re-training, only variables with inter-coder reliability (Scott's pi) over 0.7 were retained.

For reasons of space, the findings in this article are limited to comparing the following: the space each news daily gave to the Maoist movement in the context of its revenues; the framing of Maoist coverage in terms of episodic versus thematic causes–remedies analysis, the selection of topics in Maoist coverage as agenda-setting issues flagged by the paper, and the performance of the news organization on a specially designed 0–5 point index of comprehensiveness that assigned one point to articles with art (photos, graphics), one point for features and opinion articles, one point for articles which mentioned causes and remedies, and one point for articles with quotes other than from official sources.

Findings

Amount of Coverage

Table 1 presents the total number of news articles that mentioned the keywords "Naxal" or "Mao" anywhere in the article in the five dailies in the 12 months under study, along with essential revenue, market size, and readership figures. The top two rows list the Hindi- and English-language dailies, Jagran Prakashan's "main edition" designed for Delhi city and Bennett Coleman/*Times of India*'s "main edition" published in Mumbai.[5] The *Times of India*, which has a potential market of 8 percent of India who speak English and a readership of 7.6 million, published 421 articles. *Dainik Jagran*, with a potential market of 41 percent of India and a readership of 16.37 million, published 376 articles. Both these news organization are the top two revenue earners of this study which could certainly afford to pay for coverage in remote areas.

The lower three rows show the performance of the regional newspapers, in this case the highest circulation Bengali, Telegu, and Urdu regional language dailies. *Anand Bazar Patrika*, published in Kolkata in West Bengal (home to Naxalbari where the movement started in 1967), featured the highest number of articles (441). It ranks third in revenue of the five dailies and earns the highest revenue of the three regional dailies. *Munsif*, India's highest circulation Urdu daily had the lowest number of articles (110). While official data are not available on its revenues, it is likely it is the lowest of the five. *Eenadu*, India's

TABLE 1

Newspaper company revenues, potential market (speakers of the language of this edition), readership, and number of articles on the Maoist movement

Newspaper	Revenue in millions of Indian rupees[a]	Speakers of newspaper language (%)[b]	India Readership Survey, December 2012[c]	Number of articles on Mao/Naxals, July 2011 to June 2012
The Times of India (English)	47,933	2–8	7.6 million	421
Dainik Jagran (Hindi)	12,469	41	16.37 million	376
Munsif (Urdu)	Not available	5	127,000	110
Eenadu (Telegu)	4767	7	5.9 million	318
Anand Bazaar Patrika (Bengali)	7986	8	5.7 million	441

[a]The source of revenue data is annual reports for 2010–2011 submitted by individual firms to the Registrar of Companies; 2010–2011 annual reports were available for four of the five news organizations. An annual report for the year 2011–2012 was only available for Jagran Prakashan that publishes *Dainik Jagran*; no company reports were available for the Munsif organization.
[b]Data on speakers of languages is sourced from the 2001 Census since 2011 Census of India data on this topic were not available at the time of writing. Two percent of India claimed English was their first language in the 2001 Census, but given the aspirational status of English for work opportunities, social status, and also its linking function between the north and south of India, the total of first- and second-language speakers make up approximately 8 percent of the country.
[c]India Readership Survey figures are used to calculate advertising rates. December 2012 figures are used due to disputes on the calculation system introduced in 2013.

highest circulation Telegu daily, also published in Hyderabad, had almost three times as many articles on the Mao movement than its co-located Hyderabad-based newspaper *Munsif* (318). Its total readership is more than 46 times that of the smaller Urdu paper and it may be safely presumed that its revenue is much higher too. Clearly revenue is not the determining factor in amount of coverage.

Coverage of Causes and Remedies

Iyengar (1991) showed how the framing or packaging of news by journalists with or without attributing responsibility for the cause of an event resulted in differences in how audiences understood the political problem. Journalists frequently used discrete events that reflected cultural narratives to communicate with their readers, resulting in episodic presentations that did not address government responsibility to redress the problem. I hypothesized that dailies that are published by higher-revenue news organizations would have adequate staff, time, and library resources to provide qualitatively superior coverage to its readers on this important issue in terms of identification of causes and remedies when compared to dailies published by lower-revenue news organizations which might be limited to hard news based on news agency reports. Specifically, I expected that *The Times of India*, published by Bennett Coleman Company Limited with the highest revenue of the five dailies (47,933 million rupees) and a 32 percent margin of profit before taxes as reported by Guha Thakurta (2012), would publish a greater percentage of articles that framed Maoist movement activities in terms of causes and remedies, followed by *Dainik Jagran* published by Jagran Prakashan (2010–2011 revenue of 12,469 million rupees and a 25 percent profit margin before taxes reported by Guha Thakurta (2012). I expected regional newspapers would trail behind on reporting causes and remedies in order of their revenue (*Anand Bazar Patrika* group revenue 7986 million rupees, *Eenadu* group revenue 4767 million rupees, and *Munsif* no data). Table 2 compares dailies on whether and how well they framed the causes and remedies of the Maoist armed struggle (thematic framing) or whether they merely used episodic framing to describe events on the ground. This hypothesis was not supported.

Causes. Two lower-revenue regional papers, *Anand Bazar Patrika* (Bengali) and *Eenadu* (Telegu), had 23 and 14 percent of articles that mentioned causes, respectively. The higher-revenue *Times of India* and *Dainik Jagran* trailed behind with fewer articles that mentioned causes (6.18 and 7.47 percent, respectively). *Munsif* had the lowest percentage of articles with causal analyses (1.90 percent), suggesting the need for organizational interviews with the owner and editors to enquire about reasons for this lower performance: was it due to their perception that the government's perception of the Maoists as India's "greatest internal security threat" was questionable or was the issue not of concern to their Urdu-speaking Muslim market/readership?

Remedies. The daily with the highest percentage of articles that mentioned who was responsible for remedies was again the regional Bengali-language daily (21.86 percent of articles) whose linguistic market includes the Naxalbari area where the Maoist movement was born and the location of the capture and death of Maoist leader Kishanji in November 2011 during the period of the study. Lagging behind with 13.64 percent of articles that mentioned who was responsible for remedies were *Dainik Jagran*, the Hindi-language

TABLE 2
Newspaper differences in framing causes and remedies for the Maoist armed struggle (number and percentage of articles from July 2011 to June 2012): how should readers of dailies think about this issue?

	Times of India 421 articles	Dainik Jagran 375 articles	Munsif 110	Eenadu 318	Anand Bazar Patrika 439
Focus of article					
Description of situation (episodic framing)	395 (93.8)	341 (90.7)	101 (91.8)	305 (5.9)	413 (93.7)
Causes of situation (thematic framing)	4 (1.0)	8 (2.1)	1 (0.9)	1 (0.3)	1 (0.2)
Remedies (thematic framing)	13 (3.1)	26 (6.9)	6 (5.5)	10 (3.1)	22 (5.0)
Articles that mentioned causes[a]	26 (6.18)	28 (7.47)	12 (1.90)	45 (14.15)	101 (23.00)
Government causes					
Limited jobs, land, eco opportunity	18 (69.24)	13 (46.42)	4 (33.33)	4 (8.88)	20 (19.80)
Poor governance	12 (46.15	15 (53.57)	2 (16.67)	2 (4.44)	1 (0.99)
Lack basic infra (water, san, electr)	3 (11.54)	3 (10.71)	1 (8.33)	0 (0.00)	4 (3.96)
Maoist causes					
Maoist armed struggle	11 (42.31)	6 (21.43)	4 (33.33)	37 (82.22)	76 (75.25)
Maoist support for neglected dalits & tribals	4 (15.38)	1 (3.57)	1 (8.33)	3 (6.67)	8 (7.92)
Articles that named who was responsible for remedies[a]	44 (10.45)	56 (14.93)	15 (13.64)	14 (4.40)	96 (21.86)
Federal gov in New Delhi	35 (79.55)	44 (78.57)	6 (40.00)	9 (64.29)	23 (23.96)
Regional state governments	34 (77.27)	44 (78.57)	9 (60.00)	5 (35.71)	84 (87.50)
Police security military	18 (40.91)	3 (5.36)	4 (26.67)	1 (0.31)	11 (73.33)

Percentages are given in parentheses.
[a] An article may refer to more than one cause or remedy resulting in percentages that do not total to 100.

paper, *Munsif*, the Urdu-language paper with 13.64 percent, *The Times of India* with 10.45 percent, and *Eenadu* with 4.40 percent.

Clearly, just because news organizations have the revenue to pay for more time-consuming explanatory journalism does not mean that they will take the time to go beyond the Who, What, Where, and When of hard news to answer the Why question and provide context. The proprietor of *The Times of India* famously told the *New Yorker* that his company was in the advertising business, not in the news business (Auletta 2012).

Agenda-setting Topics

Following Max McCombs' (2004) work that showed how newspapers set the agenda for readers on "what to think about," I investigated the topics that were covered by the five newspapers on this supposed internal security threat identified by the ousted Congress-coalition administration and the current administration. Topics were selected for categorization by perusing several issues of each newspaper to develop an inclusive list. Table 3 shows variation between dailies in the coverage of topics, namely paramilitary forces, political parties, private industry, local citizens, indigenous communities, the capture and death of Maoist leader Kishanji, and human rights issues. The topic addressed most often in all five dailies was what government did through both policing and pro-social work to address issues in Maoist areas. Proportions ranged from a high of 72 percent government coverage in *The Times of India* to a low of 45 percent in the Hyderabad-edited *Eenadu* in Andhra Pradesh. Sevanti Ninan's (2013) reporting on The Hoot media watchdog website b19points to the increasing role of owners driving the editorial line in Andhra Pradesh (served by *Eenadu* and *Munsif* newspapers under study here) based on their caste and political party affiliation. *Eenadu*'s owner and Editor-in-Chief Ramoji Rao belongs to the Kamma caste, and supports the Telegu Desam Party and not the Congress Party that decided on splitting up the state. Attempts to obtain follow-up interviews with the news organizations under study led to no response; interviews are clearly important to understand reasons for the observed differences in coverage. Multivariate explanations for differences and similarities could range from the political interests of owner-editors in seeking favors from government for

TABLE 3

Newspaper differences in setting the reader's agenda on *what topics to think about* with reference to India's Maoist movement: differences in mentions (number and percentage of articles) between July 2011–June 2012

	The Times of India	Dainik Jagran	Munsif	Eenadu	Anand Bazar Patrika
Total number of articles on the Maoist/Naxal movement	421	375	110	318	439
Topics					
Internal/national security threat from Maoists	6 (1.43)	38 (10.13)	2 (1.82)	13 (4.09)	3 (0.68)
Government rural development and policing activities (other than paramilitaries)	302 (71.73)	308 (82.13)	69 (62.73)	14.2 (44.65)	310 (70.29)
Paramilitaries	42 (9.98)	39 (10.40)	11 (10.00)	74 (23.27)	194 (43.99)
Political parties	54 (12.83)	115 (30.67)	21 (19.09)	18 (5.66)	71 (16.10)
Private industry	30 (7.13)	6 (1.60)	4 (3.64)	4 (1.26)	2 (0.45)
Locals	102 (24.23)	86 (22.93)	14 (12.73)	73 (22.96)	223 (51.70)
Indigenous tribals/adivasis	35 (8.31)	48 (12.80)	7 (6.42)	20 (6.49)	50 (11.39)
Dalits/constitutionally protected lower castes	5 (1.19)	1 (0.27)	1 (0.92)	2 (0.65)	0 (0.00)
Marxist leader Kishanji killed in West Bengal in November 2011	27 (6.41)	31 (8.27)	15 (13.76)	43 (13.96)	49 (11.16)
"Maoist sympathizers"	35 (8.31)	27 (7.20)	9 (8.18)	16 (5.03)	34 (7.71)
Human rights	22 (5.93)	14 (3.73)	5 (4.59)	23 (7.47)	23 (5.24)
Constitution	13 (3.09)	10 (2.67)	3 (2.75)	2 (0.65)	3 (0.68)

Percentages are given in parentheses.

their other industrial ventures rather than merely maximizing economic profits for their media ventures, the role of particular advertisers for financing, to the dependence on government for newsprint and advertising.

Journalist Supriya Sharma (2012) also found news reports favored the government in her study of Chhatisgarh coverage (one of the states with high Maoist activity) in two regional Hindi dailies and two English-language dailies. Her former journalist colleagues in Chhatisgarh told her they did not represent the views of the Maoists because of the fear of police, lack of protection by their news organizations, and the perception that their readers perceived the Maoists to be villains. She concluded, "Between a constrained and partisan regional press and an uninterested and ignorant national press, the coverage of conflict in Chhatisgarh remains patchy and skewed" (52). In foreign news in the US press, Bennett (1990) found great reliance on government sources by US journalists. Privately owned US news organizations indexed their reporting to the range of views expressed by government elites, showing autonomy only when there was disagreement among government officials.

Beyond Profits: Comprehensiveness of Coverage for Informed Citizens

Assuming for a moment that improvement in the quality of news reporting for informed citizenship was a priority for a newspaper company, I also hypothesized that the highest revenue dailies would produce the most comprehensive coverage of the Maoist challenge to electoral democracy. Going beyond norms for objectivity that rose in response to US journalism history, a measure of comprehensiveness was designed to assess the comparative adequacy of representation between newspapers for voter education. Comprehensiveness of coverage was measured on a 0–5 index that summed up performance on five components: one point for each text article with art (photos, graphics), one point for each news feature and opinion (as against hard news), one point for each article which mentioned causes, one point for each article which mentioned remedies, and one point for each article with quotes from non-traditional other than official sources. Table 4 shows the Bennett Coleman Times of India Group with a 32 percent profit margin in 2010–11 and *Dainik Jagran* with a profit margin of 26 percent scored 0.66 out of 5 possible points and *Dainik Jagran* scored 0.69 out of 5. There was no statistically significant difference between *The Times of India* and *Dainik Jagran* on the comprehensiveness of the average article mentioned above or comprehensiveness weighted by the monthly average number of articles (21.58 for *Dainik Jagran* and 23.25 for the *The Times of India*). The only statistically significant difference between the two news organizations was on quotes from non-traditional sources—the *The Times of India* used them almost three times more often in 14.49 percent of their articles while *Dainik Jagran* used them in only 5.32 percent of their articles.

The low-revenue *Anand Bazar Patrika* Bengali regional daily scored the best of the five news dailies with 0.98 on the average article comprehensiveness score. It had more articles with art than the other four (44.44 percent articles with photos or graphics), more articles that listed causes than the other four (22.90 percent), and more articles that listed remedies than three of the others (15.87 percent). *Anand Bazar Patrika*'s highest performance on article comprehensiveness points to explanatory factors other than revenue size that will be addressed in forthcoming publications, e.g. the regional resonance of the issue, the status and quality of field reporters, the rapport between the chief

TABLE 4
Differences in news organization performance on the comprehensiveness of coverage index (0–5)

Components of summated index of article comprehensiveness (1 point each)	Times of India	Dainik Jagran	Munsif	Eenadu	Anand Bazzar
Text article with art (photo, graphic)	122 (28.98)	104 (27.66)	18 (16.36)	92 (28.93)	196 (44.44)
News features and opinion	44 (10.45)	47 (12.50)	3 (2.73)	7 (2.20)	25 (5.67)
Articles which mention causes	26 (6.18)	28 (7.45)	12 (10.91)	45 (14.15)	101 (22.90)
Articles which mention remedies	26 (6.18)	60 (15.96)	10 (9.09)	13 (4.09)	70 (15.87)
Articles with quotes from non-traditional other than official sources	61 (14.49)	20 (5.32)	1 (0.91)	15 (4.72)	42 (9.52)
Summated average article comprehensiveness score	0.66	0.69	0.41	0.57	0.98
Average number of articles in a month (July 11 to June 12)	35.08	31.33	9.17	26.50	36.75
Individual article comprehensiveness score weighted by monthly number of articles	23.25	21.58	3.75	15.00	36.17

Percentages are given in parentheses.

reporter and her field team during story development, and the more frequent commissioning of features and opinion columns on this issue.

The regional dailies as a group did not perform uniformly better than *The Times of India* or *Dainik Jagran*, only *Anand Bazaar Patrika* did. An F-test comparing average article comprehensiveness scores for the three regional dailies together showed very highly significant differences between them on average article comprehensiveness quality (0.98 for the Bengali daily, 0.57 for the Telegu daily, and 0.41 for the Urdu daily, $p < 0.0001$), the monthly average number of articles (36.75 for the Bengali daily, 26.17 for the Telegu daily, and 17.27 for the Urdu daily, $p < 0.0001$), and article quality weighted by the monthly average (37.17 for the Bengali daily, 14.83 for the Telegu daily, and 3.75 for the Urdu daily, $p < 0.0001$).

Pair-wise *t*-tests of significance between the two Andhra Pradesh papers showed no significant difference on comprehensiveness quality, monthly number of articles, and individual scores weighted by the monthly average. *t*-Tests comparing *Anand Bazaar Patrika* and *Eenadu* showed a very highly significant difference ($p < 0.0001$) on the average article comprehensiveness score and also article comprehensiveness weighted by the monthly average number of articles. *t*-Tests comparing averages for the Bengali paper *Anand Bazaar Patrika* and the Urdu paper *Munsif* showed significant differences in favor of *Anand Bazaar Patrika* on all three comprehensiveness measures, quality, quantity, and quality weighted by quantity of articles per month.

Writing at the turn of the century about representation of the Ram Janmabhoomi movement, Arvind Rajagopal (2001) argued that Hindi- and English-language news organizations shaped their news output differently due to differences in culture in a multilingual economically stratified society. English-language news organizations emphasized truth value for a critical rational public while Hindi news writing emphasized the narrative aspect. Vandana Pednekar-Magal's (2007) video documentary argued that India's newspapers were divided by language. The next section will discuss how newspapers were distinguished by language in this study, but also by many other forces including revenue size, their financial interests in other corporate sectors, their need to curry favor with state policymakers, and perception of their readership market's preferences.

Summary and Discussion

The purpose of this study was to provide a comparative content analysis of one major country-wide issue in Hindi, regional-language and English-language news dailies. While investors have concerns about the linguistically and regionally fragmented scale of India's newspaper markets, the focus here is on the inequality of political knowledge supplied by for-profit dailies to different linguistic constituencies in the same country.

The absolute number of articles published by news dailies differed as might be expected, given the difference in their revenues, market size, and readership figures. Reasons for these differences can only be confirmed through interviews with the news desks in each company, self-reflection that firms which live off interviews with others are reluctant to do with most researchers. There was no response from *The Times of India* Mumbai and *Dainik Jagran* Delhi to repeated offers to share these findings with them so they could help this researcher to understand the reasons for their differences.

More than 90 percent of the articles on the Maoist movement in all five dailies were framed as individual episodes or events with no explanation addressing causes, remedies, or context. Description of the event was the common frame: who, what, when, where—no why. Certainly causes were mentioned in passing in up to 23 percent of articles in *Anand Bazar Patrika* (up from a low of 1.9 percent in *Munsif* and 6 percent in *The Times of India*) but they were the predominant frame for only 0–2 percent of the articles. Who was responsible for remedies was mentioned in passing too, in 4–20 percent of articles. But remedies were the predominant frame in only 3–7 percent of articles across dailies. Ajit Dandekar and Chitrangada Chowdhry's (2012) studies for the Government of India Ministry of Local Self-government have highlighted how implementation of the Panchayat Extension Act to Scheduled Areas and the Forest Act could go a long way to remedying tribal problems: lack of implementation was not identified as a cause during this year under study. If one function of journalism is to provide political education to inform citizens, newspapers need to connect the dots repeatedly for readers, especially since market research shows Indians spend only 34 minutes a day on news and information (FICCI-KPMG 2012–14).

What *topics* should citizens of multinational India think about when they happen to think of this country-wide issue that is positioned by the state as its most important internal security threat and affects adivasis and dalits so centrally? The content analysis data show a majority of articles described what the state was doing on this issue. There was no criticism of the government for its neglect of adivasi and dalit concerns, consistent with the increase in the use of news media as a tool of crony capitalism by its owners.

Most Indians read a daily newspaper in only one language. How comprehensive then was the Bengali speaker's newspaper on this one issue as against the Urdu speaker's newspaper, and the Hindi speaker's newspaper and the Telegu speaker's newspaper? Without intending to generalize to treatment of other issues, the data show the average *Anand Bazar Patrika* article was more comprehensive in its coverage of the Maoist movement than the average article on the movement prepared for Urdu speakers by its highest circulation daily and the average article on the movement prepared for English readers of *The Times of India* and the average article on the movement prepared by *Eenadu* for its Telegu readers. Admittedly, this is one measure of comprehensiveness that privileges some components and is perforce limited to just one issue—it is hoped other researchers will develop other measures. This illustrative finding focuses attention on the multiple national constituencies of India's electoral democracy and points out the need for comparative study of other major issues.

In the British first-past-the-post electoral system that India adopted, the BJP's 31 percent popular vote in 2014 translated itself into a 52 percent absolute majority in the lower house of parliament—every vote counted because the winning candidate in any constituency had to win only one vote more than the others. Without proportional representation, India's 13.4 percent Muslim population now has its lowest ever Muslim representation in the parliament: just 4 percent of members. A Government of India report found Muslims had the lowest literacy, lowest formal-sector employment, and lowest per capita monthly expenditure in 2009–2010 (NSSO 2011). The India Human Development Report (UNDP 2011) showed the socio-economic status of the Muslim community was not improving at the same rate as other social and religious groups. The Urdu-speaking (mostly Muslim) reader of *Munsif* was served poorly by this Muslim-owned daily in terms of average article comprehensiveness on the Maoist movement that was lower than the equivalent average article comprehensiveness score of articles on the Maoist movement prepared by *Eenadu* for its Telegu readers in the same state of Andhra Pradesh. Understandably, this smaller news organization that publishes an 11-page daily supplied only a total of 110 stories on this topic compared to 439 prepared by *Anand Bazaar Patrika* for Bengali readers. Let me hypothesize that a future study will find this differential on quantity and quality will hold for these two electorates on *other issues too*. Hypotheses are formulated to be disproved. I hope I am proved wrong; this difference in access to political knowledge is not fair to the voter who can only read Urdu.

To recap: major inequalities in news supply to distinct linguistic electorates were found on one major internal security issue under study. Since this issue has existed at a low level since 1967 and has heated up since 2004, perhaps news organizations feel there is nothing analytically new here or no scoop to be had in reporting rural atrocities for the urban reader? The chief reporter may believe he has addressed variations of it in different locations over the years. In the year under study, no columns questioned the federal government on how "a diverse, scarcely unified insurgency" (Jeffrey 2010, A14) might represent "the greatest internal security threat to the country"—except perhaps in terms of battles between the federal and state governments on how to address the law and order aspects of almost 1000 incidents in some years. *The Times of India* bundled diverse Maoist incidents across states together on the same page with a black and red hammer and sickle logo as part of its attention-getting visual design. No news organization featured a Media Watch column that tracked government progress in addressing the causes of neglect of almost 30 percent of India, its tribals and dalits; it did not appear that the role of the press in holding government to account was central.

These are undoubtedly the naïve musings of an activist scholar rather than a journalist. A journalist could point to the commercial viability of the printed press in India for the next decade and give thanks that he has a job when his counterparts in the Western world have been laid off. This same journalist could repeat owner Samir Jain's comment to Ken Auletta (2012) of *the New Yorker*, "We [BCCL-Times of India Group] are in the advertising business, not in the business of journalism." How might journalism as citizen education be practiced then, given this optimism about the advertising business and the growth of India's consumer market to smaller cities, towns, and villages? Might this be an opportunity for an Indian Jeff Bezos to buy or set up a newspaper that would provide journalism for those who receive limited political education from their current newspapers? How might this daily be different from the colorful hard news bulletins that currently serve as advertising platforms?

The opportunistic piggybacking of news for public education on advertising bulletins has taken place in different locations across the world—the first printed newspaper in India in 1780 had *two* names to accommodate these distinct functions, Hickey's *Bengal Gazette* and the *Calcutta General Advertiser*. New apps of media today (e.g. Facebook and WhatsApp) continue to be financed through advertising. News organizations do not see the need for two names any longer. The journalism business model is only being reconsidered in the countries of North America and Western Europe because of the slowing of the economy and reduction in advertising. Rather than wait to find alternative funding models in India when internet penetration increases and reduces printed newspaper markets precipitously, this research presents findings that require alternative thinking now on the grounds of equal rights to informed citizenship in this multilingual federation.

NOTES

1. Panchayats (Extension to Scheduled Areas) Act, 1996 or PESA is a law enacted by the Government of India to require the creation of self-governing village councils in the tribal areas of nine states to enable them to control their natural resources consistent with their customs, religious practices, and traditional management practices of community resources not covered in the 73rd amendment of Panchayati Raj Act of the Indian Constitution. PESA requires customs, religious practices, and traditional management practices of community resources.
2. The Scheduled Tribes and Other Traditional Forest Dwellers (Recognition of Forest Rights) Act, 2006, commonly referred to as the Forest Rights Act, is legislation that enables ownership and use of forest produce by forest dwellers in an area that covers around 23 percent of the country and affects the livelihoods of around 200 million citizens, or 20 percent of the population. Such recognition of rights of use shifts administrative and resource control away from forest departments, who already exhibit a high degree of autonomy from democratic oversight and stand to lose turf.
3. Dr. Ambedkar earned two doctorates in Economics, one from Columbia University (1917) and one from the London School of Economics (1923). He was called to the Bar at Gray's Inn, London in 1923.
4. India has no "national" language listed in the Constitution, consistent with its "multiple-nation" origins spread across the sub-continent and no national paper equivalent to the United States' USA Today.
5. No newspaper has a formal "national" edition.

REFERENCES

Aalberg, Toril, and James Curran, eds. 2012. *How Media Inform Democracy: A Comparative Approach*. New York: Routledge.

Auletta, Ken. 2012. "Citizen Jains." *New Yorker*, October 8, 52–61.

Banerjee, Abhijit V., Selvan Kumar, Rohini Pande, and Felix Su. 2010. "Do Informed Voters Make Better Choices? Experimental Evidence from Urban India." November 13. http://www.hks.harvard.edu/fs/rpande/papers/DoInformedVoters_Nov11.pdf.

Bennett, W. Lance. 1990. "Towards a Theory of Press-state Relations in the United States." *Journal of Communication* 40 (2): 103–127.

Baker, C. Edwin. 2002. *Media, Markets and Democracy*. Cambridge, UK: Cambridge University Press.

Curran, James, Shanto Iyengar, Anker Brink Lund, and Inka Salovaara-Moring. 2009. "Media System, Public Knowledge and Democracy: A Comparative Study." *European Journal of Communication* 24: 5–26.

Dandekar, Ajay, and Chitrangada Choudhury. 2012. "PESA a Myth." In *More than Maoism: Politics Policies and Insurgencies in South Asia*, edited by Robin Jeffrey, Ronojoy Sen and Pratima Sen, 175–186. Delhi: Manohar.

Delli Carpini, Michael X. and Scott Keeter. 1996. *What Americans Know About Politics and Why It Matters*. New Haven: Yale University Press.

Entman, Robert. 1991. "Framing US Coverage of International News: Contrasts in Narratives of the KAL and Iran Air Incidents". *Journal of Communication* 41 (4): 6–27.

FICCI-KPMG. 2012–14. "Indian Media and Entertainment Industry Report." Kpmg.com/in.

Ghanam, Salma. 1997. "Filling in the Tapestry: The Second Level of Agenda Setting." In *Communication and Democracy*, edited by Maxwell McCombs, L. Donald Shaw and H. David Weaver, 3–14. Hillsdale, NJ: Lawrence Erlbaum Associates.

Government of India Ministry of Home Affairs. *Left Wing Extremism (LWE) Division*. http://www.satp.org/satporgtp/countries/india/maoist/data_sheets/fatalitiesnaxal05-11.htm downloaded July 26, 2015.

Guha Thakurta, Paranjoy. 2012. "More Profitable than Most—Decoding BCCL, Part II." Thehoot.org, November 19. http://www.thehoot.org/web/home/story.php?storyid=6429&mod=1&pg=1&sectonId=4&valid=true.

Harris, Gardiner, and Hari Kumar. 2014. "Rapes in India Fuel Charges of Conspiracy by a Caste." *New York Times*, May 29, 2014. http://www.nytimes.com/2014/05/30/world/asia/in-india-rape-and-murder-allegations-of-a-caste-conspiracy.html?emc=edit_tnt_20140530&nlid=47731449&tntemail0=y downloaded May 31, 2014.

IBNLive. 2010. "Arrest Me for Speaking for Naxals: Arundhati." *IBNLive*, June 3. http://ibnlive.in.com/news/arrest-me-for-speaking-for-naxals-arundhati/117722-3.html downloaded May 31, 2014.

Iyengar, Shanto. 1991. *Is Anyone Responsible? How Television Frames Political Issues*. Chicago: University of Chicago Press.

Jeffrey, Robin. 2010. "India's Maoist Revolt a Distraction." *The Straits Times*, Review, A14, February 19.

McCombs, Maxwell. 2004. *Setting the Agenda*. Cambridge: Polity.

Mody, B. 2010. *The Geopolitics of Representation in Foreign News*. Lanham MD: Rowman and Littlefield.

Ninan, Sevanti. 2013. "Divided State, Divided Media." Thehoot.org, September 19, 2013. http://www.thehoot.org/web/home/story.php?storyid=7044&mod=1&pg=1&seconId=10&valid=true.

National Sample Survey Office. Government of India 2011. *Key Indicators of Employment and Unemployment in India 2009–2010: National Sample survey 66th Round*. Document ID Number DDI-IND-MOSPI-NSSO-66-10-2011.

Patel, Aakar. 2014. "Why the Newspaper Feels Like an Anachronism." *Livemint*, August 30. http://www.livemint.com/Leisure/NBcJ2YVWkU4lqguq9lkMql/Why-thenewspaper-feels-like-an-anachronism.html downloaded September 12, 2014.

Pednekar-Magal, Vandana. 2007. *Divided by Language: India's Newspapers*. Lanham, MD: National Film Network LLC.

Rajagopal, Arvind. 2001. *Politics after Television: Hindu Nationalism and the Re-shaping of the Public in India*. Cambridge UK: Cambridge University Press.

Scroll Staff. 2014. "Anxiety about Decline in Indian Languages Is Exaggerated, Shows Readership Survey." *Scroll.in*, June 28. http://scroll.in/article/655103.

Sharma, Supriya. 2012. "Guns and Protests: Media Coverage of the Conflicts in the Indian State of Chhattisgarh." Reuters Institute Fellowship Paper. University of Oxford.

Stefan, Alfred C., Juan J. Linz, and Yogendra Yadav. 2011. *Crafting State-nations: India and other Multinational Democracies*. Baltimore: Johns Hopkins University Press.

Survival International. 2010. *Mine: Story of a Sacred Mountain*. http://www.survivalinternational.org/films/mine downloaded June 2, 2014.

United Nations Development Program UNDP. 2011. *India Human Development Report 2011: Towards Social Inclusion*. New Delhi: Oxford University Press.

OUR MEDIA, OUR PRINCIPLES
Building codes of practice for community radio in India

Kanchan K. Malik

Community broadcasting is a nascent and unique sector now operating together with the commercial and national players in India and is identified by three significant characteristics—community participation, non-profit making, and community ownership and management. The overarching philosophy of community radio, acknowledged worldwide, is that it is a tool for social justice and a platform for community voices. Community radio seeks to counter the hegemony of the mainstream media and move away from the commerce-driven negative tendencies of media and journalism such as sensationalism, tabloidization, celebrity-worship, the unrestrained use of hidden cameras and paid news. Ordinary people, through participation in management, content production and organization, produce information relevant to them, choose their own stories, express their voice and define their identity. As India witnesses an endeavour to erect a nationwide network of thousands of autonomous, locally orientated community radio stations, it becomes necessary to build a set of codes of practice for this third tier of broadcasting so that it does not become a clone of mainstream media. This paper looks at some of these principles that the community radio sector in India must hold as sacred in order to strengthen civil society, journalism practices and democracy in India.

Introduction

Community radio (CR) is known by several names globally such as participatory radio, citizens' radio, access radio, radical radio, grassroots radio, free radio, alternative radio and popular radio, among others, and takes various forms, for instance, community-based radio, development radio, campus radio, rural radio, education radio, music radio, co-operative radio and several more.

However, the overarching philosophy of CR acknowledged worldwide is that it is a tool for social justice and a platform for community voices, narratives and expression. CR seeks to counter the hegemony of the mainstream media and the negative consequences that globalization and commercialization of media and communications has had for individual and community identity, cultural and linguistic diversity, civic engagement, political participation and journalism practices. CR as a facilitator of democratic participation in social change and a platform for unheard articulations, borrows its principles and doctrines from various popular people's movements for social justice and equitable access to media and communication resources. The theoretical entry points for understanding CR worldwide are made up of academic discourses around participatory communication (White

1994; Servaes 1996), media democratization (Servaes 1999; Siochrú 2004; Rodríguez, Kidd, and Stein 2010), social movements (Downing 2001, 2008), alternative media practices (Atton 2001, 2002; Rodríguez 2001), communication rights (CRIS Campaign 2005; Gordon 2012; Thomas 2011, 113–143), public sphere (Calhoun 1992; Fraser 1992), civil society (Béteille 1999; Pavarala and Malik 2007b), and the concepts of "conscientization" (Freire 1983) and, more recently, voice poverty (Tacchi 2012; Couldry 2010).

More than 18 years after the Supreme Court of India declared that "the airwaves are public property", one witnesses today, the initial stages of a recognized CR sector in India. The second phase of the CR policy guidelines issued by the Government of India in 2006 allowed civil society organizations and community-based organizations to apply for licences to set up their own CR stations. This was seen as a major step forward by the State to promote media access and freedom of expression as well as to encourage diversity and plurality in media ownership and content. The new edition of the policy emphasized the use of radio for augmenting development efforts that were participatory and inclusive.

However, there is an underlying anxiety among CR practitioners and supporters that in order to exploit the enormous potential of community broadcasting in India, which historically positions itself as different from government-owned and market-run media, it is essential to enhance integrity to the core principles that define the sector. The CR stations in India, therefore, must adopt a set of self-regulatory norms and make ethical choices that would strengthen their social standing and credibility along with advancing the quality of delivery of their mandated agenda of participatory development, democratic deliberations, empowerment and voice to the voiceless. By following a set of ethical frameworks and conventions of acceptable behaviour that reflect the philosophical underpinnings of community media, the CR practitioners as well as advocates would also be in a convincing position to resist external regulation and also demand policy reforms that would further enable the sector to flourish. As Haraszti (2008, 7) puts it, "I see self-regulation and the promotion of quality journalism as additional safeguards of media freedom and even of media power."

This paper looks at some of the principles that the CR sector in India must hold as sacred in order to strengthen both the civil society and media democracy in India. The codes of practice profiled and recommended in this paper seek to identify self-defined acceptable norms for CR practitioners, a framework for professional conduct and responsibility with the purpose of upholding the sacrosanct ideals that characterize this sector. At any stage during the evolution of community broadcasting in India, we must not lose sight of the conventions and values that lie behind its origin, and the social role for which it has been established. Only then would the CR sector as a whole and the CR stations in particular be able to command dignity, influence and reliability in the eyes of the community, as well as the public, and achieve their designated goals.

The CR stations that are on air have, no doubt, extended the broadcast landscape in the country by encouraging marginalized voices and novel perspectives to be articulated and heard in media in both information-based as well as cultural productions. There is a tangible anticipation among the advocates of CR about the revival of the full range of radio formats and genres (not just songs and music) for an effective manifestation of local information, local identities and local culture. There have also been efforts made by government, multilateral agencies, capacity-building and advocacy groups, grassroots/civil society organizations, and associational collectives such as the Community Radio Forum of India and Community Radio Association of India to address the issues confronting the growth of the CR in India.

Several awareness and capacity-sharing workshops have been organized in different regions across India; national and international consultations have been held to enable policy reforms through advocacy and dialogue; innovative technological possibilities are being researched; financial and social sustainability studies are exploring options for setting up viable and effective CR stations; and there have been on-going endeavours to carry out research on the best practices in the country that could serve as models for upcoming CR stations.

CR for Revitalizing Civil Society

Globally, there is a widespread disillusionment and dissatisfaction with contemporary journalism practices of the so-called mainstream hegemonic media, which are increasingly concentrated in the hands of a few oligarchic multinational corporations. Media advocates and researchers maintain that the mounting influence of media globalization has eroded diversity and quality of information in the public sphere, rendering civil society increasingly ineffective (Appadurai 1997; Servaes 1999; Rodríguez 2001; Atton 2002; Siochrú 2004; Pavarala and Malik 2007a; Downing 2008). Siochrú (2004) emphasizes that the "global commodification of media outputs" that subsume media and communication "products" under general market rules are seriously hampering the critical social functions which the media must perform in a society that respects democracy.

This is true of Indian media too and it is not always easy to love the annoying negative tendencies of media and journalism, such as sensationalism, tabloidization, celebrity-worship, the unrestrained use of hidden cameras, and paid news (N. Ram, the former Editor-in-Chief of *The Hindu*, cited in Kumar 2006). As the media firms grow larger, they also become reluctant to take risks on innovative/contentious information or cultural forms that could potentially result in their losing either the advertisers or the subscribers. This is infringing upon the freedom of expression, diversity of information, and media democracy within the country (Pavarala and Malik 2007a). However, the global media juggernaut has been facing antagonism all over the world, including in India, from citizen groups, community organizations and media activists. In their effort to forge a more responsible and responsive civil society, these groups have been emphasizing the need for what Denis McQuail (1994) labels a 'democratic-participant' conception of media, which is non-commercialized, socially orientated and committed to enabling participation and, thereby, revitalizing civil society.

Traber (1985) argues when media production is placed in the hands of ordinary people with the help of minimal guidance, they can develop their own news-gathering networks and become confident reporters, writers and editors. This type of information and the manner in which it is presented will be more appropriate and more "useful" for the communities in which it is produced and distributed. This has led to the evolution of a variety of news practices in present times known variously as alternative journalism, grassroots journalism, network journalism, open-source journalism, community journalism, participatory journalism and hyper-local journalism. They go beyond the conventional understanding of news and put emphasis on greater involvement of the stakeholders in news-making and content production. Here, the public becomes a co-creator in the news/information production process.

As explained earlier, CR is a means of communication that is operated in and by the community which produces context-specific content in local languages to address the information and communication needs that otherwise remain unaddressed by mainstream media (Bonin and Opoku-Mensah 1998; Carpentier, Lie, and Servaes [2002] 2008). CR is considered crucial for the media democratization process (Wasko and Mosco 1992) as ordinary people, through participation in management, content production and organization, produce information relevant to them and choose their own messages, express their voice and define their identity. CR thus represents the major source of information for marginalized communities in the developing world where it plays the role of a mediating structure between individual's lives and the public sphere (Carpentier, Lie, and Servaes [2002] 2008; Howley 2010).

CR thus offers an opportunity for people to debate issues and events of common concern and to set counter-hegemonic agendas. Such forging of counter-publics "through a process of shifting control of media technologies to those excluded and marginalised from the dominant public sphere helps expand the discursive space, which could eventually facilitate collective action and offer a realistic emancipatory potential" (Pavarala and Malik 2007b, 209).

Community broadcasting is a nascent and unique sector now operating together with the commercial and national players in India and is identified by three significant characteristics, i.e. community participation, non-profit making, and community ownership and management. As India witnesses the endeavours to erect a nationwide network of thousands of autonomous, locally orientated CR stations that have varied profiles as well as practices, it becomes necessary to build a set of codes of practice for this third tier of broadcasting so that the sector as a whole does not lose its primary and fundamental philosophy, purpose, and essence of inclusivity and diversity. In order to move the CR movement to the next level, it is essential to take stock of the principles that ought to define the burgeoning CR sector in India and keep it on the right track.

CR stations being established in India may differ significantly depending on the communities that they intend to serve, but all of them are mandated to be community-driven, and their operations managed and controlled locally with a view to reflecting local realities, strengthening cultural identity and giving a voice to the marginalized. Although diversity is the *raison d'être* and the soul of CR sectors worldwide (see Malik 2007, 16–19), they must adhere to certain universal principles and practices that are non-negotiable so that the CR stations do not become clones of mainstream media and defeat their rationale and scope.

The codes of practice outlined, described and recommended in the paper have been derived through an analysis of the core characteristics and essential features that define CR, and from a review of norms globally acceptable for independent or people's media. Community broadcasting in India is governed by a legal framework as reflected in the CR guidelines issued by the Ministry of Information and Broadcasting, which also elucidate the role the CR sector is expected to play and the policies for programming, ownership and funding that it must adopt. These guiding principles and legal obligations have also been taken into account while formulating the list of practices which the author refers to as the "Codes of Practice for Community Radio in India".

Recommended Codes of Practice for CR in India

The "Codes of Practice for Community Radio in India" recommended in this paper are general principles relevant for safeguarding the fundamental nature of the CR sector in

India. They are complementary to any other guidelines that govern good media/community media practices and are not intended to replace or substitute them. They may be embraced, in part or whole, as guidelines by CR stations individually, if appropriate, with an objective to promote accountability while at the same time protecting their freedom and ensuring their firm existence. This paper argues that the specific codes of practice/conduct that each CR station in India ought to adopt need not be imposed or mandated by an external regulator from the outside. Instead, they may be developed by and from among practitioners themselves, and be espoused voluntarily by the stations that identify themselves as CR.

What follows are the 13 possible codes of practice synthesized and put together through an analysis of:

- "Policy Guidelines for Setting Up Community Radio Stations in India" (2006).
- Characteristics of CR as recognized by the World Association of Community Radio Broadcasters (AMARC): a global network of stations, federations and community media stakeholders, the United Nations Educational, Scientific and Cultural Organization (UNESCO) and other multilateral agencies.
- Codes of conduct/practice being followed in various countries (desk-based review of the international codes of practice instruments of countries such as Nigeria, Australia, Canada, Nepal and Thailand, and selectively South Africa, Ireland, the United Kingdom and the United States) that have a durable and entrenched CR sector; and
- Academic discourses surrounding CR globally.

In addition to the public and policy documents mentioned here, the author also draws from her experience of conducting academic as well as field and policy work and research in this area for over a decade and the understanding of the sector developed during her doctoral work on community radio (Pavarala and Malik 2007a).

As stated in the Introduction, the codes of practice for CR in India listed and explained in this section of the paper have been coalesced through a systematic study of an assortment of documents to serve as guiding principles for the community broadcasting sector and the CR stations in India. The author has endeavoured to provide the theoretical context for interpretation and the line of reasoning for inclusion of each code. As is true for all ethical codes, the policy makers, the licence holders or other stakeholders are not legally obliged to follow them. These 13 codes seek to reflect the fundamental values, for example, participation, independence, diversity and self-reliance, and their interpretations that ought to determine the operational and normative standards for CR broadcasting in the country. Following are the recommended codes of practice for CR in India:

1. Ensure community ownership and management.
2. Serve a recognizable community and be not-for-profit.
3. Reflect diversity and sensitivity in programming content.
4. Reinforce content development leading to social change.
5. Enhance community participation.
6. Strengthen capacity building/training opportunities.
7. Protect and augment cultural and linguistic diversity.
8. Provide voice to the voiceless and encourage inclusivity.
9. Promote right to communicate and contribute to democratic communication.
10. Espouse self-sustainability mechanisms.

11. Exercise editorial independence.
12. Advocate for an enabling policy environment.
13. Facilitate adherence to codes of practice.

Ensure Community Ownership and Management

The policy guidelines released by the Government of India in 2006 require that any organization desirous of operating a CR station should be explicitly constituted as a non-profit organization and also have a proven record of at least three years of service to the local community. The Indian policy guidelines as well as the internationally accepted norms of CR also call for CR stations to adopt ownership and management structures that are reflective of the community. This code of practice seeks to posit CR as providing an alternative to the profit-orientated agenda of the mainstream media, which ought to be necessarily backed by steadfast experience of working in the social sector. It also underscores that a CR station must truly represent all the people of a community in its ownership, control and decision-making structures. The CR ownership and management codes of practice of the countries referred to in this paper all endorse that the CR stations should promote community ownership, access and participation in station operations and governance. CR stations are expected to provide for membership, management and operation of the station by the community served and encourage localism, diversity and minority/historically disadvantaged groups' representation in ownership. Community broadcasting should be, in the words of the African Charter on Broadcasting (2001, 2), "broadcasting which is for, by and about the community, whose ownership and management is representative of the community, which pursues a social development agenda, and which is non-profit".

Serve a Recognizable Community and be Not-for-profit

The CR policy guidelines in India indicate that the stations in the CR sector must serve a specific well-defined geographical community. This entails that the primary accountability of the CR stations should be to their territorial or geographical community. The CR stations must ensure that they adequately represent all community interests and broadcast programmes catering to the local needs. The codes of conduct in various countries make it obligatory for programming to be relevant to the community being served and for the CR station to play to its listenership, develop an interactive and informed audience, and encourage their active participation in production, media utilization and awareness. Besides this, the service of the CR stations must be provided with the intent of social gain rather than private financial profit. The activities of the CR station ought to be motivated by community well-being, not commercial considerations. For the purpose of ascertaining whether stations are providing community broadcasting services for the benefit of the community and their operations are not commercially driven, a mechanism must be designed to receive feedback on a continuous basis from different groups within the community and public hearings or social audits may also be performed. Viewed in the wider context of media democracy, CR must work towards reclaiming some of the broadcast spectrum for the communities and utilize it to foreground pluralism of ideas, free flow of information and freedom of expression. In this manner, CR can serve as a channel to give expression to the needs of the local population and to reconnect with the civic and cultural lives of the communities.

Reflect Diversity and Sensitivity in Programming Content

The primary content guideline in the existing Indian CR policy instructs that programmes should be of immediate relevance to the community and reflect the special interests and needs of the local community. Philosophically, as well as structurally, CR stations must therefore, as aptly stated in Codes of Conduct in Canada as well as Australia, enhance the diversity of local programming available to the public and present programmes that expand the variety of viewpoints broadcast. This calls for working towards a variety of programming choices as well as formats produced so that they can cater to a listenership that may be diverse in ethnicity, culture, gender, language, sexual orientation, age, and physical and mental ability. The National Campus and Community Radio Association (NCRA) Codes of Conduct in Canada also recognize

> that media can in many instances reinforce the social and economic inequities that oppress marginalized groups in our society and, as a result, we recognise our responsibility to serve the needs of socially, culturally, politically and economically disadvantaged groups in our communities. (NCRA 2011, 3)

The programming content ought to promote harmony and diversity and contribute to an inclusive and cohesive community. The relevant provisions in the Indian CR policy on this matter, which include that the permission holder must adhere to the All India Radio codes for advertising and programming, among others, are fairly explicit and must be adhered to by all CR stations in India (see "Content Regulation & Monitoring" in the "Policy Guidelines for Setting Up Community Radio Stations in India" 2006).

Reinforce Content Development Leading to Social Change

According to a narrative report of the National Broadcasting Policy Stakeholders' Forum by the National Broadcasting Commission (2010, 5), the stakeholders in the broadcasting sector must recognize "the difference between decentralized state broadcasting (the establishment of state/government-owned broadcasting stations in communities) and genuine community broadcasting, which is the establishment and management of broadcasting stations by communities for the purpose of their own development". The roots of the struggle for the CR sector in India and other South Asian nations lie in it being regarded as a tool for development. In the developing countries, as a Rockefeller Foundation report asserts, CR is "one of the best ways to reach excluded or marginalized communities in targeted, useful ways", and in giving them a "voice" that matters most in development communication (Dagron 2001). The provision in the CR policy too affirms that, "The emphasis should be on developmental, agricultural, health, educational, environmental, social welfare, community development and cultural programs" ("Policy Guidelines for Setting Up Community Radio Stations in India" 2006). CR stations must give highest priority to programmes that encourage the empowerment of communities through appropriation of CR for progressive social change and sustainable, democratic and participatory community development.

Enhance Community Participation

Participation of the community must be enhanced in all aspects of station operations, including identification and definition of issues, programme planning and production, as well as management. Only then would CR serve as a vehicle of participatory democracy (see McQuail 1994) and generate a renewed appreciation of local voices, public access and community involvement in broadcasting. Participation is at the heart of social sustainability of a CR station and the Indian CR policy also mandates that at least 50 per cent of content shall be generated with the participation of the local community for which the station has been set up. CR as a medium for generating an autonomous, democratic, localized and community-based communication environment must strengthen a democratic, dialogical and participatory process of programme production. The codes of practice endorsed by the Community Broadcasting Association of Australia (CBAA) seek to ensure that all CR stations must have written policies and procedures in place that encourage community participation,

> Our station will make sure that people in our community who are not adequately served by other media are encouraged and assisted to participate in providing our service. We will have in place policies and procedures to support this commitment. We will document evidence of our efforts to encourage community participation. (CBAA 2008, 5)

All international policies and codes advocate that effort to enhance participation of volunteers must be backed by principles that oppose and break down prejudice on the basis of ethnicity, race, language, gender, sexuality, age, physical or mental ability, occupation, religious, cultural or political beliefs.

Strengthen Capacity Building and Training Opportunities

Traber (1985, 3) argues that mass media marginalize the role of the "simple man and woman" and foreground the elite and the powerful whereas for alternative media, such as CR, "the aim is to change towards a more equitable social, cultural and economic whole in which the individual is not reduced to an object but is able to find fulfilment as a total human being". Traber argues when media production is placed in the hands of ordinary people with the help of minimal guidance, they can develop their own news-gathering networks and become confident reporters, writers and editors. This type of information and the manner in which it is presented will be more appropriate and more "useful" for the communities in which it is produced and distributed. Thus, in addition to promoting access to media facilities, it is also important that members of the communities are provided training facilities as a primary step towards full democratization of the communication system. For the CR sector to prosper, CR stations must offer the opportunity to any member of the community to initiate communication and participate in programme making, content production and evaluation. This is possible if models of training and mentoring are developed that will enable participation in the station tasks at a variety of levels. The in-house training of paid staff and volunteers must ensure that everyone is aware of, understands and complies with the legal obligations, policies and the codes of practice, and is able to participate effectively in providing the service.

Protect and Augment Cultural Linguistic Diversity

The CR sector can serve as an example of how alternative media spaces act as powerful sites for nurturing local language and culture and building identity. The radio programmes produced in the local dialect make communities identify strongly with the language of the programmes and produce a feeling that the programmes are their own. The local content and their "own" language of broadcast promote active listenership by clearly evoking a sense of pride in local culture and identity. The programmes of CR stations should, thus, be in the local language and dialect(s) and feature local talent and indigenous experts. CR stations must ensure that suppressed local artistic talents come to the fore and women caught up within feudal social structures find a voice of their own. The Nepalese Code of Conduct for Community Radio Broadcasters (2008: available as a poster in the office of the Association of Community Radio Broadcasters Nepal) emphasizes that there must be "special focus on the preservation, dissemination, development, and celebration of local languages, art literature, culture, folk music, talent and originality. Language must be kept simple and respectful". Encouraging local creative talent, local language and fostering local traditions makes the programmes geographically and culturally more intimate to the lives of the communities.

Provide a Voice to the Voiceless and Encourage Inclusivity

Hamilton (cited in Atton 2002, 25) contended that there must be "de-professionalization, de-capitalization and de-institutionalization" of alternative media such as CR to distinguish them from mainstream mass media. In other words, alternative media must be available to ordinary people without excessive cost, with negligible professional training and their structure must offset other media institutions. Thus, CR stations must follow management, programming and employment practices which oppose discrimination and uphold the values of democracy, equality, inclusion, social justice and human rights. The CR programmes must raise a voice in favour of the weak, deprived and vulnerable, and amplify the voices of the excluded and marginalized whose issues are not adequately represented in other media. They ought to facilitate the inclusion of women and other excluded sectors of society through CR. In contrast to mainstream media's liberal democratic ideal of the informed citizenry, alternative media promote the participatory democratic ideal of the mobilized citizenry. By opposing mass media's hierarchy of access (Atton 2001) and being self-managed (Downing 2001), non-hierarchical (Atton 2002), or collectivist-democratic (Hochheimer 1993), alternative media aim to include people normally excluded from mainstream media. This means alternative media encourage

> such access, where working people, sexual minorities, trades unions, protest groups—people of low status in terms of their relationship to elite groups of owners, managers and senior professionals—could make their own news, whether by appearing in it as significant actors or by creating news that was relevant to their situation. (Atton 2001, 5)

Promote Right to Communicate and Contribute to Democratic Communication

The "AMARC Community Radio Charter for Europe" (1994) states that the CR sector must "promote the right to communicate, assist the free flow of information and opinions, encourage creative expression and contribute to the democratic process and a pluralist society". There ought to be full interaction between the producers and receivers of messages. Features such as interactive, two-way communication; pro-active feedback mechanisms; complaints-handling; and internal conflict resolution between staff and volunteers are indispensable for maintaining free, independent and pluralistic media that promote harmony and diversity and contribute to an inclusive, cohesive and culturally diverse milieu. For building meaningful democratic spaces, it is crucial to create a listening environment in which everyone from the community gets access to CR programmes and enters into deliberations. Organizing regular group listening sessions to elicit feedback would give people an opportunity to analyse their problems collectively, decide on the changes that affect their lives and become active in implementing these changes. Such an interactive process prompts people to express their viewpoints, share their knowledge and also moves them to participate in programmes. This has been successfully achieved in initiatives where a culture of popular, local participation in development efforts has been integrated over the years. Streitmatter (2001) argues that alternative media have the potential to serve as conduits for the political agendas and have helped ignite social movements through their advocacy of various disenfranchised social groups.

Espouse Self-sustainability Mechanisms

CR stations are non-profit-distributing ventures and have limited commercial options. The CR sector is distinctive in terms of its sources of revenue and funding. In most countries, advertising and/or sponsorship is permitted on CR stations but confined within specified norms. The policy in India allows CR stations to seek funding from multilateral aid agencies. Sponsored programmes are not permitted except those by central and state governments. Limited advertising and announcements relating to local events, local businesses/services and employment opportunities are allowed for a maximum duration of five minutes per hour of broadcast. Thus, economic viability and sustainability continues to be the major challenge for CR stations in India. The CR stations run by larger, well-endowed non-governmental organizations (NGOs) may manage to draw parts of their cost from the organization's funds, but are then obliged to reflect the NGO's programmatic agenda in their broadcasts. Such vulnerability to NGO-ization must be avoided by exploring new ways to generate revenue and seek neutral funding to accomplish self-sustainability. Communities must look at an assortment of options such as community contributions, no-strings-attached grants from aid agencies, donations, limited advertisements, local announcements, cost-effective technology choices and other innovative methods to reduce dependence on external sources. An emphasis ought to be placed on funding from a diversity of sources to ensure that, primarily, the community served determines the programming. It is also desirable that the government supports this sector, meant to empower the poor and marginalized, with appropriate public investments. Internationally, there are several examples of governments setting up an autonomously administered Community Radio Support Fund to which people could apply for grants, both to help in establishing a station as well as for meeting operational expenditure.

Exercise Editorial Independence

AMARC lays down that CR stations should be editorially independent of government, commercial and religious institutions, and political parties in determining their programme policy. The Nepalese Code of Conduct for Community Radio Broadcasters, mentioned earlier, adds that, "Radio stations should be neutral and impartial and should remain free from the influences of any person, group, organization or party". The guidelines of the

Community Radio Coalition, Nigeria specify that CR stations should be guaranteed management and editorial independence and be subject to better public oversight. The CBAA codes of practice emphasize that CR stations ought to, "Demonstrate independence in programming as well as in editorial and management decisions" and ensure that editorial decisions affecting the content and style of individual programmes or overall station programming are not influenced by programme or station sponsors. It further specifies that CR stations

> will attempt to avoid censorship where possible. However, in our programming decisions we will consider our community interest, context, degree of explicitness, the possibility of alarming the listener, the potential for distress or shock, prevailing Indigenous laws or community standards and the social importance of the broadcast. (CBAA 2008, 6)

The NCRA/ANREC Codes of Conduct in Canada encourage stations to develop their own policies and procedures that relate to their programming and operations and resist attempts at censorship that would erode independence, and not accept financial compensation from those who seek to influence programming content or policies (NCRA 2011). They favour encouraging representation from all members of the community in all aspects of station governance and policy making. Ramasoota (2010, 39) report titled "Building a Democratic Regulatory Framework for Community Radio in Thailand" clearly articulates that there should be clear guidelines with respect to who should and should not be allowed to make public contributions and to maintain independence; "controversial figures" such as politicians, businesses and business entrepreneurs should be kept at arm's length from supporting CR. In order to maintain transparency and accountability of CR station in financial planning, it is essential to properly acknowledge all public contributors. NCRA/ANREC Codes also mandate that all on-air sponsorship messages and advertising must be distinguishable from other programming content.

Advocate for an Enabling Policy Environment

CR stations must organize themselves into a network with a view to advocate for and facilitate the establishment of an enabling legal environment for CR development. Efforts must be put in place to address the barriers that hamper access to communications infrastructure by citizens and communities such as: insufficient or inappropriate spectrum allocation; market failure to deliver new systems based on appropriate technology at affordable costs; unreasonable processing levies; socio-cultural barriers to access; and unfriendly public policy frameworks. There should be incentives by the government that support local expertise in the production of broadcasting equipment and software. Thus, there ought to be appropriate policy environment for sustained growth of the CR sector in the country. Laws, historic charters and pronouncements such as "Article 19 of the Universal Declaration of Human Rights", the "Beijing Platform of Action", "People's Communication Charter", "AMARC Gender Policy for Community Radio", the "Right to Information Act", and others, which enhance the practice of independent and free media, must be recognized and propagated. There is a growing need for synergizing CR with the other new social movements, such as the Right to Information movement, food security initiatives and even disaster management, so as to amplify and intensify the use of CR resources for public good, freedom of expression and information, and the empowerment of historically marginalized and poor sections of society.

Facilitate Adherence to Codes of Practice

Among other legal obligations such as preserving logs of all programme broadcasts for three months, as community broadcasters, it is the responsibility of the CR station to abide by all legislative requirements in its programming and advertising content as well as in its operations. Each station must also formulate (in a participatory manner) and follow a set of internal codes and policies (including the voluntary codes of practice) that steer their day-to-day activities, such as programming, advertising, volunteering and sponsorship, and support the governance, management, financial and technical operations of the station with the intent of maintaining certain values and principles of conduct. For example, the CBAA codes of practice include the norm that:

> We will not broadcast material that is likely to stereotype, incite, vilify, or perpetuate hatred against, or attempt to demean any person or group, on the basis of ethnicity, nationality, race, language, gender, sexuality, religion, age, physical or mental ability, occupation, cultural belief or political affiliation. The requirement is not intended to prevent the broadcast of material which is factual, or the expression of genuinely held opinion in a news or current affairs program or in the legitimate context of a humorous, satirical or dramatic work. (CBAA 2008, 3)

Similarly, the CR stations could formulate specific internal policies about content aimed at children; related to portrayal of women; concerning the kinds of advertising the station will broadcast; in matters that affect health; or those that pertain to environmental issues to facilitate decision making by the staff in these matters. The CR stations ought to put in place a system to ensure that their staff and volunteers are aware of all codes and legal requirements that must be respected within the station.

Conclusion

As community-driven, volunteer-run, not-for-profit organizations, the CR sector in India must position itself differently in its process, approach, style and substance in comparison to the state-owned and commercial broadcasters. It is possible for CR stations to challenge the hegemony of the mainstream media and its programing methods only through developing rigorous and appropriate codes of conduct and practice in the spirit of self-regulation. By espousing self-regulation and ethical practices, the CR stations voluntarily commit to abiding by a code of practice that they can themselves compose and verbalize. They can also establish an in-house complaints redressing mechanism that deals with the alleged breaches of the code. It must be pointed out here that self-regulation is about safe-guarding ones freedom; it is not censorship and not even self-censorship. It is about establishing minimum principles on ethics, accuracy, personal rights and so on, while fully preserving editorial freedom on what to report and what opinions to express.

The "Codes of Practice for Community Radio in India" that the author has tried to build here are generalized tenets derived from a selection of universal core values that media activists, academics, grassroots organizations, CR broadcasters and even some of the policy makers consider as being indispensable for the CR sector to sustain its relevance in India or anywhere else in the world. They may be used as an inventory for reference and are open to being adapted and adopted by different stations in the form and measure that the stations may deem proper. After all, there is no single model that fits all. Each community has its own priorities and practices and they must find a system of practices that is best for them without compromising on the principles such as freedom of expression, equality and access for the disempowered.

DISCLOSURE STATEMENT

No potential conflict of interest was reported by the author.

REFERENCES

"African Charter on Broadcasting (ACB)." 2001. May 3–5. Accessed July 22, 2015. http://portal.unesco.org/ci/en/files/5628/10343523830african_charter.pdf/african%2Bcharter.pdf.

"AMARC Community Radio Charter for Europe." 1994. Accesed July 17, 2015. http://www.amarceurope.eu/the-community-radio-charter-for-europe/.

Appadurai, Arjun. 1997. *Modernity at Large: Cultural Dimensions of Globalisation*. Delhi: Oxford University Press.

Atton, Chris. 2001. "Approaching Alternative Media: Theory and Methodology". Paper presented to ICA pre-conference Our Media, Not Theirs, The American University, Washington, DC, May 24. Accessed July 22, 2015. http://mediaprof.org/ourmedia/omwebsite/papers/om2001/Atton.om2001.pdf.

Atton, Chris. 2002 *Alternative Media*. London: Sage.

Béteille, Andre. 1999. "Citizenship, State & Civil society." *Economic and Political Weekly* 34 (36): 2588–2591.

Bonin, Marie-Hélène, and Aida Opoku-Mensah.1998. "What is Community Radio?" Accessed July 22, 2015. http://www.amarc.org/documents/manuals/What_is_CR_english.pdf.

Calhoun, Craig, ed. 1992. *Habermas and the Public Sphere*. Cambridge, MA: MIT Press.

Carpentier, Nico, Rico Lie, and Jan Servaes. [2002] 2008. "Making Community Media Work: Community Media Identities and their Articulation in an Antwerp neighborhood Development Project." In *Communication for Development and Social Change*, edited by J. Servaes, 247–373. Paris: UNESCO.

CBAA (Community Broadcasting Association of Australia). 2008. "Codes of Practice." Accessed July 22, 2015. http://cbaa.org.au/sites/default/files/codes_of_practice_3.12.08_LR.pdf.

Couldry, Nick. 2010. *Why Voice Matters: Culture and Politics after Neoliberalism*. London: Sage.

CRIS Campaign. 2005. *Assessing Communication Rights: A Handbook*. London: World Association for Christian Communication.

Dagron, Alfonso Gumucio. 2001. *Making Waves: Stories of Participatory Communication for Social Chang*. New York: The Rockefeller Foundation.

Downing, John. 2001. *Radical Media: Rebellious Communication and Social Movements*. Thousand Oaks, CA: Sage.

Downing, John. 2008. "Social Movement Theories and Alternative Media: An Evaluation and Critique." *Communication, Culture & Critique* 1 (1): 40–50.

Fraser, Nancy. 1992. "Rethinking the Public Sphere: A Contribution to the Critique of Actually Existing Democracy." In *Habermas and the Public Sphere*, edited by Craig Calhoun, 109–142. Cambridge: MIT Press.

Freire, Paulo. 1983. *Pedagogy of the Oppressed*. New York: Continuum.

Gordon, Janey, ed. 2012. *Community Radio in the Twenty-First Century*. Switzerland: Peter Lang.

Haraszti, Miklós. 2008. *The Media Self-regulation Guidebook: All Questions and Answers*. Vienna: Organization for Security and Co-operation in Europe.

Hochheimer, John L. 1993. "Organizing Democratic Radio: Issues in Praxis," *Media, Culture & Society* 15 (3): 473–486.

Howley, Kevin. 2010. "Notes on a Theory of Community Radio." In *Understanding Community Media*, edited by K. Howley, 63–86. Thousand Oaks, CA: Sage.

Kumar, S. Nagesh. 2006. "Balancing Freedom and Social Responsibility." October 23. Accessed July 22, 2015. www.thehindu.com/todays-paper/balancing-freedom-and-social-responsibility/article3064459.ece.

Malik, Kanchan K. 2007. "Community Radio: Concept and Worldwide Practice." *Vidura: Journal of the Press Institute of India* 44 (1, January–March): 4–7.

McQuail, Dennis. 1994. *Mass Communication Theory: An Introduction*. 3rd ed. London: Sage.

"National Broadcasting Commission (NBC) narrative report on Broadcast Policy Stakeholders' Forum." 2010. Held in Abuja, Nigeria, January 26. Accessed July 22, 2015. http://www.imesoimeso.org/wp-content/uploads/2013/04/Broadcast_Policy_Stakeholders_Forum.pdf.

NCRA (National Campus and Community Radio Association). 2011. "The NCRA/ANREC Codes of Conduct in Canada." Accessed July 22, 2015. http://www.ncra.ca/advocacy-files/NCRA-proposed-codes.pdf.

Pavarala, Vinod, and Kanchan K. Malik, eds. 2007a. *Other Voices: The Struggle for Community Radio in India*. New Delhi: Sage.

Pavarala, Vinod, and Kanchan K. Malik, eds. 2007b. "Revitalising Civil Society: Forging Counter-publics with Community Radio." In *Other Voices: The Struggle for Community Radio in India*. 183–209. New Delhi: Sage.

"Policy Guidelines for Setting up Community Radio Stations in India." 2006. Accessed July 22, 2015. http://mib.nic.in/writereaddata/html_en_files/crs/CRBGUIDELINES041206.pdf.

Ramasoota, Pirongrong. 2010. *Building a Democratic Regulatory Framework for Community Radios in Thailand*. New York: Social Science Research Council. http://mediaresearchhub.ssrc.org/grants/funded-projects/building-ademocratic-regulatory-framework-for-community-radiosin-thailand-1/building-a-democratic-regulatory-frameworkforcommunity-radios-in-thailand (URL valid at time of writing).

Rodríguez, Clemencia. 2001. "Chapter 1: 'From Alternative Media to Citizens' Media'." In *Fissures in the Mediascape: An International Study of Citizens' Media*, 1–24. Cresskill: Hampton Press.

Rodríguez, Clemencia, Dorothy Kidd, and Laura Stein, eds. 2010. *Making Our Media: Global Initiatives Toward a Democratic Public Sphere, Volume One: Creating New Communication Spaces*. Creskill, NJ: Hampton Press.

Servaes, Jan. 1996. "Linking Theoretical Perspectives to Policy." In *Participatory Communication for Social Change*, edited by Jan Servaes, Thomas L. Jacobson, and Shirley A. White, 29–43. New Delhi: Sage.

Servaes, Jan. 1999. *Communication for Development: One World, Multiple Cultures*. Cresskill, NJ: Hampton Press.

Siochrú, S. Ó. 2004. *Social Consequences of the Globalization of the Media and Communication Sector: Some Strategic Considerations*." Working Paper No. 36. Geneva: World Commission on the Social Dimension of Globalization: International Labour Office.

Streitmatter, R. 2001. *Voices of Revolution: The Dissident Press in America*. New York: Columbia University Press.

Tacchi, Jo. 2012. "Digital Engagement: Voice and Participation in Development." In *Digital Anthropology*, edited by H. Horst and D. Miller, 225–241. Oxford: Berg.

Thomas, Pradip Ninan. 2011. *Negotiating Communication Rights: Case Studies from India*. New Delhi: Sage India.

Traber, Michael. 1985. *Alternative Journalism, Alternative Media. (Communication Resource, 7 October)*. London: World Association for Christian Communication.

Wasko, Janet, and Mosco, Vincent, eds. 1992. *Democratic Communications in the Information Age*. Toronto: Garamond Press & Ablex.

White, Shirley A. 1994. "The Concept of Participation: Transforming Rhetoric to Reality." In *Participatory Communication: Working for Change and Development*, edited by Shirley A. White, K. Sadanandan Nair, and Joseph Ascroft, 15–32. New Delhi: Sage.

Index

Note: **Boldface** page numbers refer to figures and tables and page number followed by 'n' denotes endnotes

Adam, John 15, 16
Administrative Staff College of India (ASCI) 60
advertising industry on trial 71–4
"Advertising Man of the Century" 72
Aeropagitica of Indian history 16
African Charter on Broadcasting 141
AMARC *see* World Association of Community Radio Broadcasters
Ambedkar, B.R. 122, 133n3
Anand Bazaar Patrika 123–31, **125**, **127**, **128**, **130**
ASCI *see* Administrative Staff College of India
Asian News International 97, 99

Banerjee, Mamata 56
Bangal Gejeti (Roy) 15
Bayley, W. B. 16, 19
Bennett Coleman Company Limited 42
Big Bad Male World, women reporters in 86–9
Bombay Times 54
Brazil, Russia, India, China, and South Africa (BRICS) grouping 39
Buckingham, John Silk 12

Calcutta Journal 12, 14, 15
Calcutta, origin of Indian journalism 13
CBAA *see* Community Broadcasting Association of Australia
CBI *see* Central Bureau of Investigation
Center for Media Studies (2014) in Delhi 44–5
Central Bureau of Investigation (CBI) 55, 57
Central Chronicle 96–8

CGNet Swara (Chhattisgarh) 6; citizen journalism and 94–8, 101; civil society, unconnected to 102; democratizing journalism 102; emergence of 93; inaccuracy of 98–100; information access 92–3; interactive voice response technology 93; issues and views of professionals 98–9; lingual diversity, issues with 101; professional journalists working with 94, 96, 101–2
Chit Fund Scam 55–7
Choudhary, Shubhranshu 93
cine-journalism 23–34
Cinema Cinema 30
cinematic civic consciousness 30–3
citizen journalism 94–8, 101
civil society and media 3
codes of practice for community radio 7; adhering to legal requirements 147; communication rights 144–5; community capacity building 143; content diversity and sensitivity 142; cultural linguistic diversity 143–4; editorial independence 145–6; enabling policy environment 146; inclusivity and "voice to the weak" 144; ownership and management 141; participation of community 142–3; progressive social changes 142; providing training opportunities 143; self-sustainability mechanisms 145; serving as not-for-profit ventures 141; serving recognizable community 141
communication revolution in India 3
communication rights 144–5
community broadcasting 139, 141
Community Broadcasting Association of Australia (CBAA) 143, 147

INDEX

community capacity building 143
community participation 142–3
community radio (CR): codes of practice *see* codes of practice for community radio; overview of 7, 136–8; revitalizing civil society 138–9; stations 146
constitutional agitation 11
content diversity and sensitivity 142
CR *see* community radio
crony capital in news media space: Chit Fund Scam 55–7; Enforcement Directorate official 54–5; NewsX Sale Case 59–60; Sahara blackmail case 54–5; Tejpal business empire 57–8, **58**; Zee extortion case 53–4
crowd-sourcing 27–8
cultural linguistic diversity 143–4

Daily Chhattisgarh 96–7
Dainik Bhaskar 97, 99
Dainik Jagran 123–31, **125**, **127**, **128**, **130**
dalits, Maoist movement 122–3
delegative democracies 38, 46
Delhi Times 54
Democracy as a Universal Value 43–6
democratic communication 144–5
democratizing journalism 102
Deshbandu 97–8
Dwyer, Rachel 34, 34n1

early phase of Indian journalism 94–5; Calcutta as "white town" 13–14; Hicky's journal 13–14; Marquess of Hastings 15; print journalism, emergence of 14–15; Rammohun Roy, contributions of 13, 16, 20–1; Wellesley's contribution to Indian journalism 13
economic inequality 2, 5, 41–3
editorial independence 145–6
ED official *see* Enforcement Directorate official
Eenadu 123–31, **125**, **127**, **128**, **130**
Enforcement Directorate (ED) official 54–5

FDI *see* foreign direct investment
Filmfare 23, 24, 26
film magazine journalism 23–34
FIR *see* First Information Report
First Information Report (FIR) 53

foreign direct investment (FDI) 59
Forest Areas Act (2006) 122, 133n2
Friend of India 18

Global Media Monitoring Project 80
GramVaani 95

Hari Bhoomi 97, 98
Hicky, James Augustus 13–14
Hindu, The 55, 56
Hoot Reader:Media Practices in the Twenty-first Century, The 52

India Against Corruption 107, 115
India Grows at Night (Das) 1
Indian Express 51
Indian general election (2014) 10–11
Indian Information and Broadcasting Ministry 39
Indian news media 5, 94–5; delegative democracies 38; Democracy as a Universal Value 43–6; inequality in society 41–3; private media 38–41; social, political, and economic inequality 37
India's growing "crisis of governability" 1
"India Shining" 107
India Today 55, 57
interactive voice response (IVR) technology 93
internet infrastructure in India 93
IVR technology *see* interactive voice response technology

Jindal, Naveen 53, 54
Jindal Steel and Power Ltd (JSPL) 53, 54
journalism education 95
journalism's supply of political knowledge 6; discussion and conclusion 131–3; India's Maoist movement 122–3; political context of India 121; research design and findings 123–31
JSPL *see* Jindal Steel and Power Ltd

Knight International Journalism Fellowship 93
Kumar, Arvind 23–4

liberalised media, structure and economics of 81
literary coverage of cine-journalism 28–30

INDEX

Macaulay, Thomas B. 12
Madhuri (cine-journalism) 5, 23–7; civic consciousness 30–3; crowd-sourcing 27–8; Hindi literary coverage 28–30
mainstream hegemonic media 138; and CGNet 96, 99
"manufacturing news" 52
Maoist movement and journalism's knowledge supply 6; agenda-setting 127–9, **128**; amount of coverage **125**, 125–6; comprehensiveness of coverage 129–31, **130**; coverage of causes and remedies 126–7, **127**; dalits 122–3; selection of dailies 123–4
Marquess of Hastings 15, 16
media organizations, emergence of 94
media ownership, complex field of 50–3
member of the state legislative assembly (MLA) 85
@mentions, Twitter communication 110, 112, 113, **113**
Merinews.com 95
Metcalfe, Charles 21
Mirat-ul-Akhbar, closure of 4, 19–20
MLA *see* member of the state legislative assembly
"multi-national" electoral democracy 121, 133n4
Munsif 123–31, **125**, **127**, **128**, **130**
"Murdochization" of Indian journalism 11, 94

National Campus and Community Radio Association (NCRA) 142, 146
national public affairs television program *see* We the People
NCRA *see* National Campus and Community Radio Association
Nepalese Code of Conduct for Community Radio Broadcasters 144, 145
NewsX Sale Case 59–60
Nigeria Community Radio Coalition 146
not-for-profit organizations, community radio station 141, 145

open communication platform 111

Padamsee, Alyque 71–3
"paid news" 11, 52, 94

Panchayat Extension to Scheduled Areas (PESA) Act 122, 133n1
participation of community 142–3
PCI *see* Press Council of India
phantasmagoria 50
phantom journalism 5, 49–50; crony capitalism and news net *see* crony capital in news media space; media ownership, complex field of 50–3
political context of India 121
political democracy 2
power structures, external/internal management 85
Pratidin 56–7
Press Council of India (PCI) 61; report on paid news 94
Press Ordinance (1823) 16–19
print journalism, emergence of 11, 14–15
professional journalists, work with CGNet Swara 94, 96, 101–2
programming content: diversity and sensitivity in 142; progressive social change 142
public journalism 95

Rammohun Roy 13, 16; contribution to Indian journalism 16, 20–1; *Mirat-ul-Akhbar* 19–20; Press Ordinance (1823) 16–19
Ray, N. 99
Reliance Industries Ltd (RIL) 52
retweets, Twitter communication 111, 112
RIL *see* Reliance Industries Ltd
rural/tribal communities, CGNet Swara for 92–3, 95

SABC *see* South African Broadcasting Corporation
Sahara blackmail case 54–5
Scheduled Tribes and Other Traditional Forest Dwellers Act 133n2
self-sustainability mechanisms 145
Sen, Amartya 43–4
Serious Fraud Investigation Office (SFIO) 59
SFIO *see* Serious Fraud Investigation Office
Shama-Sushma 26, 28
Sharma, Supriya 129
small-town reporting 84–6
social inequality 2, 5, 41–3

INDEX

social media connectivity 112, 116

South African Broadcasting Corporation (SABC) 40

South African media 5; delegative democracies 38; Democracy as a Universal Value 43–6; inequality in society 41–3; private media 38–41; public sphere 38; social, political, and economic inequality 37

Srinivas, S. V. 34, 35n7

Study on Cross Media Ownership in India 60

Tejpal business empire 57–8, **58**

Telecom Regulatory Authority of India (TRAI) report 61

three Cs of Indian journalism 4

Times of India, The 54, 123–31, **125**, **127**, **128**, **130**

TMC *see* Trinamool Congress

TRAI report *see* Telecom Regulatory Authority of India report

Trinamool Congress (TMC) 56

Twitter communication, Delhi rape (2012) 6; activists and journalists 108–15; mobilization and activism 106–8; public communication 106

"Un-fair Obsession, An " 66

Wellesley, Richard 13

We the People program: advertising industry on trial 71–4; beauty norms, ugliness of 68–71; episodes of 66; possibilities and limits of 74–6; skin-lightening products 67–8; "Un-fair Obsession, An " 66

women reporters 5; in Big Bad Male World 86–9; electronic news media 78; local reporter 82–4; organisation selection process 80–1; participation and roles in media 79–80; small-town reporters 81–2, 84–6; urban and rural media practitioners 79

World Association of Community Radio Broadcasters (AMARC): Community Radio Charter for Europe 144; Gender Policy for Community Radio 144

Zee extortion case 53–4